A Therapist's Guide to the Multidisciplinary Treatment of Eating Disorders

The book provides an orientation to the diagnoses of eating disorders along with current information about evidence-based practices for multidisciplinary treatment. Unlike other books on eating disorders, this book conceptualizes eating disorder treatment as a team effort, focusing on the psychotherapist and their role as a member within a comprehensive treatment team.

Keane and Mendes identify the primary components of an eating disorder-specialized multidisciplinary "treatment team": a therapist to provide ongoing psychotherapy and care coordination, a medical provider to oversee medical complications and general medical stability, and a registered dietitian to provide nutrition counseling and manage nutritional status. It is increasingly common that adjunctive disciplines, such as integrative therapists, couple's counselors, school counselors, and other therapeutic support, are also involved in the treatment team. Through the experiences of seasoned eating disorder experts, readers will learn the basic tenets of eating disorder treatment, diagnostic differences between disorders, effective treatments, case examples, and sage clinical advice. Chapters are written from the perspective of a psychotherapist, as well as from that of a registered dietitian and a medical physician.

Designed to prepare both experienced and novice psychotherapists, as well as master's and doctoral students, for providing eating disorder treatment, this easy-to-read book is a must for any psychotherapist considering work with eating disorders.

Robert J. Keane, PhD, is a senior behavioral health administrator and Assistant Vice President of Program Development and Training at Walden Behavioral Care. He has over 40 years of experience treating diverse populations within the mental health community.

Kameron M. Mendes, LMHC, has clinical and administrative experience across a range of treatment settings, including psychiatric inpatient hospitalization, residential care, and intensive outpatient programs. He provides outpatient therapy at Renovated Wellness in Lynnfield, MA, while earning his PhD.

"With over 30 years of experience in the treatment of eating disorders, I find this therapist guide to be a long-overdue and invaluable contribution to the field. Bob Keane and Kam Mendes have created a resource that bridges the critical gap between clinical curiosity and practical competence, offering therapists a clear, compassionate, and evidence-informed roadmap for engaging with this complex population. Their emphasis on multidisciplinary collaboration and foundational knowledge aligns with the integrative principles I've long advocated. This book is not just a guide, but an invitation to join a movement of thoughtful, well-equipped clinicians ready to meet the urgent needs of those struggling with eating disorders."

James Greenblatt, *MD, founder and CEO of Psychiatry Redefined,*
author of several books, including Answers to Anorexia *and*
Finally Hopeful: The Personalized, Whole Body Plan to
Find and Fix the Root Causes or Your Depression

"This book is a tremendous gift to anyone entering or already established in the field of eating disorders treatment, no matter the discipline. Written by highly experienced providers using well-informed yet humble and compassionate voices, each chapter offers case vignettes to illustrate the nuances of complex interdisciplinary eating disorders care. You will be able to immediately apply this information to your practice, given digestible soundbites, articulate action plans, and the empowerment packed into each chapter. Written in a conversational tone, you can feel the mentorship coming through the pages, making this an efficient and effective training resource for any clinician."

Paula A. Quatromoni, *DSc, MS, RDN, Associate Professor of*
Nutrition and Epidemiology, Boston University

"We finally have a book that breaks down gatekeeping in the eating disorder community. This book warmly welcomes the therapists we need in the field and equips them with the knowledge and skills to move beyond individual silos and collaborate with other disciplines. It is a priceless collaboration reflecting decades of experience available in one bite-sized package. I wish this book were available far sooner for clinicians and supervisors alike!"

Sarajane Mullins, *LMHC, NCC, Clinical Director of*
Mullins Counseling Collaborative, Inc. and Clinical Eating
Disorder Consultant at Eliot Community Human Services

A Therapist's Guide to the Multidisciplinary Treatment of Eating Disorders

Edited by Robert J. Keane and
Kameron M. Mendes

Routledge
Taylor & Francis Group

NEW YORK AND LONDON

Designed cover image: Getty Images

First published 2026
by Routledge
605 Third Avenue, New York, NY 10158

and by Routledge
4 Park Square, Milton Park, Abingdon, Oxon, OX14 4RN

Routledge is an imprint of the Taylor & Francis Group, an informa business

For Product Safety Concerns and Information please contact our EU representative GPSR@taylorandfrancis.com. Taylor & Francis Verlag GmbH, Kaufingerstraße 24, 80331 München, Germany.

ISBN: 978-1-032-98816-0 (hbk)
ISBN: 978-1-032-98098-0 (pbk)
ISBN: 978-1-003-60077-0 (ebk)

DOI: 10.4324/9781003600770

Typeset in Galliard
by KnowledgeWorks Global Ltd.

Contents

Preface

Robert J. Keane and Kameron M. Mendes

Welcome to the world of eating disorder treatment. We need you. Eating disorders (ED) are being diagnosed now more than ever, and consequently, the gap between ED-specialized therapists who can provide high-quality care is widening. Although outpatient treatment is the backbone of the mental health system, therapists are in short supply, and for those who are available, training is often variable. Additionally, for us, it has never settled well that so many great clinicians shy away from working with eating disorders. We hear concerns from providers about the complexity each case entails, and just as loudly, a need for specialized training, which seems impossible to find.

This book was born out of countless hours of conversations just like these. As therapists and administrators in an acute care eating disorder facility, we were tasked with training therapists of all experience levels to work with individuals with severe eating disorders. Some therapists came with a wealth of personal or professional experience with EDs; however, more often than not, we trained therapists without any background or ED-related experience. And we saw this as a strength – a fresh perspective, an open mind, and a genuine curiosity.

Similarly, in our roles, we were responsible for the care of everyone receiving treatment at our facility. We spent hours each day in clinical rounds discussing clients' progress, case formulation, unique challenges, barriers, complicated family matters, and housing instability. So, it's safe to say we've seen a lot. And yet – we don't profess to be experts. We resist the label of "expert" because in this work, there is so much we don't yet know, and always so much more to learn.

Inevitably, after hiring a new-to-the-field therapist, the first question we're always asked is: "What should I read to learn more?" Of course, we refer them to the eating disorder world's greatest hits, books like: *Sick Enough, Life Without Ed, Survive FBT, Telling Ed No!, Nutrition Counseling in the Treatment of Eating Disorders, Answers to Anorexia*, among others (see the end of this chapter for references). However, when it came to books that describe the specific role of the psychotherapist within a multidisciplinary team, we haven't found any to recommend. Amazingly, a book that instructs therapists on how to facilitate individual therapy, as well as how to operate within a multidisciplinary team – the gold standard for eating disorder treatment – just doesn't exist. Particularly for our new therapists, who receive several weeks of training before building a client caseload, having access to this kind of information would have been invaluable. And in our minds, this kind of book could be similarly helpful for any therapist with an interest in working with eating disorders or who has inadvertently found themselves treating someone with an eating disorder.

So it was that we set out to write such a book. One in which a therapist (of any experience level) can learn how to apply the skills you already possess to those with eating disorders. We aimed to create a text that weaves the experience of seasoned ED clinicians alongside empirical evidence in an easy-to-read format. However, although the ideas we'll advance in this book are "easy-to-read," it does not mean that they are simple. The goal of this book was to shy away from writing a dense, jargon-filled textbook, in favor of something more approachable, while still providing the fundamental and practical knowledge you'll need to be an effective eating disorder therapist.

As such, it's important to note that this book is merely a starting point in your work with eating disorders. It can serve as a reference guide to ED assessment and common medical or nutritional issues you'll likely encounter. It will also get you acquainted with how to apply widely taught therapeutic techniques in your individual work. All the ideas we present are foundational concepts that you will take with you throughout your work with EDs. If you've found yourself working with someone with an eating disorder (or suspect they may have one), our hope is that this book can bring you up to speed in short order.

With that said, the learning curve for providing care to those with eating disorders is steep. There is no way you can learn everything overnight. As we mentioned, despite our years of experience working exclusively with those with eating disorders, we still do not profess ourselves to be experts. Because of this, it is important that you are aware of your shortcomings. Doing the work first-hand will be the greatest learning experience – by far – because if you say the wrong thing (which will inevitably happen), you'll be corrected, in vivo. We suggest that you don't resist this dynamic; instead, embrace it.

For the content of this book, we have asked a group of outstanding, actively practicing ED-specialized clinicians to impart their knowledge and experiences into the important areas that a new-to-the-field ED therapist will need to know. All of our providers have had many years of experience treating primarily eating disorders in a variety of treatment settings. While most everyone we've worked with across disciplines has come to this work with talent and dedication, we've wondered what it would be like to work once again with truly remarkable clinicians. It is in that spirit that we asked the authors of the chapters that follow to contribute to this book. We asked them to try to capture the essence of their approach to treating eating disorders and to communicate that to you, the reader, in a user-friendly and engaging manner. We invite you to read through these pages. There is a lot to learn, but we believe that once done, you will feel more prepared (and dare we say excited) to begin this fulfilling work.

Contact Us

For more information about the book, authors, and how to contact us, please visit *EDTherapistGuide.com*.

References

Ganci, M. (2016). *Survive FBT: Skills manual for parents undertaking family based treatment (FBT) for child and adolescent anorexia nervosa.* LMD Publishing.

Gaudiani, J. L. (2018). *Sick enough: A guide to the medical complications of eating disorders.* Routledge.

Greenblatt, J., Nakip, A. & Dimino, J. (2018). *Answers to Anorexia* (2nd ed.). Friesen Press, Manitoba, Canada.

Herrin, M. & Larkin, M. (2013). *Nutrition counseling in the treatment of eating disorders.* Routledge, New York, United States.

Kerrigan, Cheryl. (2011). *Telling Ed No!: And other practical tools to conquer your eating disorder and find freedom.* Gurze Books.

Schaefer, J., & Rutledge, T. (2014). *Life without Ed.* McGraw-Hill Education.

About the Authors

Karli Bresnahan, MSW, LICSW, is a Licensed Independent Clinical Social Worker who has diverse clinical experience including working in inpatient psychiatric settings, integrated behavioral health programs in primary care, and outpatient private practice. Karli also held a leadership position as a Clinical Director of a residential eating disorder treatment program in Massachusetts. Across all of these roles, she has worked with individuals ranging in age from 10 to 75 years old and has supervised clinical interns and fellow clinicians. She enjoys working with clients of all ages and presentations but specializes in working with individuals with eating disorders. Karli's current position is working as a psychotherapist at Renovated Wellness in Lynnfield, MA.

Christina Brothers, MSW, LICSW, is a Clinical Social Worker originally from Mobile, Alabama. She has a bachelor's degree in psychology from the University of Alabama in Tuscaloosa and received a master's in social work from Salem State University in 2011. Much of the foundation of her training and early years as a clinician was spent on an inpatient eating disorder and psychiatric unit. She now works at the Massachusetts Institute of Technology in their Student Mental Health and Counseling Center and has an active outpatient private practice. She specializes in working with those with eating disorders, OCD, or other high-risk presenting concerns. Christina enjoys working with adolescents, families, and young adults in her private practice and integrates curiosity, humor, and a relational treatment style, often pulling from an ACT framework. She currently resides in Boston, Massachusetts, with her husband and young daughter.

Lachlan Crawford, ND, is a naturopathic doctor with advanced training in integrative psychiatry and contemplative psychotherapy. A graduate of the Canadian College of Naturopathic Medicine, she also completed a certificate in Contemplative Psychotherapy from the Nalanda Institute and an advanced fellowship in Integrative Psychiatry with

Dr James Greenblatt and sits on the board of the Psychiatric Association of Naturopathic Physicians. Dr Crawford brings a whole-person, trauma-informed approach to mental health care and is currently the Director of Integrative Medicine for an inpatient and residential center for eating disorders.

Rachel S-D Fortune, MD, is the Executive Medical Director of Monte Nido Walden, which she joined after several years working in both academic Adolescent Medicine at Yale University School of Medicine/Yale New Haven Hospital and private residential mental health treatment at Newport Academy. She is board certified in Pediatrics and Adolescent Medicine and has devoted her career to caring for adolescent patients, particularly those struggling with eating disorders. Dr. Fortune graduated with her MD in 2004 from Wake Forest University School of Medicine and completed a Pediatrics residency at Nationwide Children's Hospital in 2007 and Adolescent Medicine fellowship at Children's Hospital Colorado in 2012. Dr. Fortune brings her enthusiasm, passion, humor, and no-nonsense clinical approach to her patients and is appreciated for her approachable leadership style.

Marcia Herrin, EdD, MPH, RDN, FAED, has a doctorate in nutrition education and a master's in public health nutrition. She is the founder of Dartmouth College's nationally renowned eating disorder treatment program and is a Clinical Professor at Dartmouth's Medical School with an appointment in the Adolescent Medicine Faculty and provides training to Pediatric Residents at the Children's Hospital at Dartmouth. Dr. Herrin has treated eating disorder patients for over 35 years and is the author of *Nutrition Counseling in the Treatment of Eating Disorders* (2013) and *The Parent's Guide to Eating Disorders* (2007).

Robert J. Keane, PhD, is a Senior Behavioral Health Administrator and Clinician with more than 40 years of behavioral health experience. He has worked for the past 11 years in an acute care setting for the treatment of eating disorders, and prior to that, he worked in both inpatient and outpatient treatment settings. Formerly the Deputy Commissioner at the Department of Mental Health and the Regional Director for Boston at the Massachusetts Behavioral Health Partnership (MBHP), Dr Keane has a sound understanding of the behavioral health system. With Stuart Koman, PhD, he is co-author of *Designing and Operating a System of Care in Behavioral Health* (2025). Dr. Keane earned his master's degree and PhD from Boston College Graduate School of Social Work and is currently a member of the faculty.

Cheryl Kerrigan, MSW, LICSW, is a Published Author, Speaker, Eating Disorder Survivor, and Licensed Clinical Social Worker specializing in eating disorder recovery. She is the author of *Telling Ed No and Other Practical Tools to Conquer Your Eating Disorder and Find Freedom* and is a contributing author to multiple national magazines and eating disorder recovery books. Cheryl serves as a member on an Ethics Committee, consults with various providers, and "brings recovery to life" by speaking at treatment facilities, workshops, schools, and conferences. Cheryl shares her expertise and insights to inspire hope, healing, and recovery.

Stuart L. Koman, PhD, is the Co-Founder, Former President, and Former CEO of Walden Behavioral Care, one of the nation's first systems of care for individuals with eating disorders. Stu is a skilled family therapist and strong advocate for parents and families in all treatment settings. He is co-editor with Marsha Pravder Mirkin, PhD, of the *Handbook of Adolescents and Family Therapy* (1985) and co-author of *Designing and Operating a System of Care in Behavioral Health* (2025) with Robert J. Keane. He holds a BS from Trinity College in Connecticut and a PhD from Duke University.

Jacquelyn "Jac" MacDougall, LMHC, is a Licensed Mental Health Counselor who specializes in eating disorders and trauma. Over the past decade, she has worked in clinical and leadership roles across all levels of care in eating disorder treatment. She is the founder of Two Truths Counseling, a practice that provides treatment using an eclectic skills-based approach that is grounded in building an authentic and trusting relationship. Jac is also an EMDRIA-trained EMDR therapist. In her free time, she loves live music, spending time in nature, and reading silly fantasy novels.

Amy Mayer, PsyD, is a Clinical Psychologist who has worked in the eating disorder field for the past 25 years. She received a doctorate from William James College and completed her clinical internship at Mass Mental Health Center, Harvard Medical School. Dr. Mayer has worked with people of all ages in every level of care, as a clinician and as a supervisor, and has been a part of a multidisciplinary peer supervision group for two decades. As an extrovert who works with colleagues who mostly identify as introverts, Amy loves the challenge of building and contributing to eating disorder treatment teams and groups of all kinds.

Caroline Mendes, MS, RDN, CEDS-C, is a Registered Dietitian with over a decade of experience specializing in the treatment of eating disorders. She is the founder of Renovated Wellness, an integrated outpatient group practice of dietitians and therapists, where she provides nutrition counseling, clinical supervision, and professional consultation. Caroline is a Certified Eating Disorder Specialist and Consultant through the International Association of Eating Disorder Professionals. Her clinical work focuses on adolescents and families, drawing on the principles of

Family-Based Treatment (FBT). She earned her master's degree in dietetics from Boston University, where she also serves as a guest lecturer.

Kameron M. Mendes, LMHC, is a Licensed Mental Health Counselor with clinical and administrative experience across a range of treatment settings, including psychiatric inpatient hospitalization, residential care, partial hospitalization, intensive outpatient programs, and outpatient practice. Previously, he served as the Clinical Director of a 52-bed psychiatric inpatient hospital that specializes in the treatment of eating disorders, and has extensive experience supporting adolescents, adults, couples, and families with concerns related to mood and anxiety disorders, trauma, relational and communication challenges, and other complex mental health issues. Currently, he provides outpatient therapy at Renovated Wellness in Lynnfield, MA, and is earning a PhD in the School of Social Work at Simmons University. He received his master's degree in counseling psychology at William James College in Newton, MA.

Contributors

Karli Bresnahan, MSW, LICSW
Renovated Wellness, Lynnfield
Boston College School
   of Social Work
   Boston, MA

Christina Brothers, MSW, LICSW
MIT Student Mental Health &
   Counseling; Private Practice
   Newton, MA

Lachlan Crawford, ND
Monte Nido Walden
   Dedham, MA

Rachel S-D Fortune, MD,
   FAAP, CEDS
Monte Nido Walden
   Dedham, MA

Marcia Herrin, EdD, MPH,
   RDN, LD, FAED
Geisel School of Medicine
   at Dartmouth
   Hanover, NH

Robert J. Keane, PhD
Monte Nido Walden, Boston
   College School of Social Work
   Boston, MA

Cheryl Kerrigan, MSW, LCSW
Author; *Telling Ed No!*
   Boston, MA

Stuart L. Koman, PhD
Hesperia Capital, Boston, MA;
   William James College
   Newton, MA

Jacquelyn "Jac" MacDougall,
   LMHC
EMDR Therapist, Two
   Truths Counseling
   Hingham, MA

Amy Mayer, PsyD
Private Practice
   Brookline, MA

Caroline Mendes, MS, RDN,
   CEDS-C
Renovated Wellness, LLC
   Lynnfield, MA

Kameron M. Mendes, LMHC
Renovated Wellness, LLC,
   Lynnfield, MA
Simmons University
   Boston, MA

Acknowledgments

By Robert J. Keane

Age is a funny thing. After years in behavioral health and over a decade working in the eating disorder field, I began to think a lot about what I have learned and what I really know about this work. The results were humbling. Perhaps as with many things in life, with time and experience one begins to see not how much one knows, but rather how much there is still to learn. After some thought, I reasoned that while I may not know all I hoped, I do know some things, and perhaps as important, I know really good people who also know some things. I felt I had an obligation to put all that together and that is how this book began.

I deeply appreciate the work of the contributors. When we approached them, each readily agreed and despite full work schedules worked diligently to put into writing their remarkable talent and hard-earned experience. They have been generous with all they know and gracious with the pressures of getting this whole effort to fruition. For my own training in eating disorders, I am indebted to Stuart Koman, Jim Greenblatt, and Paula Vass. They were my first teachers in this area and afforded me an opportunity to work and learn from them. I always felt welcomed and appreciated. I thank my family who have supported me over the whole of my career, and especially for their encouragement and sacrifice. And I feel so much gratitude to the hundreds of behavioral health professionals and many clients I have known over the years. Your willingness to allow me to hear your stories and work alongside you has been an honor.

And last, I want to thank my co-editor, Kam Mendes. Putting together a book like this is a huge undertaking and Kam has been an exceptional partner. It is fun to work with him. I value him as a friend and see him as a true scholar and a gifted writer. He is someone I work well with and look forward to future projects.

By Kameron M. Mendes

I never thought I would write a book, yet here it is – and I could not have done this alone. To my wife, Caroline, whose love and unwavering support carried me through this long process, and to my children, Ollie and Frankie, you are my inspiration, reminding me every day why this work matters. To my parents and in-laws, your guidance and willingness to step in when life demanded allowed space for me to dedicate the time and focus needed for this project. Without all of your help, this book would not exist in its present form.

I am deeply grateful to all the clients I have had the privilege to work with; your courage and trust have taught me more than any book or classroom ever could have. I hope this work honors your voice and experiences. I am equally thankful to our co-authors, who generously shared their expertise to make this a truly collaborative work, as well as to the many wonderful clinicians I've had the pleasure of practicing alongside over the years.

Finally, I owe an immense debt of gratitude to my co-author, mentor, and friend, Bob Keane. Without you, I would not have had the opportunity to pursue this deeply fulfilling work or the many meaningful projects we've taken on together. Your insight, generosity, and dedication have not only shaped the words on these pages but have also shaped me as a thinker and clinician.

Part I

Introduction to Eating Disorders

Chapter 1

A Few Things to Know as You Start Out

Robert J. Keane and Kameron M. Mendes

Though eating disorders present diagnostic similarities, as therapists it is important to remember that each client is different and that your approach will need to vary creatively to meet each individual's needs. Because of this, it is hard (and maybe foolhardy) to declare anything about eating disorder treatment with absolute certainty. For one thing, we simply don't know enough yet. Eating disorders are a class of disorders which incorporate one's genetic makeup, psychological strengths and vulnerabilities, and the ever-changing social environment in which they live. For a therapist, this means that there is never one clear path nor linear road to recovery. As an eating disorder therapist, you must be flexible in your approach and able to adapt what you do as you learn from, and with, your clients.

What follows in this chapter are some important topic areas for you to consider as you approach this important work. These themes reflect lessons we've learned through years of practice, and you'll find that they will be woven throughout the book in the chapters ahead. Our hope is that they will serve as a meaningful starting point for your own work.

Eating Disorders Are Serious Business

At the outset it's important to acknowledge that eating disorders are serious. They can cause grave bodily injury and can be deadly. For instance, eating disorders have amongst the highest all-cause death rate of all mental illnesses (Chesney et al., 2014). Similarly, Van Hoeken and Hoek (2020) report that as a group, eating disorders create a significant reduction in quality of life and result in healthcare costs almost 50% higher than those without an eating disorder. We have found that clients who enter treatment early have a better chance of improving their relationship with food and are more likely to return to normal eating. However, for those who struggle with an eating disorder over years, these illnesses can be all-encompassing, never allowing freedom from the obsessive thoughts that rule nutrition and activity. But for anyone that struggles with an eating disorder, the consistent

DOI: 10.4324/9781003600770-2

presence of a treatment team throughout the eating disorder journey can be lifesaving. People recover from eating disorders and treatment provides the greatest hope for recovery and a full and better life.

You Can Do This

At the hospital, we got a lot of calls from lots of folks – clients, parents, other family members – desperately looking for an eating disorder therapist, and by the time they get to us, they're exasperated. They tell us that they've called everyone on their insurance panel and scoured therapist search engines. What usually happens is predictable: When our caller finally finds someone who specializes in eating disorders, there is almost always some sort of barrier. Many times, the therapist is busy or aren't accepting any new clients. Even if they are, there's a long waitlist and, of course, treatment can't wait. Oftentimes, they are told that the therapist doesn't accept their insurance plan. Barriers like these are becoming increasingly common and, for some, requires that treatment be paid out of pocket which is out of reach for most.

At the same time, we field many calls from therapists in the community once their client has been admitted. They tell us that their client, who initially entered their practice to treat depression or anxiety, was misdiagnosed. They really have an eating disorder. Regretfully, the therapist explains, had they known the client had an eating disorder they never would have accepted them into their practice to begin with. They tell us they know nothing about eating disorder treatment and inform us that they will no longer be available to treat the client. In short, they are dropping the case. Nothing we say can dissuade them. From our perspective, the therapist has a preconceived notion, often based on fear, of eating disorder treatment and can't seem to hand off (or abandon) the client fast enough.

This is an unfortunate situation. It is our belief that many therapists already possess the necessary skills to treat eating disorders. The presenting behaviors with food and eating are good information for the therapist to have but is best left to a Registered Dietitian or Medical Doctor to tackle. In fact, many times as a treating therapist, you may be unaware of recent medical information, like weight, vitals, and labs, which is not necessarily a bad thing. We have seen, time and again, inexperienced eating disorder therapists get overly attached to these numbers, as if they are black-and-weight symbols of their effectiveness, especially since our work does not often deal with tangible measures of progress. And if weight is down or labs are unstable, they feel an urge to spend vast amounts of time trying to convince the client to correct them – but this is a fool's errand. Of course, it is important to be aware of the general trends of these numbers and know what they mean. But remember, they are not a reflection of your effectiveness, and you do not possess the skills to provide guidance on correcting one's weight or labs.

The real job of a therapist in eating disorder treatment is not to immerse themselves in the nutrition and activity side of behaviors, but rather to come to understand the "why" of eating behaviors. This involves learning how someone thinks about their body and ultimately understanding with the client significant life events like trauma, loss, and isolation that have fueled the eating disorder. Like all therapists, eating disorder therapists spend a lot of time helping clients develop motivation to change behaviors. This often includes hard discussions about what an eating disorder has taken from a client's life and what is perpetuating the illness.

Importantly, the shortage of therapists willing to work with eating disorders is real, and as the need grows, we hear therapists talk about their lack of education and general fear about how to begin to treat an eating disorder. Certainly, one of the main points we hope to convey in writing this book is our belief that effective treatment for an eating disorder requires the skills and commitment that you already have, although with an important caveat; effective treatment does not happen through the efforts of one therapist, rather it requires a team of professionals who are willing to work together.

It Takes a Team

We believe in the power of a team because even with the best intention, due to the complexity that is often present in eating disorders, a solo practitioner can be easily overwhelmed and ultimately feel ineffective. The attention and involvement of other disciplines is essential. A multidisciplinary team creates a small holding system for the client and the opportunity for each provider on the team to consult and learn from one another on a regular basis. Eating disorders are body-brain illnesses, and each member of the team comes with a distinct area of expertise that holds a certain piece in treatment. It is through the collaboration among this team that a path for treatment is established.

But teams can be counterintuitive for many therapists. Much of our professional training and practice does not occur in a team, in fact, for many, outpatient practice usually occurs in relative isolation. We meet with one client at a time in an office with the door closed with only rare opportunities to consult with other disciplines. Practicing in isolation is so ingrained in us that many therapists think of it as a hallmark of professional autonomy; and sometimes, perhaps out of pride in our independence, we neglect opportunities to collaborate with others, even in our own discipline.

When treating an individual with an eating disorder, it is important to break out of that siloed thinking and welcome the involvement of other professionals. The interdisciplinary collaboration of a team is an essential part of treatment, and when accepting a client with an eating disorder, it is important to identify all the other providers who are also involved in the client's care. Usually, this group will include a medical provider, and a registered dietitian.

Eating Disorders Are Complicated

Effective eating disorder treatment requires a therapist who can practice with curiosity and creativity. We've interviewed a lot of therapists over the years, and we try our best to screen for both. For example, in a first job interview, we often ask a favorite question, "are you intelligent?" While it's certainly an odd question and one most people have never been asked before in a job interview, after an initial look of puzzlement and a deep breath, the response has become oddly predictable. Almost all applicants say "yes."

Of course, given that we're in a job interview, it makes sense to say yes. Anything other than an affirmative answer might not be wise, but it is usually clear that the interviewee is slightly uncomfortable acknowledging their own brilliance. Once we can move past the discomfort of the question, a second question follows, "how do you know?" This is the point at which things get interesting. Most people find it quite difficult to identify how they know they're smart, so again, there is almost always a pause (maybe even longer than the first question). Some candidates will say they know they are smart because they did well in school, and because they did well in school, they have enough information to believe they are smart. Others, maybe those who didn't do so well in school, say they have a type of intelligence that taps into areas that are not so measurable in conventional terms. They might talk about their interests, like how they can play the guitar, emphasizing that it is a very complicated instrument. Some talk about what we might call social intelligence and tell us that they can read people well and hence are good in social situations. They may make the case that their social intelligence is what makes them smart and is also what will make them a natural as a therapist.

Regardless, at some point during our interview, we pivot our questioning from intelligence to what we are really interested in. We ask, "are you curious?" And more specifically "is your sense of curiosity something you can apply to your work?" And that gets to what we are looking for. We want to know if the candidate can look at a challenge or a problem (or a behavior) not as an obstacle but rather with interest and wonder. If you can, is it possible to be creative and persistent in trying to understand that problem?

Curious people don't get put off by things that don't make immediate sense. They tend to believe that there are reasons for things to work the way they do, even if those things appear maladaptive. They wonder. And we love that quality in a therapist who wants to work with eating disorders. If you focus too much on the behavior of an eating disorder, or are put off by it, you will miss the point entirely. True curiosity allows a therapist to go past the presenting behavior and into the client's mind, looking for the "why" in a set of disorders that we really know very little about. For treatment to progress, curiosity must be front and center.

We tend to believe that most eating disorders have developed due to a combination of multiple factors, each impacting a client's life. So as a treater, it is important to resist the often-wishful thinking that these illnesses are simple and have one or two limited and defined causes. Most likely, the client is managing a confluence of things in their environment that, working in concert, have resulted in an eating disorder. And it makes sense as this plays out diagnostically. Eating disorders have a high co-morbidity with trauma, substance use, depression, and anxiety. As a result, the clinical presentation of an eating disorder may seem ominous, but in truth, it will be familiar. But it's not simple. As a golden rule, "all eating disorders are all complicated."

Recovery

Recovery is a term that refers to the process of healing from an eating disorder. Rarely will it be painless, predictable, or straightforward. Rather, it is fraught with discomfort, temptation, and seemingly insurmountable obstacles. But the only way to get through it is through it. We find that recovery is often stymied by avoidance or trying to find an "easier" way out, but that approach almost always leads back to the disorder. Recovery does not necessarily take stoicism or emotional strength (though they can help); rather, it takes resilience, persistence, and determination.

We like to think of recovery as a cumulative process – a series of actions – not simply something that is to be achieved. Often, we hear clients, early in their recovery, declare, "I'm in recovery," said as if they've arrived at a destination, although they continue to engage in day-to-day battles with ED behaviors. Some providers hear this declaration and disregard it, thinking that it is too premature to assign the "recovery" label when ED behaviors are still so present. However, we think about this differently. If a client truly believes they are taking steps or making decisions aligned with recovery, we do not dismiss their perception simply because they are still struggling. At the same time, it remains our responsibility to explore whether their steps, actions, or decisions are effective in moving them toward recovery's end.

As a new-to-the-ED-world therapist, it's important to remember that you are not the arbiter of what is or isn't recovery. We often see novice therapists get frustrated that their clients aren't doing what they tell them to do and therefore are not engaging in recovery. But your client's journey will last much longer than any one therapeutic relationship. It's far too easy to fall into the trap of believing that if your clients aren't doing what you suggest, they must want to stay stuck in their disorder; however, it's more often the case that they just haven't found another way yet. And don't assume that it's your responsibility to provide them with that alternative. As a therapist, it's our job to question the foundation upon which decisions are made – recovery oriented or not – along with what defines a "good" choice or behavior. For instance, if bingeing is related to intolerable feelings of distress, is it our responsibility to make them stop bingeing, or is it to help them conceptualize and manage their distress in a way that doesn't feel so overpowering?

One of the most common questions you'll hear from clients, parents, and others seeking your help is whether "full recovery" (i.e., the complete and permanent end of eating disorder symptoms) is possible. There is no agreed-upon answer to this question, as opinions vary widely and often conflict.

As for our perspective, we believe that "full recovery" is possible, but it's much more complicated than simply the cessation of behaviors. Full recovery involves a comprehensive awareness of the internal (e.g., psychological and biological) predispositions and external experiences that have contributed to the ED's development. Without this deeper understanding, the same factors that gave rise to the eating disorder may continue to draw those striving for recovery back into disordered patterns.

With such a wide range of perspectives, it's no wonder that the path to recovery is profoundly individual. This book will emphasize the importance, and, in many cases, necessity, of treatment in pursuing recovery. However, this may not be the case for everyone:

I met Henry in my outpatient practice. He was in his late thirties, with a loving wife and a successful career. He wasn't coming in for help with current eating disorder symptoms; instead, he was looking to process the trauma related to his eating disorder from nearly two decades prior.

What I would come to learn was that, for Henry, sitting in my office and saying aloud the words "my eating disorder" was a profound act of recovery. Although he had not engaged in eating disorder behaviors for over 15 years, he had never spoken openly about that chapter of his life. Apart from his wife, no one else really knew. Only once at the very beginning of his ED had he mentioned it to his parents, while quickly assuring them that he was OK.

Henry spent years trapped in cycles of restriction and purging and made several serious attempts to recover. These efforts usually began with a promise to himself to stop, managing to abstain for several months, only to find himself drawn back into the disorder. Restriction was often the first step, but purging would soon follow. However, it wasn't until a passing comment from a college friend he hadn't seen in years, "You need to eat a sandwich," that Henry made a lasting change. The remark struck a nerve, triggering an intense fear that someone had quickly discovered his closely guarded secret, and with it, his shame. He said of this, "I wondered to myself who else knew? So much of my ED had to do with control, but I realized I had actually lost control, and that scared me." This experience is all too common among those with eating disorders, particularly men experiencing restrictive patterns, as cultural stereotypes frame these disorders as problems that primarily affect women, chiseling away at one's masculinity.

When I first met Henry, I noticed he possessed remarkable emotional depth and insight. He was reflective, open, self-aware; qualities that, at one time, had been muted by his disorder, yet would be essential to his healing. At first, he described his recovery as happening "cold turkey," but in truth, it was years in the making. The decision to stop was swift, but the process of recovery unfolded slowly, over time. It wasn't until 15 years later that he would return to this part of his life, "My history with an eating disorder can't continue to be a skeleton in my closet. Suppressing it worked for a long time, but it's not sustainable for me to have that amount of shame buried deep down."

Now, Henry is doing the difficult work of looking back, but this time, it isn't to dwell in shame or fear; rather, it's to take back his story, so it no longer has to live in the shadows. Instead of seeing his past as a source of weakness, he's starting to see it as something that has shaped and strengthened him. The struggle to understand and reclaim this incredibly formative chapter in his life continues; however, he now possesses the courage to try to embrace it, rather than avoid it; "I want to have empathy for my eating disorder, my past; because I need empathy for myself."

Henry's story, while uniquely his own, reflects a common reality for many with eating disorders – a silent, isolated struggle. In clinical practice, you will encounter many such stories, and you will be invited to play a part in your clients' recovery journeys. Supporting someone through recovery is an extraordinary privilege that is both rewarding and challenging. As such, it is essential that you lean on the multidisciplinary team to share the responsibility of treating these life-threatening illnesses. Together, you can help clients face their pain and write new chapters that are no longer ruled by food, shame, or silence.

Eating Disorders Are Integrated Illnesses

In most graduate training programs, we're indoctrinated into the biopsychosocial model, a comprehensive way of conceptualizing any case from three very different yet interrelated realms; the biologic aspects of a person, the psychological workings of the mind, and the social influences of a life and time. Unfortunately, most therapists are not comfortable moving between all three domains. We really work in just two: the psychological aspects of a person and the societal influences from our environment. We know very little about the biological or medical side of human experience. Our education and our work orient us to a large divide between the psychological/social side of a human life and the biological/medical side. And as a result, we tend to think about the underlying drivers of behavior in the context of the psychology of the mind and the social experiences one encounters during one's life.

It gets a bit more confusing because somewhere down the line, we heard that most behavioral health treatment should be "integrated." That means that since the body and mind are connected, treatment should ideally involve behavioral health and medical treatment occurring at the same time. Of course, in our current healthcare service system this rarely happens. In practice, medical care and behavioral health services are rarely integrated; instead, each operates in its own silo with little communication or collaboration among providers.

This doesn't work when treating an eating disorder. Unlike most other behavioral health illnesses, eating disorders demand that both sides of the healthcare system work together. With an eating disorder, the mind and body are truly linked and impacted. For instance, if you are working with someone who is malnourished, there is a very clear impact on the physical workings of the body. Simply addressing the lack of nutrition and accompanying loss of body weight in a medical silo misses the need to treat underlying psychological causes. And similarly, if you are moving ahead in therapy, but oblivious to the effects of malnutrition on the brain and body, your efforts will invariably fail. Eating disorders require that behaviors be assessed and treated simultaneously with medical and behavioral health providers working together.

As a therapist treating eating disorders, it is important to stretch how you've practiced in the biopsychosocial model. It will be essential to truly include, as equal partners, the different disciplines who treat the biology, psychology, and social aspects of a case. A person with an eating disorder may have started using eating disorder "behaviors" due to several underlying psychosocial stressors, but make no mistake, each behavior has a significant impact on the body, in fact, likely multiple systems in the body. Effective treatment will require a coordinated effort between behavioral health providers and medical specialists; less things dissolve into a disorganized effort of chasing symptoms while leaving the root causes unaddressed.

There Is No Secret Formula

We meet many new therapists who come freshly minted from a graduate program and are enthusiastic to work in the eating disorder field. They are smart and dedicated and have a strong foundation in evidence-based treatments. They can speak eloquently about the basics of Dialectical Behavioral Therapy, Cognitive Behavioral Therapy, Cognitive Processing Therapy, and Motivational Interviewing, to name just a few. They begin this work with great enthusiasm and a willingness to use the tools they know so well; however, within six months of working with our clients, we receive an exasperated call. The new therapist tells us nothing is working. They are distraught and feel completely overwhelmed.

We meet, and almost every time, a familiar story emerges. They tell us that their eating disorder clients are resistant to making progress or, even worse, simply don't want to get better. We hear that despite their best efforts, their clients are not accepting any attempt at skills training that our young therapist is so prepared to offer. In reviewing case after case, our new therapist tells us that their client has no interest in learning a skill to help with emotional regulation and is especially resistant to any offer of a strategy that will decrease eating disorder behaviors. In some cases, if the therapist happens to be unusually hard on themselves, they start to question why they even went into the field in the first place. There is a hard lesson here; there is no secret formula in eating disorder treatment and there are certainly no quick fixes.

We remind our young therapists that the treatment of eating disorders is not predictable or linear. And most importantly, effective treatment demands building a trusting relationship with your client before any evidence-based treatment can really take hold. Without a solid, trusting relationship, treating eating disorders can be fool's gold. Part of that work involves slowly learning what motivates a client to begin to address the behaviors that encompass their eating disorder. In truth, much of the work we do with our eating disorder clients is about motivation. Once we can understand what truly motivates someone, good things can start to happen.

For example, Susan H. was an adolescent when her eating disorder began and, over time, she found it to be an ever-present companion. When we met, she was 22 and said she was ready to really work on her eating disorder. When asked about her struggle, she fondly spoke about her eating disorder, referring to it several times as her best friend. She recounted times she had used her disorder when she felt highly stressed and said it helped her make sense of and cope with her world. Although others saw that the behaviors she was using were taking a toll on her body, she didn't seem to notice and reported that she thought she looked and felt "fine."

The focus of our work was clear: to help her recognize her "friend" for what it was, a destructive force that was limiting her in life, not helping her. But to begin to explore that painful message we had to build a strong bond of trust between us. That happened over time, and in one powerful session, she was able to begin to talk about the sacrifices she had endured for her eating disorder. She was able to recount some of the significant losses she had experienced and sadly recalled the loss of a cherished boyfriend who ultimately ended their relationship because he felt too much of his life had become accommodating her needs. She tearfully told a story of a final fight in which they argued about where (or if) to go out to dinner, an issue she conceded was driven by her eating disorder and a frequent cause of friction. Despite her sadness, it became apparent that Susan had reached an important stage in her treatment: ambivalence (i.e., starting to question, and maybe even consider challenging, her eating disorder – although there were no guarantees that action against the eating disorder would occur). With this shift, she became much more interested in learning strategies to manage the anxiety and stress in her life.

While there is no set formula for success, once motivation to create even a small change is established, things start to happen. Treatment usually begins as an effort to help the client find motivation and hopefully moves into learning specific skills or strategies to manage intense feelings. To be sure, the skills we are teaching therapists in graduate schools do work, just not always right away. Clients often come into our office saying, "I just need skills and strategies to get over this eating disorder" – welcome words to our young therapists. However, even after giving them an entire toolbox of skills, they inevitably still struggle. They then go on searching for even more skills because the last ones "didn't work." But what they fail to realize is that skills are on the other side of motivation. We often tell therapists that it is a privilege to be asked by a client to teach them a skill, and when clients start putting their skills to work, it is a signal that the relationship is strong, as the client is taking steps to move away from the safety of their eating disorder.

Think Beyond Behavior

When we first began working in the eating disorder field, it was important to think through eating disorder "behaviors." Whatever the client is doing or not doing with food is a "behavior," and the job of a therapist is to learn and ultimately understand with the client the meaning that is behind the behavior. The real work is not to get bogged down by the minutia of what one is or isn't eating, or the mechanics of the behavior; rather, as a therapist, you must work with the client to understand the bigger picture: what drives the behavior and how to assist in the effort to push back. A talented colleague reminded us once that "it would be a mistake to think that eating disorders are about food." In a field filled with an abundance of objective information about one's eating (calories, percentages, weight, etc.), our work is the search for the meaning beyond the presenting behavior, not to get caught up in the metrics.

Ask Thoughtful Questions

In the first interview, many therapists begin with some sort of form or a survey to capture basic information. But past the formality of an introductory tool, it is a good idea to have a cache of questions that will help you begin to build an understanding of your client's eating disorder and provide clues that can inform the best way to move ahead. We often use a series of three questions.

The first one is disarmingly simple: we ask a client to tell us the story of how their eating disorder started. Interestingly, almost everyone can recall the point in their life when they first used an eating disorder behavior and even exactly where they were. And there's usually a compelling story to be told. If there's a common thread to all the stories, it would have to be that almost all seem to begin with good intention, often with a genuine interest in getting healthy or healthier. For instance, a client might say that their eating disorder started with a recommended diet or with the start of a new exercise program. A 14-year-old client told us "I wanted to go running with my mom" and a 30-year-old woman proudly recalled, "Food has always made me feel better." Each story helps a therapist understand the client's narrative and is worth revisiting later in treatment as it often creates in the mind of the client the belief that they are at fault for their eating disorder. Sadly, a part of the shame our client's experience often harkens back to their belief that when "this all started" in their effort to improve themselves, look better, or perform better, they caused or welcomed this illness.

After a bit of a pause, we follow up with a slightly harder question. We ask the client when they realized that their eating disorder was out of control. This tends to make people a bit more uncomfortable perhaps as it is a painful realization and because it implies an acknowledgment of the idea that things are, in fact, out of control. But like the first question, most clients do remember when their eating disorder (which they thought was helping them) turned into something that they can now (sometimes begrudgingly) concede is not. Some will talk about a dramatic shift from a point where they thought of their eating disorder as a helpful friend to a point at which they fear their eating disorder. Some clients will even acknowledge that their eating disorder at this point controls them and can express fear at how the eating disorder has grown in power. In essence, many clients can talk about how the well-intentioned goal they had enthusiastically set has shifted, and now there's a quiet sense of desperation that they are controlled by the very thing that they firmly believed was there to help them. Some may even verbalize that they need help in trying to turn the tide back, and that's why they are reaching out to you.

Our third and last question often forms the basis for a clinical formulation. We ask the client to tell us about their theory on why they have an eating disorder. Somewhat of a surprise to us, most everyone has a theory. It usually encompasses some of the stressors they have experienced in their life; most know that their eating disorder did not randomly drop out of the sky and land on their shoulders. With some guiding questions, a rich life story can emerge. As a therapist, you can begin to understand the events that have influenced the eating disorder, and it is sometimes an opportunity to add a "learning point" about eating disorders. For instance, after hearing a client's theory on their eating disorder, to move into the work ahead, a therapist might add some information, like "as you've learned, eating disorders are complicated and that it makes sense to think through those events in your life."

One last thought is that at some point we routinely ask about social media use. This is particularly relevant for adolescent and young adult clients. Although we suspect that many will underreport, it's a good idea to ask how many hours a day your client is on social media, and second, to learn what apps they frequent. We have been alarmed since the pandemic by the number of hours per day many adolescents with eating disorders are online. It is not unusual for us to hear reports of double-digit hours a day, often late into the night. In some cases, we learn that an adolescent essentially lives in a virtual world that has seemingly replaced one of human connection.

In 2023, the American Psychological Association published a health advisory for adolescent social media use. In it, they cited the detrimental effects of social media for adolescents with, or at risk of developing, eating disorders. Pro-ana websites (i.e., pro-anorexia) provide active encouragement and information for engaging in eating disorder behaviors, and glorify weight loss (i.e., thin-spo, or thin-inspiration). Directions on how to lose weight can easily be found, but it doesn't stop there; some sites even teach you how to hide the behaviors in order to deceive those that care about you from finding out. It is also not uncommon for those with eating disorders to post pictures of themselves seeking "mean-spo" (i.e., mean inspiration) or negative comments about their body from internet strangers to help them continue engaging in their eating disorder. Similarly, many provide graphic before and after pictures that create comparisons between one's body to others. In sum, the internet can be an extremely dangerous place for those with eating disorders, and this is in addition to the barrage of health and weight-related content that's normally found on these platforms.

Take Time to Examine Feelings

Many of the clients that we have worked with could be described as highly talented, hardworking, goal driven, and disciplined. These qualities, when applied to many things in life, are a formula for success. Many tend to be serious students and highly competent professionals. But for some, these qualities can be fertile ground for an eating disorder and create a great injustice; the skills and talents a person possesses draw them away from something that enhances life toward something that is destructive and ultimately life-threatening.

An individual who once excelled as a student may eventually find that they are unable to focus on school, and they may even lose interest in advancing academically. Despite a passion for learning, the energy once directed toward academics goes instead toward the ever-increasing focus of a demanding and aggressive eating disorder. Similarly, an accomplished professional who at one point was poised to excel in their career can become lost in their eating disorder to the point that their job performance suffers and impacts their career aspirations.

In addition to the skills and talents many of these individuals possess, rest assured that somewhere behind their eating disorder, which fills them with self-doubt and insecurity, there are feelings that they are powerful and confident. A lot of our work as therapists is to assist a client in identifying and legitimizing these hidden feelings. But this is hard work. It can be helpful to use a structure at the beginning of an individual session or group to take an inventory of how your client is feeling, and to learn with your client the power that each feeling holds for them.

For example, we ran adolescent group therapy for adolescents struggling with eating disorders and created a structured introduction at the beginning of each session. Sitting in a circle, we asked the group members to go around and for each to say their name, preferred pronouns, and how they are feeling today. It may seem like a simple exercise, but in practice it was quite challenging. It was common for adolescents to struggle with identifying how they were feeling, and for some, even if they had a feeling at all. Some needed help labeling their feelings and all shared the perception that some feelings are good, and others are bad.

This structure accomplished several goals: first, it got the members of the group to begin speaking (something characteristically difficult for many adolescents). Second, it challenged each member to take an inventory of how they were doing at that moment and pair that with a feeling state, and with that, promoted a sense of ownership of the feeling. And last, but very important, speaking how you feel out loud invites comments or reactions from others in the group, an important piece of the interrelatedness that group members need to experience. For many with eating disorders, saying how one feels out loud is a bold step in unfamiliar territory, as eating disorders tend to stifle, or numb, feelings. A structure is not a necessary component to identifying feelings; however, it can be a useful one.

Talking Is Great, but There Must Be Action

There's an ingrained belief among many clinicians that talking is the currency of a cure. We've learned that talking about distressing things in life and making connections to how we feel creates a shift in our thinking; and that over time, whatever malady that existed before seems to dissipate. But it really doesn't work like that with eating disorders.

Unlike other mental illnesses, talking, even with ample insight, doesn't by itself create change. That's because, in addition to talking about the hard things in life (some of which are no doubt related to the eating disorder), eating disorder treatment requires action steps. And in almost all cases, that action involves taking specific steps to address nutrition. Depending on the presenting behavior, that may mean decreasing bingeing or purging episodes or increasing the amount of food consumed.

Action is an enormous challenge for an individual with an eating disorder. But it also requires a change in thinking for the therapist. Therapy is often not paired with a required behavioral action. In fact, we are often quite kind about the absence of behavior change and would rather explore one's resistance than hold someone accountable to meeting even a small goal. But, in eating disorder treatment, every session is tasked with moving from talking to doing.

This doesn't negate the importance of conversation to develop a deep understanding as to the why of an eating disorder, but does require consistently assessing the level of motivation an individual has and then shifting to "and what are you able to do today to make a step forward?" If a shift in eating behavior doesn't happen, then that becomes a source for discussion in the next session along with the work of building motivation.

After providing training on eating disorders to providers at a large community mental health agency, a young therapist approached us and asked, "This work is so direct. It just sounds so un-therapeutic. How do you do it?" And in response, we simply said, "Well, the alternative can be dire." Holding our clients accountable to challenging this life-threatening illness is incredibly important, and it doesn't have to seem un-therapeutic. Remember, all of this work relies on a strong therapeutic alliance – and there's a reason that client is sitting in front of you. Whether they sought treatment of their own accord or not, something brought them there.

Case Vignette

At the age of 32, Susan entered outpatient treatment for a restrictive eating disorder. In the first meeting with her therapist, she said that her eating disorder had been a burden throughout much of her adult life and that she wanted to start therapy to address it. She talked about being incredibly motivated and how she was ready to make a real change in her life. She talked about how much she enjoyed individual therapy and presented herself as an articulate and thoughtful client. Susan always arrived on time and came prepared to talk about serious life issues. She was often insightful and made connections between the issues she brought into therapy and how they related to her struggle with her eating disorder behaviors. In short, she was an invested and motivated client.

Except nothing happened. When Susan left treatment after almost a year, she was at the same weight as when she had entered treatment and was as active in her eating disordered behaviors as when she started therapy. Despite the insightful sessions, including hours of talking and making seemingly wonderful connections, there had been no change in her behavior. Looking back, her therapist recognized that she had allowed herself to be seduced by what seemed to be engaging therapy with great conversation and wonderful insights, but little or no action.

There's a lot to be learned from this case. When working with eating disorders, talking is very important, but it means little if not accompanied by real change in behavior. This does not mean that every change has to be a big leap forward or that each session results in a tangible step forward, but rather that in the course of treatment, there is a consistent effort to create incremental steps toward a clear goal that can be measured over time. And when it seems as though movement is not happening, it is very important to name that and to work to understand what might be holding the client back. Talking alone does not create a recovery.

Eating Disorders Devastate Families

We often think of eating disorders as individual illnesses that impact just the person with the illness, but that is far from the truth. Eating disorders impact families in a profound way. When a family member is struggling with an eating disorder it creates a crisis, and the entire family system becomes activated. It is common for parents or caretakers to struggle with a sense of disbelief at the onset of the disorder and often find themselves struggling with self-blame, a general lack of knowledge about eating disorders, and confusion about what to do to help.

Despite seeing their child daily, many parents and family members are caught off guard when an eating disorder is identified, and in many cases, tell us that they were unaware that their child was struggling. This makes sense for adolescents in particular, who are masters at hiding their bodies in baggy clothes making sometimes drastic changes in weight undetectable. When the eating disorder does become known, it is not uncommon for it to be unceremoniously communicated by a relative or family friend who hasn't seen the child in a while, or maybe someone from their child's school, or in the office of a pediatrician at an annual physical. Parents often feel embarrassed and blamed.

Most parents can lovingly recall feeding their child in infancy and over the years working to build a positive relationship with food through family dinners, favorite meals, and holiday gatherings. Parents recall countless celebrations over the years in which food was a centerpiece and, in many cases, a proxy for the love they feel for their children. The notion that their child is rejecting food (or their love and caring) is devastating and almost incomprehensible. Parents struggle through a series of feelings about their child's struggle with an eating disorder beginning with a great sense of fear. With that, some will mobilize and learn as much as they can about eating disorders, resolved to do all in their power to end them.

Parents reach out to the mental health community desperately searching for help, always with an urgent wish to "fix" the problem and return to normalcy as soon as possible fearing that their hopes and dreams for their child are slipping away. Frustration develops as parents learn that an eating disorder is rarely a quick fix, especially when attempts at treatment end in perceived failure; "They're not better yet!" This frustration can often turn into anger and the mantra that treatment is a journey seems woefully inadequate for the child and family that is suffering.

As a clinician it is critical to join with a family in a non-judgmental manner and to identify and assess a family's strengths in treatment. While certainly there may be issues within a family related to food or appearance that may impact your client's eating disorder, remember that recovery from an eating disorder always requires support from important people in the client's life. Most often, these critical individuals are family members. As hurt and uninformed as a family member might feel, behind their affect is a powerful source of support and caring. Use it.

Language Is Powerful

The words we use to describe our experiences carry weight. As you may have already noticed, in the ED-world, we use distinct language to describe similar concepts. Take, for instance, *weight gain*. For many with eating disorders, this term can evoke feelings of fear, shame, or dread. However, when framed as *weight restoration,* it can help bypass the fear associated with gaining weight, since "restoration" implies that something necessary has been lost and needs to be regained. Further, the word *food* is often referred to as nutrition, energy, fuel, or power. These alternatives shift the focus from distress to necessity and strength. Likewise, *eating* can be referred to as intake, nourishment, or even challenging oneself. For instance, you may say to a client, "Overcoming an eating disorder means challenging yourself with new foods" implying that eating is a courageous act, instead of a shameful one.

You'll also find throughout this book language intended to externalize the illness (i.e., referring to the illness as a separate entity). For instance, rather than saying, "Johnny is afraid of pizza," we might say, "Johnny's eating disorder is afraid of pizza" or simply, "The eating disorder is afraid of pizza." Externalizing the illness can play an essential role in treatment, as many with eating disorders feel that they are their illness. By distinguishing the person from the eating disorder, the therapist can join with them and work together to challenge the eating disorder. However, not all you encounter will embrace this distinction. Some may resist the idea that they are separate from their eating disorder; however, when it works, it can be a powerful therapeutic tool.

The Continuum of Care

Eating disorder treatment exists on a continuum, with outpatient treatment acting as its backbone. Higher levels of care (HLOC) are short-term, targeted treatment interventions designed to align severity of ED symptoms with the appropriate level of treatment intensity. HLOCs consist of medical admissions, psychiatric inpatient units, residential treatment, partial hospitalization programs (PHPs), and intensive outpatient programs (IOP). Each level of care provides varying degrees of structure, support, and supervision. As you progress through the levels of care (think about this like going down steps on a ladder, from medical hospitalization at the top to outpatient at the bottom), the client assumes more autonomy over their recovery. That is, they are spending more time managing ED symptoms in the community, rather than in structured programming.

HLOC programs are designed as an intervention for clients whose eating disorder severity requires close medical and behavioral supervision. These are typically short-term interventions, whereas outpatient treatment supports a client over the long term. A client may be referred to a PHP or IOP, and upon discharge, resume working with their outpatient team. This cycle can be repeated multiple times, even at different organizations that provide similar services; however, the idea is for the outpatient team to oversee the client's treatment before, during, and after these short-term interventions.

Although this book is geared toward outpatient treatment, it is important for you to know each level of care and what they entail.

- *Medical hospital:* Reserved for individuals with serious medical complications that cannot be safely managed in the community. These stays are typically brief and aimed solely at medical stabilization.
- *Psychiatric inpatient:* Offers 24/7 supervision and medical oversight. Usually lasts longer than a medical admission. It addresses both acute medical issues and behavioral components of the eating disorder.
- *Residential treatment:* Provides 24/7 therapeutic structure while incorporating community-based interventions that allow clients to begin practicing recovery skills in the community along with the support of a highly structured environment.
- *Partial hospitalization programs (PHPs):* Also called day programs, PHPs typically meet five days a week from morning to late afternoon. They are structured around group therapy, supervised meals, and other therapeutic activities.

- *Intensive outpatient programs (IOPs)*: These programs meet several times per week, often in the evening. They typically offer group therapy and one supervised meal per session. IOP is considered the most flexible and least intensive HLOC option.

Not all with an eating disorder require HLOC treatment. Many clients can thrive in the community with outpatient treatment alone. However, it is important to know that these options exist, and when a client is no longer making progress, or getting worse, in outpatient care, then HLOC should be considered. And importantly, these decisions should never be made in isolation. Because decisions involve behavioral and medical issues, use the multidisciplinary team to determine whether a transition to HLOC is appropriate.

Take Care of Yourself

Almost any therapist you speak with will warn about burnout and the high level of stress associated with working in the mental health field. We hear that clients are sicker, expectations are higher, and the behavioral system itself is increasingly fractured and difficult to navigate. For a therapist working with clients struggling with eating disorders, the high lethality rate and diagnostic complexity can even heighten this anxiety. We believe that to work effectively in this field, you must be cognizant of the emotional stress of your work and, most importantly, you must take deliberate steps every day to take care of yourself.

We encourage all therapists we work with to establish boundaries in their work and to develop a plan for what each can do to nurture themselves. And this can be a big challenge. Taking care of yourself may sound simple, but the truth is that most of us are not so good at it. We feel much better about taking care of others and easily become engrossed in our work, often losing sight of the other side of our lives. We have known many talented therapists who begin their careers with good intentions for self-care, only to see those intentions wane as months and years pass by. Eventually feeling tired and overworked, many look to their employer for support and become disillusioned and angry when that doesn't happen in the time and manner that they might hope. We encourage you to think carefully about what you will do in your life to help you manage the stress and anxiety of your work, to make sure you are healthy and balanced in your life. Here are a few tangible recommendations to start with:

1 Arrive at work on time and leave on time
    There are two points of the day that you can control (mostly). The first is what time you arrive at work, and the second is when you leave.

In truth it is harder to manage the second (when you leave) than the first, and even with the most predictable of jobs there will be times that warrant working late. But in general, create a clear daily boundary for yourself and bookend your workday.

2 Find interests outside of your work that are tangible and doable

It is really the task of a lifetime to find interests that you enjoy and are capable of shifting your attention from work-related stress at the end of the day. While some of us are born with an apparent interest or talent that may make this easy, most of us are not and must search for an interest or passion that gives us a sense of personal satisfaction and pleasure. We encourage you to begin your search right away and to lean toward things that are tangible and doable (which are often very different from the work you do) as well as affordable and accessible. For instance, it's wonderful if sky diving works for you, but in addition to being a bit risky, it's not something you can likely do or afford every day.

And really consider the tangible point. By that we mean something that has a beginning and an end and is measurable in some way. Our work in behavioral health often lacks concrete measures of success or progress. Our clients certainly don't rate us every day, and awards for a job well done are unfortunately infrequent. It is up to you to find that in your personal life. Look toward things like hobbies, regular exercise, and group activities that allow you to learn new things. Most importantly, find something that requires your mind to focus rather than drift into the work you did today.

3 Recognize when you need a break

With our clients, we talk a lot about an observing ego, and it's not bad advice for us. Developing an observing ego is essentially creating a willingness to check in with yourself from time to time to see how you are feeling and to consider where you are on your journey as a therapist, and, importantly, how you are taking care of yourself. As a part of this, notice when you are beginning to become irritated or overly critical of work, yourself, or people in your life. Pay attention to how and what you are saying, and if your affect is telling you that you need a break.

Know that time away from work is as important to your career as the time you spend at work. Although it is difficult (and in some organizations even frowned upon) regular time away from work is critical to your longevity as a therapist and general well-being. Pay close attention to your vacation time and be sure to use it. Most of us get a degree of enjoyment (and relief) from knowing that we have a break coming up and can anticipate our next days away. That feeling of anticipation is an important part of the fun of a vacation. To preserve that, it is always good practice to return from one vacation with a plan for when you will be taking your next days off.

References

American Psychological Association. (2023). Health Advisory on Social Media Use in Adolescence. American Psychological Association. https://www.apa.org/topics/social-media-internet/health-advisory-adolescent-social-media-use

Chesney, E., Goodwin, G. M., & Fazel, S. (2014). Risks of all-cause and suicide mortality in mental disorders: a meta-review. *World Psychiatry*, 13(2): 153–160.

Van Hoeken, D. and Hoek, H.W. Review of the burden of eating disorders: mortality, disability, costs, quality of life, and family burden. Current Opinion Psychiatry, 2020, 33:521–527.

Chapter 2

Diagnosis Meets Practice

A Crash Course in Eating Disorder Assessment

Kameron M. Mendes and Karli Bresnahan

Eating disorder (ED) diagnoses serve a practical purpose, but they often fail to reflect the full complexity of one's relationship to food, eating, or their body. As is the case with any illness, conducting an accurate assessment and obtaining a clear understanding of the client's chief complaint is vital. Alongside this, developing differential diagnoses can help shape the contours of the identified problem as well as possible alternative explanations. However, not every client seeking your help will have a deep, robust, or even accurate understanding of their presenting problem. For example, clients with Anorexia Nervosa (AN) may initially cite bingeing as the problematic behavior that they want, or *need*, to stop, and although their self-reported binge episodes may appear to meet clinical criteria (e.g., consuming an objectively large amount of food, experiencing a loss of control (LOC)), outside of those instances, they engage in severe restrictive behaviors. In this case, would it be accurate to try to resolve the client's bingeing when it could be the natural result of starvation? Therefore, it is essential that the therapist has a deep understanding of each eating disorder's clinical criteria and becomes a skilled assessor by asking the right questions and reviewing important clinical markers.

In contrast, while diagnosis is important for identifying and understanding what you're treating, eating disorder diagnoses provide notoriously little information. It is simply an acknowledgement of a symptom, and plainly, the current state of eating disorder diagnosis provides little insight into the issue at hand. In clinical practice, you'll find that non–eating disorder-informed providers label any disturbance in eating as an "eating disorder," resulting in a wide range of presentations. This variability highlights the importance of understanding the *motivation* behind the behavior, which can be multi-layered. For instance:

Is the client restricting due to a fear of weight gain or drive for thinness?
Does it provide them with a sense of control, safety, or accomplishment?
Are they overeating when they are sad, angry, or lonely?

DOI: 10.4324/9781003600770-3

Do they believe that eating the "wrong" foods will lead to something bad happening? Is this fear justified?

Could their mood be increasing or diminishing their appetite?

Does the client believe that, with every bite of food, their stomach is being filled and that it has nowhere to go?

We have encountered all of these scenarios, each rooted in different underlying issues: major depressive disorder, obsessive-compulsive disorder, psychosis, borderline personality disorder, trauma. At times, it can be difficult to determine the primary diagnosis, as eating behaviors can serve a multitude of emotional or psychological functions.

As is the case with any behavior, eating disorder symptoms are subject to change. A client who presents with an initial diagnosis of Atypical Anorexia Nervosa (i.e., OSFED) can shift to Bulimia Nervosa (BN) or Binge-Eating Disorder (BED) based on several changes in behavior. As it stands, ED diagnoses will give you information about specific behaviors, but not much more. For instance, bulimia, a term that dates back to the late 1800s, translating to simply "nervous ravenous hunger," only characterizes one aspect of the disorder, completely missing that bulimia is comprised of cycles of both bingeing followed by compensatory behaviors (often self-induced vomiting, or *purging*). Moreover, terms like anorexia and bulimia are highly stigmatized in our society, often leading those experiencing an eating disorder to hide in shame, rather than seek treatment (Foran et al., 2020).

You might be asking yourself, "Why do we diagnose eating disorders the way we do?" or "Why keep such stigmatizing terms that may hinder one's motivation to pursue treatment? We should change these things!" There are no easy answers to these questions. Those in the DSM workgroups assume the important and difficult task of quantifying and labeling human behavior, which is particularly difficult to do for behaviors as diverse as eating patterns. In short, they are tasked with an impossible mandate. Partly because of this, protecting consistency (or tradition) while introducing incremental, but meaningful, changes may help to push the field forward slowly over time. For instance, mental health parity laws have helped expand coverage for all feeding and eating disorders to be reimbursable diagnoses by insurance companies – a herculean feat – and drastic changes to this could harm access to care. Likewise, changing eating disorder's conceptualization or terminology when we have such a rudimentary understanding of them should be approached cautiously. However, all of this underscores the importance of understanding ED's diagnostic criteria *and* the behavior's motivation.

In this chapter we will review the following diagnoses as seen in the Diagnostic and Statistical Manual for Mental Illnesses V-TR (APA, 2022): Anorexia Nervosa (AN), Bulimia Nervosa (BN), Binge-Eating Disorder (BED), Avoidant Restrictive Food Intake Disorder (ARFID), Other Specified

Feeding and Eating Disorder (OSFED), Unspecified Feeding or Eating Disorder (UFED). We'll also briefly review the non-clinical diagnoses of Orthorexia and Diabulimia. We will focus primarily on how each diagnosis appears in real-world clinical settings based on our professional experiences as well as supportive research. Finally, we'll present factors that may be helpful to consider as you organize your clinical assessment and contextualize the presenting behaviors. Although this chapter will review notable diagnostic criteria for each diagnosis, we still recommend that you review the DSM-5-TR's (APA, 2022) section on Feeding and Eating Disorders directly.

Anorexia Nervosa

Anorexia Nervosa (AN) is often misunderstood, minimized, or even encouraged. Policies aimed at curbing the "obesity epidemic" in the United States, such as making caloric values on restaurant menus easily identifiable, have led to unhelpful (at best) and harmful (more accurately) consequences that have negatively impacted this vulnerable group. Anorexia is characterized by a restriction of nutritional intake, leading to significantly lower weight than would be expected, which is driven by an intense fear of weight gain. Further, disturbances in the way one views their body's weight or shape, and the over-evaluation of the body on one's self-concept, are also defining features of anorexia.

There are two primary subtypes: Restricting Type (AN-R) and Binge-eating/Purging Type (AN-BP). Restricting-type anorexia is when weight loss is sought through fasting, dieting, or excessive exercise. In binge/purge-type anorexia, cycles of bingeing and purging are the methods used to satisfy the disorder's characteristic drive for thinness. In clinical practice, you will most likely see these two subtypes co-occur. In these cases, we often use the diagnosis that best describes the most prominent behavior over the last several months. For instance, it would be wise to apply the restrictive subtype if a client is only engaging in restriction, or when purging behaviors are sparse or intermittent. In cases where a client is engaging in both restriction and bingeing/purging, but it's unclear which is the primary behavior, assign the binge/purge subtype as it is typically understood that nutritional restriction is also likely to be occurring with an anorexia diagnosis. When assigning severity, research has indicated that the body mass index (BMI) severity specifiers as outlined in the DSM-5-TR (APA, 2022) may not adequately capture severity levels for those with anorexia (Zayas et al., 2018); thus in clinical practice, we're often using clinical symptoms, such as frequency of behavior (i.e., restriction, bingeing, purging, etc.) or medical status (which can include laboratory abnormalities, concerning vital sign readings, among others) to assign severity. Importantly, *biologically appropriate weight* or *target treatment weight*, which both refer to an estimated weight range that is determined by the PCP and

RD of where someone's body weight would be healthiest, is often used in place of BMI to determine weight status and severity.

A common myth about restrictive-type anorexia is the total elimination of food or eating. The reality is that those with AN-R rarely stop eating entirely. It is far more often the case that caloric intake is decreased to an amount that will lead to weight loss and *feel safe*. For example, you may encounter clients who intentionally limit their daily caloric intake to an amount that would lead to weight loss (e.g., eating only 1200 calories per day as opposed to 2000 calories per day); however, this number is subject to change day-to-day, and often downward, based on the severity of eating disorder thoughts or urges. It is also common that, prior to the start of the eating disorder, those with AN-R greatly enjoyed food or eating, although since the ED, the prospect of consuming those once-beloved foods instills a sense of fear, guilt, or anxiety.

In these cases, although food or calories are often the "problem," we need to dig beneath that, and upon deeper inspection, we see that it is not the food they are afraid of, but the consequence of eating it (e.g., perceived weight gain). As therapists, we're not necessarily equipped to argue with an eating disorder about food and nutrition – we are going to lose that battle every time. But conversations about food or eating have less to do with our lack of expertise, and more to do with the fact that we're not actually talking about food or nutrition: we're talking about *fear*–and we therapists know a thing or two about how to explore and manage fear. So, try not to fall into the "food trap." That is, if you find yourself arguing about nutrition with a client or getting into an unending and impossible conversation about food or eating, shift to talking about the fear that's associated with food or eating.

Motivation

Increasing motivation for recovery is often a key therapeutic goal for those with anorexia. In clinical practice, you will encounter various levels of motivation toward recovery. Anorexia is often characterized by a lack of motivation to recover or *ambivalence*. That is, to those with anorexia, the benefit of engaging in restrictive or compensatory behaviors to lose weight far outweighs the negative aspects of engaging in the behaviors (things like hunger pangs, family discord at the dinner table, medical complications, challenges at work or school, or the unpleasantness of purging). To the eating disorder, these negative side effects are seen as the costs of doing business in the service of the more important goal of being thinner or not gaining weight.

This speaks to the ego-syntonic nature of anorexia. The term *ego-syntonic* refers to thoughts, feelings, and behaviors that are in harmony with a person's self-image and values. This is when there is an alignment between the eating disorder's thoughts or urges and the client's sense of self and goals, which typically does not cause the client distress or create a desire for change. In contrast, ego-*dystonic* traits are those that conflict with a person's self-concept and cause them anxiety or stress. Those with anorexia perceive that these behaviors, albeit maladaptive, serve a purpose and fulfill an unmet need.

It is often the case that those with anorexia minimize the severity of their illness. Even those that require a higher level of care treatment, exhibit critical lab values, dangerously low weight, long medical or psychiatric hospitalizations, experiencing cardiac events, or receiving nutrition through feeding tubes will often say it "wasn't *that* bad." Any one of these examples could be classified as "hitting rock bottom"; however, to an ED, it could always be worse. And despite pursuing treatment (whether of their own accord or at the urging of family, friends, or providers), it is common for those with anorexia to remain ambivalent toward recovery (e.g., unsure they want to relinquish their ED). You will likely hear clients say, "I want to get better, but I also don't want to get fat." As a therapist, you're going to want to tease apart the meaning of "I want to get better," since the drive for thinness or fear of weight gain (i.e., "I don't want to get fat") is a core element of anorexia. What does "get better" mean? Is it possible to "get better" from anorexia, while holding on to its core component? This approach is likely to result in a pseudo-recovery where food, weight, and body image continue to dictate one's decision-making around eating or food. Full recovery under these conditions is unlikely to occur.

Body Mass Index

There is lively discussion in the eating disorder world about whether body weight should factor into diagnosis for anorexia. There are those who argue that because anorexic symptoms are seen in all body types, weight, shapes, and sizes, body weight should not play a role in its diagnosis. However, being low weight has traditionally been linked with the way anorexia was conceptualized. Any individual who meets all of the other diagnostic criteria for anorexia but is not considered low weight is classified as Atypical Anorexia Nervosa in the diagnostic category of Other Specified Feeding or Eating Disorder (OSFED). Although the DSM-5-TR (APA, 2022) uses BMI to denote the severity of the illness, being "low weight" continues as part of the topline diagnostic criterion that many practitioners argue has little to do with anorexia.

Although the distinction between Anorexia and Atypical Anorexia Nervosa (e.g., experiencing all symptoms of anorexia, except being at a normative or above-normative weight; see more about this in the OSFED section) continues, recent research has highlighted that there are few physiological and psychological differences between the two diagnoses (Walsh et al., 2023).

For instance, you will likely encounter severely emaciated individuals that are considered *medically stable* (e.g., vital signs and labs are within normal limits), and conversely, you will find individuals with higher BMIs that have dangerous lab values, such as low potassium, sodium, or phosphorus, marking severe malnutrition. While it may be true that, with continued ED behaviors or weight loss, the individual who is emaciated may experience similar medical complications, the individual with a higher BMI is experiencing those complications *now*. Therefore, it is important for you to know that both of these presentations, regardless of one's weight, require immediate intervention.

Case Vignette: Anorexia Nervosa

Sarah is presenting to your practice due to worsening restriction. She is the star athlete on her college's cross-country team, and during the season, she is running upwards of 20 miles per week, strength training with the team on non-run days, and routinely staying after practice to get in further training miles (e.g., compensatory behaviors). Despite the characteristic drive for thinness and fear that weight gain may negatively impact her cross-country performance, she is able to eat most of her meal plan and is clear that this is only so that she doesn't pass out at practice. During the offseason, she decides that she no longer needs to eat what her meal plan dictates (e.g., restriction) because she's not training as much, although she continues to train more than is required by her coaching staff (e.g., continued compensation). After a while, she develops microfractures in her ankles, making her unable to train or compete at all. Suddenly, she finds that the restriction worsens, and bouts of purging emerge as she's unable to engage in exercise.

In this case vignette, Sarah's presentation aligns with a restrictive eating disorder, specifically Anorexia Nervosa, Restricting type. Restriction and compensatory behaviors (i.e., excessive exercise) are evident, as well as the ego-syntonic nature of her illness (e.g., believing that thinness will help her performance, or conversely that gaining weight will negatively affect her performance). Physical injuries are common in those who are malnourished and over-exercising, which consequently puts them in the position of being unable to engage in physical compensatory behaviors, often resulting in worsening or changing ED behaviors. Sarah's vignette highlights how behaviors can change in response to life circumstances, which may require a change in diagnostic specifier if purging continues.

Bulimia Nervosa

BN is characterized by recurrent cycles of binge eating followed by compensatory behaviors aimed at preventing weight gain. Binge eating involves consuming an objectively large quantity of food within a short period, accompanied by a loss of control (LOC). In response, individuals with bulimia engage in various maladaptive weight control strategies, such as self-induced vomiting, excessive exercise, or the misuse of laxatives, diuretics, or other medications. Importantly, compensatory behaviors are not unique to bulimia, as individuals with anorexia may also engage in similar compensatory behaviors, like purging or excessive exercise routines.

Individuals with bulimia often tie their self-worth to body weight, shape, and size, and frequently experience a fear of weight gain. However, unlike those with anorexia, individuals with bulimia typically maintain a weight within or above the normal range. This distinction in weight status can be a useful diagnostic marker: when a client is engaging in bingeing behaviors followed by compensatory weight control measures and their body weight is significantly below the expected range, a diagnosis of anorexia should be considered.

Among the compensatory behaviors, purging, or self-induced vomiting, is the most common. It is typically done in secret, and because individuals with bulimia often appear to be within a normal weight range, the behavior can go unnoticed (especially if unreported). While purging is rarely described as pleasurable, many individuals characterize it as addictive, due to the immediate sense of relief following the purging episode. This temporary reduction in distress is often related to the perception that the act of purging has averted weight gain; however, this relief is often short-lived and may be followed by ongoing distress, particularly if the individual does not feel "empty enough," which may result in continued purging until their metrics of "empty" and "enough" are satisfied. Likewise, it is common that intense feelings of shame and guilt are present following a purge episode.

Repeated purging can lead to serious medical complications. Over time, purging may become easier or even involuntary, as is sometimes observed in cases of *rumination*, where food is involuntarily regurgitated and re-swallowed. In contrast, others may find their ability to purge becomes increasingly difficult as their gag reflex diminishes, leading them to adopt more extreme methods to induce vomiting. For example, when fingers are no longer effective, some may resort to using tools such as spoons or toothbrushes. In cases where purging appears involuntary, intervention can become more challenging due to the perception that the client cannot control it – but these behaviors still qualify as purging and require targeted treatment.

Motivation

Individuals with bulimia often experience similar motivational challenges as those with anorexia nervosa. Compensatory behaviors, although unpleasant, are frequently viewed as necessary, effective tools to ward off the intense fear of weight gain or becoming "fat," and are oftentimes described as "addictive." More specifically, self-induced vomiting is perceived as a quick fix, offering immediate relief and a reduction in distress after binge eating. Yet, this does not necessarily mean that individuals *want* to be engaging in these behaviors. The urge for immediate relief can be so powerful that even harmful actions like purging become seen as necessary.

In contrast to anorexia, bulimia is typically ego-dystonic, as there is an awareness that self-induced vomiting or medication misuse is dangerous and does not align with their values. In today's internet age, access to health information makes it easier than ever to research the risks; however, minimization of the illness's severity is still common. Phrases like "It's not that bad," "It used to be way worse," or "Purging makes me feel better" reflect a mindset that downplays the seriousness of the behavior and serves to sustain it. Consequently, the idea of giving up compensatory behaviors (without a perceived alternative means of controlling weight) can feel threatening and provoke resistance.

Severity

The DSM-5-TR (APA, 2022) classifies the severity of bulimia on a spectrum from mild to extreme, based on the weekly frequency of compensatory behaviors. In clinical practice, however, symptom frequency often fluctuates. Many individuals with bulimia experience periods of consistent compensatory behaviors that last weeks or months, followed by stretches of minimal engagement that may fall below the diagnostic threshold. Conversely, some clients purge daily or even after every meal or snack. In such cases, it is essential to collaborate closely with the medical provider on the multidisciplinary team to assess and monitor the client's medical stability.

Distinguishing Bulimia from Anorexia and Binge-Eating Disorder

In practice, bulimia and anorexia, binge/purge subtype (AN-BP), can be difficult to distinguish due to the significant overlap in presenting symptoms. Both often involve periods of dietary restriction followed by binge eating and compensatory behaviors. Additionally, self-evaluation based on body weight and shape is central to both diagnoses, further complicating their differentiation.

Cross-over between diagnoses is common. Eddy et al. (2008) found, in a sample of 216 women whose treatment was followed over the course of 7 years, that it was far more likely that those with an intake diagnosis of anorexia transition to bulimia, rather than from bulimia to anorexia (about one-third of their sample transitioned from anorexia to bulimia, whereas only 14% transitioned from bulimia to anorexia). They also found that over 85% of those with AN-BP experienced cross-over to either restrictive-type anorexia or bulimia, raising questions about the utility and clarity of current diagnostic subtypes, given this frequent overlap.

In contrast, distinguishing bulimia from restrictive-type anorexia and BED is more straightforward, as both AN-R and BED do not include overt compensatory behaviors, such as purging. However, the picture is not always clear: individuals with restrictive-type anorexia may engage in excessive exercise, which can serve a similar compensatory function. Likewise, they may also report episodes of *subjective binge eating* (i.e., perceiving a normal amount of food to be incredibly large, while also perceiving a LOC). This is believed to be a response to starvation and losing control of their ability to maintain extreme restrictive behaviors, rather than the LOC that is typical of binge-eating. These nuances underscore the importance of careful assessment and observation in establishing accurate diagnoses.

Case Vignette: Bulimia Nervosa

Robert is a 52-year-old divorced white cisgender male referred to your practice after meeting with his new PCP due to longstanding bingeing and purging behaviors. Robert's bingeing and purging started when he was 18 years old after a difficult experience transitioning into college several states away from his family and friends. Being isolated and having trouble making friends in this new environment, Robert started working out, thinking that if he looked better, people would like him more. Over the years, his symptoms endured, although there had been several instances where he went a couple of years without engaging in any bingeing or purging. Recently, during a high-conflict divorce, the behaviors returned. Usually, bingeing starts in the evening after dinner, followed by several rounds of purging late into the night before going to bed. Upon waking, he feels guilty and remorseful, vowing to himself that he will never binge or purge again, and that he will start out "fresh" this morning by having only an English muffin for breakfast and a salad for lunch in an effort to assuage his guilt over what had occurred the previous evening.

As can be gleaned from this case vignette, Robert's behaviors would recede for a time before coming back into his life in response to significant life stressors. Self-evaluation of his body was central to the formation of the disorder; for instance, he started working out, thinking that people would like him more if his body conformed to societal ideals. He also used restriction (i.e., the next day following purging) as a means of coping with the guilt and regret he was experiencing, attempting to use food to remedy his feelings of disgust; however, this will likely only set him up for another binge, or at least make it more likely.

Binge Eating Disorder

BED is one of the most common of the eating disorders in the United States as prevalence rates are estimated to be nearly double that of anorexia and bulimia, combined (Qian et al., 2021). Officially added to the APA's

DSM-5 in 2013, it constitutes a relatively new diagnosis, although it was originally introduced in the 1950s.

The DSM-5-TR (APA, 2022) breaks down the behavioral component of a "binge" into two parts: the first is how long the binge lasts and how much is eaten, and the second is a perceived LOC. The quantity of food consumed in a two-hour period of time must be "definitely larger" than what others may eat, given similar time parameters. This doesn't mean that a binge *has to* last two hours; rather, within that time, a LOC is experienced, and an objectively large amount of food is consumed.

In clinical practice, it is not uncommon that bingeing episodes are shorter than the two-hour benchmark. Schreiber-Gregory et al. (2013) found, in a study that aimed to measure binge eating duration using a technique called ecological momentary assessment (e.g., where participants provide real-time updates about binge eating behaviors, usually using a cell-phone app or similar device), that the average binge eating episode lasted 42 minutes, and ranged from 2 minutes to 2.6 hours. Also, they found that the length of a binge did not impact symptom severity, as those with longer binge episodes exhibited similar eating disorder symptoms to those with shorter binge episodes, and that binges are more likely to occur on weekdays, rather than weekends, typically in the afternoon or evenings (Schreiber-Gregory et al., 2013).

The second component of binge-eating is experiencing a LOC, or an overwhelming feeling that one cannot avoid a binge or stop eating once underway. Pollert et al. (2013) identified LOC as a distinguishing feature of binge-eating, finding significantly higher levels of LOC reported among individuals with binge eating disorder compared to those without. Additionally, LOC has been shown to contribute to the psychological distress associated with binge-eating, including elevated rates of depression and poorer overall mental health (Colles et al., 2008). In clinical practice, LOC can manifest in various ways: clients may report memory lapses during binge episodes, experience intense and intrusive urges to eat, or feel heightened anxiety around specific foods that trigger these urges.

Importantly, LOC is not simply a matter of willpower (despite societal fat-phobic narratives that suggest otherwise), and you may find that clients have differing perceptions of what constitutes a "binge" and "loss of control." For example, Gloria stated, "I binged last night. I ate 3 scoops of ice cream and finished my partner's bowl which was another 2 scoops. I just couldn't help myself." Does Gloria's statement qualify as a binge? Even though the quantity of food she consumed is not necessarily larger than what others would eat?

Binge-eating is not necessarily limited to eating large portions. The DSM-5-TR (APA, 2022), outlines five patterns typically seen in binge-eating episodes, requiring a minimum of three to be present for formal diagnosis: eating very quickly, eating to the point of uncomfortable fullness, eating substantial amounts of foods when not experiencing physical hunger cues, avoiding eating with people due to embarrassment about amount of food eaten, experiencing feelings of self-disgust, sadness, or intense guilt after eating.

In Gloria's case, to determine whether or not her description meets the criteria for a binge episode, further questions are necessary. Does the statement "I just couldn't help myself" describe a LOC? Has there been significant weight gain that may hint at other instances of uncontrollable overeating? How did the extra two scoops of ice cream make her feel – disgusted, embarrassed, guilty? Are there other episodes of eating large amounts in secrecy, such as hoarding food, eating very quickly, eating food that has spoiled or been thrown out, or family members finding food wrappers hidden away? Whether Gloria ate an objectively large amount of food is not the only necessary factor for diagnosis. If the client perceives their eating to be out of control and is causing them distress, these are indicators to find out more about their relationship with food and what is contributing to their perception that their eating behaviors are problematic.

Interestingly, binge-eating has been thought to be a result of dietary restriction, although supporting evidence on this idea is mixed. In a study examining eating patterns in those with BED, Harvey et al. (2011) found that fewer than 10% consistently ate all three meals per day, with breakfast being the least likely meal to be consumed, and dinner being the most likely. Likewise, Zunker et al. (2011) found in an EMA study examining those with bulimia that recent restriction increased the likelihood of a binge episode. Conversely, another study looking at those with bulimia found that those who ate frequent, small, or low-calorie meals were less likely to binge (although this study used self-report measures that asked about eating behaviors over the past month, which are not as accurate as EMA studies, which ask about behaviors in real-time daily). Recently, in an EMA study of those with BED, Bartholomay et al. (2024) found no evidence that dietary restriction led to binge-eating, concluding that although restriction may play a role in binge-eating for other diagnoses (like bulimia), it may not be as pronounced in those with BED. Despite these mixed findings, the point remains that those with BED maintain a chaotic and inconsistent relationship with food, often leading to feelings of shame, guilt, or embarrassment. Unfortunately, these feelings can prevent those in need from reaching out for help or talking with the people closest to them. Instead, as is the case with most eating disorders, the tendency is to hide the behaviors, which only serves to reinforce them.

Lastly, it's important to be aware that the term "binge" is commonly used in a variety of contexts in our culture to describe engaging in an abundance of something: "I binged my favorite Netflix show for hours last night" or "I binge drank last weekend." Because this word is used so commonly used and in differing situations, it may not always be an accurate depiction of what someone is experiencing. Thus, providers should take care to ask clarifying questions while also being mindful of the ways in which they're using these terms. Referring to "bingeing" a TV show when talking to a client who is experiencing severe distress from this behavior may show a lack of empathy that could harm the therapeutic alliance.

Case Vignette: Binge-Eating Disorder

Lucy is a 15-year-old female who presents to your outpatient therapy practice at the recommendation of her pediatrician due to gaining 30 lbs in the last 10 months while also experiencing low mood and becoming increasingly withdrawn from her friends. In the intake session, Lucy disclosed eating large amounts of food, 2–3 times per week – typically in secret, and often late at night – followed by intense feelings of guilt and shame. She endorsed feeling "out of control" during these times and would only stop when she felt physically ill. Her mother has also found hundreds of food wrappers in her bedroom. These behaviors started about a year ago, around the same time that Lucy witnessed her father have a heart attack. Additionally, Lucy endorsed extremely low self-esteem and high levels of body dissatisfaction, citing bullying from peers over the past several years as the primary reason with her recent weight gain exacerbating these feelings. When asked how she coped with these external stressors, she said, "eating helps get my mind off things that are upsetting, even if it's just for a little while."

Lucy meets the diagnostic criteria for binge-eating disorder (i.e., eating large amounts of food in a short period of time, and experiencing a LOC). She can insightfully describe the psychosocial stressors that have contributed to these behaviors, and that eating, albeit distressing and at times physically uncomfortable, provides an escape from these uncomfortable feelings. When we hear stories like Lucy's, we think: *without this eating disorder, how would Lucy have coped with all of this?* In practice, you will hear stories very much like Lucy's, and the answer to that question will often be a combination of support, validation, and skills building to help Lucy cope in more effective ways.

Avoidant Restrictive Food Intake Disorder

Avoidant Restrictive Food Intake Disorder (ARFID) was added to the DSM-5 in 2013. Often characterized as "extreme picky eating," ARFID typically presents early in life and maintains throughout the lifespan. Even those seeking treatment later in life report longstanding selective eating issues dating back to their youth. With this in mind, at face value, ARFID may seem static or unchanging; however, we have found that with treatment (and persistence), once narrow food options can be increased to adequate levels. Suffice to say, those with ARFID are unlikely to ever achieve "foodie" status; however, their relationship with food can markedly improve.

The Three Types

ARFID is an eating disturbance with three main presentations: aversive food experiences, sensory difficulties, and a general lack of interest in eating or food (APA, 2022). Aversive experiences refer to events that create fear or anxiety around eating, leading to the avoidance of specific items or entire categories of food; for example, a child choking on a hot dog or hard candy may no longer eat foods that are cylindrical or round. However, aversive events do not necessarily have to be overtly related to food. Experiencing a severe illness, food poisoning, or stomach virus that involves an inability to tolerate eating without vomiting can also qualify as aversive experiences. Similarly, children who have experienced significant medical issues, requiring feeding tubes or gastrointestinal issues like severe acid reflux, may also be at increased risk.

The second type of ARFID presentation revolves around sensory difficulties related to food or eating. Sensitivity around food's texture, smell, taste, or a combination of these things leads to feelings of disgust and revulsion, making eating these foods intolerable. These sensitivities are not merely preferences, but can provoke intense aversion and anxiety, leading to a significantly limited range of acceptable foods. Many with ARFID experience heightened sensory processing, making certain textures feel overwhelming or certain smells intolerably strong. Sensory avoidance can make it difficult to tolerate new foods or even variations of familiar ones, contributing to nutritional deficiencies. Further, sensory difficulties seen in ARFID are also often seen in individuals with autism or ADHD, and may further exacerbate food sensitivities (Watts et al., 2023).

Finally, lack of interest in food or lethargy around eating is the third type of ARFID. Disengagement or disinterest in food or eating can manifest as a general lack of appetite, low motivation to eat, or an absence of hunger cues. In practice, these individuals may simply not feel compelled to eat, may forget meals entirely, or view eating as a chore that can lead to a cycle of inadequate nutrition leading to fatigue, reduced energy, and lower cognitive and physical functioning, which further decreases the drive to consume food. Impairments of hunger and fullness (i.e., satiety) cues are common among this population.

Regardless of presentation, "preferred foods" are often hedonic, bland, and consistent in texture, such as French fries, chicken fingers, pop-tarts, cereal, or pizza. However, these preferences vary by individual, so it isn't uncommon to encounter somewhat unusual preferences, such as dried seaweed chips, fish eggs, or cheese-whizz. Preferences can also be highly specific with some individuals only eating certain brands of food, or preferring a particular item from one specific restaurant, or requiring that food be prepared in a very precise manner.

As is the case for anyone eating the same foods over and over, it is common that those with ARFID cycle through foods. Eating large amounts of the same thing can get boring; however, with ARFID, this boredom can lead down a slippery slope if the client does not similarly add foods into their repertoire. This can contribute to an increasingly narrow variety of acceptable foods. For instance, if they were relying on four or five foods for the bulk of their nutritional intake, any reduction in variety without replacing it with another food of similar or greater nutritional value can be dangerous.

Motivation

ARFID is interesting when it comes to motivation. Unlike anorexia and bulimia, those with ARFID can be either highly motivated or completely disinterested in addressing this issue. Fear and disinterest around food are likely to be the most significant barriers to improvement. Celebrating a completed challenge does not necessarily come with feelings of guilt, which is common in anorexia, so as a therapist, you may find that you're able to celebrate the client's feat with positive affirmations and praise, rather than the more muted approach that is typical of anorexia.

ARFID and Anorexia

Because ARFID involves intentional restriction, it is important to distinguish it from anorexia. Similar to anorexia, those with ARFID are often underweight–either they have fallen off their growth curve or have maintained their weight on the low end of the growth curve for most of their lives. However, those with ARFID do not experience the drive for thinness that is characteristic of anorexia; in other words, a desire to be skinnier or fear of weight gain does not play a central role behind ARFID's restrictive eating patterns. On the contrary, those with ARFID often agree that they need to gain weight and can easily and enthusiastically align with that goal. If the fear of weight gain, or a desire to be thin, appears to be a core driver of restriction, an ARFID diagnosis should be reconsidered in favor of anorexia or other-specified feeding or eating disorder. However, as we've mentioned before, clinical practice is rarely as well defined as the DSM. We can, and do, see ARFID and body image disturbance (or fear of eating due to calorie or body change concerns) co-occur. In these instances, it is often the case that kids who develop ARFID at a young age start to experience body image concerns in late childhood or early adolescence that contribute to their already problematic restrictive eating patterns. Of note, pathological fear of weight gain or drive for thinness is different from "normative" body dissatisfaction or striving for societal ideals of beauty, which may appear in those with ARFID as it would in any individual.

Case Vignettes: ARFID

Isabelle is an 8-year-old female, referred to your practice by his outpatient pediatrician for concerns about her eating after ruling out the possibility of an underlying medical condition for her symptoms. Since a young age, Isabelle has always had difficulty eating. Her parents describe a child who would "eat anything" as they first introduced foods, but as she grew into toddlerhood, she became increasingly picky, preferring bland, single-textured, carb-heavy foods. She typically only eats five foods and can eat them every day for months on end. Isabelle has been unable to eat at a restaurant without significant preparation, such as researching the menu before going or calling to ensure they can make food that she would eat or bringing a separate meal. Despite these challenges, Isabelle has tracked well on the growth curve; however, after transitioning into a new school, Isabelle has stopped eating several of her preferred foods and has lost several pounds as a result.

In this case vignette, Isabelle is in quite a predicament! She is struggling with sensory and texture issues related to food with an onset at a very young age and associated psychosocial impairment (Criterion 1D) and weight loss (Criterion 1A). Her condition was seemingly exacerbated by the transition into a new school, which often occurs, as stress tends to worsen ARFID's restrictive behaviors.

Rick is a 47-year-old single, cisgender male referred by his outpatient psychiatrist due to concerns about his lack of food variety and psychosocial impairment. Rick has been eating six foods for as long as he can remember. He has not eaten any food that is cylindrical since choking on a hot dog when he was seven years old. He reports that his parents never had any concerns about his eating until after the choking episode, when he started experiencing anxiety when eating. Days can go by with little intake, often forgetting to eat or just "not feeling like it." Recently, he and his long-time partner broke up after arguing about where to go to eat – an all-too-common argument throughout their relationship. Since then, he has been having difficulty dating, as he typically orders from the children's menu, leading to feelings of shame and embarrassment.

In this vignette, Rick's presentation is a combination of disinterest in food, seemingly after experiencing an aversive food-related event. He is also experiencing significant psychosocial stress (Criterion 1D), as he recently lost a relationship, in part, related to this issue, and has also been experiencing difficulty dating. Because he was referred by a physician, we can assume that his condition is not a result of an underlying medical issue, although we might recommend a follow-up with his primary care physician if his medical standing is unknown. In the context of differential diagnoses, we may also be thinking about post-traumatic stress disorder related to his aversive choking experience as well as attention deficit/hyperactivity disorder, as lack of appetite is a common symptom of ADHD.

Other Specified Feeding or Eating Disorder

Other-Specified Feeding or Eating Disorder (OSFED) is the most common eating disorder diagnosis (Micali et al., 2017). It occurs when an individual exhibits symptoms that are typical of a feeding or eating disorder, which causes significant distress or interferes with daily functioning. A collection of five "subthreshold" diagnoses, they do not meet the full diagnostic criteria for "full threshold" disorders, such as anorexia, bulimia, or binge-eating disorder.

1 *Atypical Anorexia Nervosa*: Meeting all criteria for anorexia nervosa, but (even in the presence of significant weight loss) weight remains within or above normal range.
2 *Bulimia Nervosa (Low Frequency/Short Duration)*: Bulimia symptoms that occur less than once weekly or under three months.
3 *Binge-Eating Disorder (Low Frequency/Short Duration)*: Binge episodes that occur less than once weekly or under three months.
4 *Purging Disorder*: Purging (i.e., self-induced vomiting, laxative/diuretic misuse, etc.) to control weight/shape without binge eating.
5 *Night Eating Syndrome*: Regular eating after waking or late evening with awareness, causing distress.

OSFED gives clinicians the ability to note why the presentation does not meet the full criteria for a particular disorder by recording "other specified feeding or eating disorder," followed by the reason (e.g., "binge-eating disorder, short duration").

Lastly, as previously mentioned, Atypical Anorexia Nervosa is hotly contested in the eating disorder field, as it prevents providers from making a full-threshold anorexia diagnosis based solely on the client's weight, something that has little to do with the illness's severity or associated medical complications. As such, it's important not to underestimate OSFED. Whether labeled "sub" or "full" threshold, the psychological, functional, and medical consequences can be just as severe. Again we are reminded of the difficulty in diagnosing a *behavior*, as our behaviors can shift rapidly in response to many factors.

Unspecified Feeding or Eating Disorder

UFED is intended to be used when there are clearly symptoms related to feeding or eating that are causing significant distress or functional impairment, but there is not enough information to make a more specific diagnosis. This is in contrast to OSFED, where there is enough information to make a specific diagnosis (i.e., OSFED), but the symptom profile does not meet the clinical criteria of a full-threshold ED. In UFED, impairment due to a feeding or eating disorder is evident, but you lack enough information to make a more formal diagnosis. UFED can be used as a "placeholder" or initial diagnosis, such as upon admission to an acute care facility, wherein a UFED diagnosis is made with the intention to update it to something more specific once more information has been gathered.

Orthorexia and Diabulimia

Orthorexia and Diabulimia are not diagnoses contained within the DSM; however, they are well-known within the eating disorder community. A term coined by Bratman and Knight (1997), Orthorexia is characterized by an unhealthy obsession with eating foods perceived as "pure" and "clean" and restricting foods that do not meet these criteria. Koven and Abry (2015) describe:

> Orthorexia individuals are typically concerned by the quality, as opposed to the quantity, of food in one's diet, spending considerable time scrutinizing the source (e.g., whether vegetables have been exposed to pesticides; whether dairy products came from hormone-supplemented cows), processing (e.g., whether nutritional content was lost during cooking; whether micronutrients, artificial flavoring, or preservatives were added), and packaging (e.g., whether food may contain plastic-derived carcinogenic compounds; whether labels provide enough information to judge the quality of specific ingredients) of foods that are then sold in the marketplace.
>
> (p. 386)

Like anorexia, individuals with orthorexia may significantly restrict their food intake, eliminate entire food groups, follow rigid food rules, or experience anxiety, guilt, or shame when they deviate from their self-imposed standards. However, unlike anorexia, orthorexia is primarily driven by a desire for health, control, or moral virtue through dietary choices instead of weight or body image concerns. In practice, it is common to see a combination of weight or body image-related concerns and extreme "clean" eating. In other words, it's common to find those with anorexia experience significant orthorexic components.

Diabulimia is an informal term used to describe an eating disorder in individuals with Type 1 diabetes who intentionally restrict or omit insulin in order to lose weight. Manipulating insulin is a medically dangerous behavior. Without sufficient insulin, the body is unable to absorb glucose for energy and instead begins breaking down fat and muscle, leading to rapid weight loss. Individuals with diabulimia may exhibit classic eating disorder symptoms, such as body dissatisfaction, a preoccupation with weight, and restrictive eating, alongside patterns of intentional insulin restriction. Diabulimia is a highly dangerous eating disorder subtype that can lead to immediate and severe consequences. Those with diabulimia are likely to have frequent episodes of diabetic ketoacidosis (DKA). It is best to involve the usual components of the multidisciplinary team (physician and registered dietitian), along with the client's endocrinologist (who usually collaborates directly with the physician and dietitian).

References

American Psychiatric Association. (2022). Diagnostic and statistical manual of mental disorders (5th ed., text rev.). https://doi.org/10.1176/appi.books.9780890425787

Bartholomay, J., Schaefer, L. M., Forester, G., Crosby, R. D., Peterson, C. B., Crow, S. J., Engel, S. G., Wonderlich, S. A. (2024). Evaluating dietary restriction as a maintaining factor in binge-eating disorder. *International Journal of Eating Disorders*, 57(5), 1172–1180. DOI: 10.1002/eat.24094

Bratman, S., Knight, D. (1997). Health food junkie. *Yoga J*, 136(1), 42–50.

Colles, S. L., Dixon, J. B., O'Brien, P. E. (2008). Loss of control is central to psychological disturbance associated with binge eating disorder. *Obesity*, 16(3), 608–614. doi:10.1038/oby.2007.99

Eddy, K. T., Dorer, D. J., Franko, D. L., Tahilani, K., Thompson-Brenner, H., Herzog, D. B. (2008). Diagnostic crossover in anorexia nervosa and bulimia nervosa: implications for DSM-V. *American Journal of Psychiatry*, 165(2), 245–250.

Foran, A. M., O'Donnell, A. T., Muldoon, O. T. (2020). Stigma of eating disorders and recovery-related outcomes: A systematic review. *European Eating Disorders Review*, 28(4), 385–397.

Harvey, K., Rosselli, F., Wilson, G. T., DeBar, L. L., Striegel-Moore, R. H. (2011). Eating patterns in patients with spectrum binge-eating disorder. *International Journal of Eating Disorders*, 44(5), 447–451. doi:10.1002/eat.20839

Koven, N. S., Abry, A. W. (2015). The clinical basis of orthorexia nervosa: emerging perspectives. *Neuropsychiatric disease and treatment*, 385–394. https://doi.org/10.2147/NDT.S61665

Micali, N., Martini, M. G., Thomas, J. J., Eddy, K. T., Kothari, R., Russell, E., Bulik, C., Treasure, J. (2017). Lifetime and 12-month prevalence of eating disorders amongst women in mid-life: a population-based study of diagnoses and risk factors. *BMC Medicine*, 15, 1–10. DOI 10.1186/s12916-016-0766-4

Pollert, G. A., Engel, S. G., Schreiber-Gregory, D. N., Crosby, R. D., Cao, L., Wonderlich, S. A., Tanofsky-Kraff, M., Mitchell, J. E. (2013). The role of eating and emotion in binge eating disorder and loss of control eating. *International Journal of Eating Disorders*, 46(3), 233–238. doi:10.1002/eat.22061

Qian, J., Wu, Y., Liu, F., Zhu, Y., Jin, H., Zhang, H., ... Yu, D. (2021). An update on the prevalence of eating disorders in the general population: a systematic review and meta-analysis. *Eating and Weight Disorders-Studies on Anorexia, Bulimia and Obesity*, 1–14. https://doi.org/10.1007/s40519-021-01162-z

Schreiber-Gregory, D. N., Lavender, J. M., Engel, S. G., Wonderlich, S. A., Crosby, R. D., Peterson, C. B., Simonich, H., Crow, S., Durkin, N., Mitchell, J. E. (2013). Examining duration of binge eating episodes in binge eating disorder. *International Journal of Eating Disorders*, 46(8), 810–814. doi:10.1002/eat.22164

Walsh, B. T., Hagan, K. E., & Lockwood, C. (2023). A systematic review comparing atypical anorexia nervosa and anorexia nervosa. *International journal of eating disorders*, 56(4), 798–820.

Watts, R., Archibald, T., Hembry, P., Howard, M., Kelly, C., Loomes, R., Markham, L., Moss, H., Munuve, A., Orcos, A., Siddall, A., Rhind, C., Uddin, M., Adman, Z., Bryant-Waugh, R., Hübel, C. (2023). The clinical presentation of avoidant restrictive food intake disorder in children and adolescents is largely independent of sex, autism spectrum disorder and anxiety traits. *EClinicalMedicine*, 63. https://doi.org/10.1016/j.eclinm.2023.102190

Zayas, L. V., Wang, S. B., Coniglio, K., Becker, K., Murray, H. B., Klosterman, E., Kay, B., Bean, P., Weltzin, T., Franko, D., Eddy, K., Thomas, J. J. (2018). Gender differences in eating disorder psychopathology across DSM-5 severity categories of anorexia nervosa and bulimia nervosa. *International Journal of Eating Disorders*, 51(9), 1098–1102.

Zunker, C., Peterson, C. B., Crosby, R. D., Cao, L., Engel, S. G., Mitchell, J. E., & Wonderlich, S. A. (2011). Ecological momentary assessment of bulimia nervosa: does dietary restriction predict binge eating? *Behaviour Research and Therapy*, 49(10), 714–717.

Chapter 3

A Recovered Person Speaks to Therapists

Cheryl Kerrigan

Is being fully recovered even possible? Will I always be in recovery? Does anyone fully recover from their eating disorder, or do they just learn to manage it? These are some questions you will be asked from clients, parents, relatives, friends, or loved ones. Separately, you might have asked yourself the same questions as it relates to your clients and contemplated the answers. Well, I am here to assure you that being fully recovered from an eating disorder is possible and does exist. In this chapter, I will share with you my background, experience, wisdom, and guidelines to help you help your clients believe it for themselves. And for you to believe it too, for yourself and for them.

First, let me begin by telling you about myself, my background, and how I got here. A key to note for clarity as you read this chapter is that what is discussed throughout is my perspective of my eating disorder. It is based on psychotherapist Thom Rutledge's method of identifying the eating disorder as a destructive relationship with a person named Ed rather than a condition. Thom was one of my therapists during my recovery, and his "separation metaphor" of personifying my eating disorder as a unique entity was instrumental in my success. I will speak about specifics on how this happened for me later in the chapter. Also note, I will refer to my eating disorder as Ed during my early life, as well. I have done this for the sake of clarity.

When It All Began

I came into the world two and a half months early and weighed only three pounds. The doctors didn't think I would survive, but I did. I heard my birth story many times, so I knew I had been born a preemie. Family members doted over me and commented on my small stature. I felt early on that being small was like my own superpower and made me unique in so many ways – a truth I heard that made me feel special. Unfortunately, I wasn't the only one listening; Ed heard it too.

My struggle with eating disorder thoughts began when I was five years old. Ed told me if I wanted to be loved, special, and unique, I needed to

DOI: 10.4324/9781003600770-4

listen to his rules about food and do certain behaviors that he instructed. I wanted all the things he promised, so I began to listen to what Ed told me and did what he asked. As elementary school progressed, I came face to face with low self-esteem, anxiety, and negative thoughts. I lost my home due to a fire when I was seven and had to move to a new town and a new school. It was hard. Thoughts of not making new friends, that my new home would burn down too, being alone at recess, wondering if the teachers would like me, and whether I am smart enough went through my head. Ed told me that if I restricted certain foods, the things I feared would not come true. So, I began to control what I put in my mouth in hopes my fears would be just that, fears, and not my reality.

Middle school came, and life felt more difficult. Cliques – how to get in one and make sure it was the right one, having "cool" clothes, the pressure to excel in school, picking the "right" extracurricular activities, pushing down and hiding my sexuality as I knew I liked girls, my body developing and changing, and more. How is a young person to cope with all these pressures and changes? Never fear, Ed was right by my side with comforting words and rules to follow. He said he loved me, understood me, and wouldn't let me down, and that if I did what he asked, I would excel in school, have lots of friends, choose the right activities to do, and that I'd be thin and happy. In believing what he promised, I did as I was told. My food restriction increased, my exercise increased, and my behaviors and rituals were dominant. I was able to merge my behaviors and rituals into my everyday life and blend in so as not to stand out from anyone else. Ed taught me well.

High school came, and Ed was by my side every step of the way. Ed came with me to choir practice, singing lessons, drama, and color guard. He sat beside me at every test I took and with every homework assignment I finished. I had rules to follow as I was striving to be thin, to be a perfect straight A student, an outstanding achiever in my extracurriculars, a friend everyone could rely on, a daughter to be proud of, all the while living life as a heterosexual person, even though I knew I wasn't, but my religion told me I had to be. I was doing exactly what Ed said in hopes all the things I desired and hoped for would come true. I could not disobey. If I did, I would feel like a disappointment – and that was not an option. During these years, my moods were up and down, and my weight was dropping. Ed was my best friend, my identity, my normal, and was carefully woven into all aspects of my life, yet my life was not my own, it was Ed's.

After high school, life continued with the pressures and stress of college and adulthood, all the while Ed was by my side every step of the way. As time went on, I got a job, got married – to a man – and built a house. I was the President of my adult choir, had a full-time job, which I loved, had a dog, lots of friends, and family close by. Ed led me to believe the only reason good things were happening in my life was because I was listening to his advice and doing exactly what he said. I was still restricting, over-exercising, self-injuring, taking laxatives and diet pills, and could fit into girls' size clothes.

From the outside looking in, my life looked great; however, Ed wore my body and brain down so much that I had to enter treatment. It was my first hospitalization, and I was 29. My health was compromised, I couldn't concentrate, my body was giving out, and I was depressed. I was scared and did not know what to expect, nor did I want to let go of my best friend. I had known Ed for so long, and the thought of him being gone was debilitating. Ed knew me better than anyone, even better than I knew myself.

Ed's voice was louder in the hospital because he did not like the fact that one of my treatment goals was weight restoration. He told me the staff didn't know what they were talking about and that they didn't know me like he did. He assured me they were lying and only wanted me to get fat. He also said I didn't have a problem and wasn't sick at all. They are the enemy, he said. While in treatment, I participated in groups and eventually followed my meal plan. Despite being a bit proud of myself, I was unsure of this entire process but did it anyway, all the while I was terrified of leaving Ed behind. I was released from the hospital and participated in outpatient therapy with my entire treatment team consisting of my physician, therapist, registered dietitian, and psychiatrist.

After my discharge from the hospital, life was hard learning how to eat, feel, and live. Ed was still with me, and I was fighting to keep Ed and eat at the same time. Life got harder for me when one of my best friends suddenly passed away. I was devastated, sad, lonely, and angry. Instead of turning to friends and family for help, I turned to Ed to help me feel better. I knew he could comfort me. Things went from bad to worse, and I relapsed.

I ended up in the hospital again and felt like a failure. The recovery cycle continued onward. When I was discharged this time, my weight was up, but my mind and thoughts were with Ed, and I was still struggling. I was not committed to recovery. It seemed too overwhelming, too scary, too much to learn, and the magnitude of all I had to do was paralyzing.

As I entered my thirties, a divorce from my husband happened, I came out of the closet, and a new life began. I was at the same job with the same company and loved it. Ed was right there too. No matter what I was going through, good or bad, I knew I could count on him. His voice was loud, demanding, manipulative, and relentless, and yet felt comforting as it was what I knew and felt safe, but I wasn't. What I didn't realize then was that he didn't care about me at all, and I was never going to achieve or receive what he promised.

As time went by, I married a woman and life was good. I went back to school, at night, at 33 years of age, to get my bachelor's in business; however, Ed never failed to remind me who was in control and that all of this could change if I disobeyed him, so I continued to listen and obey. Years went by, and I was on autopilot. I couldn't understand why I felt so unfulfilled and lonely. I had a job, a wife, a home, friends, and family, and I was doing exactly what Ed said, yet I still felt I wasn't doing enough. I had to do better. My behavior became even more extreme with restriction, self-injury, exercise, and diet pills. My weight was the lowest it had ever been, and my health was failing. My days consisted of going to work and coming home to be alone with Ed. I was isolating myself even more from friends and family. Ed dominated every thought, every feeling, and every moment – until my family stepped in.

On a Thursday night in March 2006, my family held an intervention. We sat at the table as each of them told me how they felt, what they saw, and how scared they were. They told me they loved me, and I needed to get help. I yelled back that I was fine and didn't have a problem. I felt attacked and angry. I explained to them I had a job, a home, and friends, and if I were sick and had a problem, I would never have all that. Tough love was shown, and ultimatums were given. Treatment was being offered, and I had 24 hours to decide – I was 37 years old.

Those 24 hours were fraught with so many questions and emotions. Fear, anger, loneliness, doubts, excuses, denial, and so much more. Ed was right next to me telling me my family didn't understand – only he did. My body and brain's fight between with my family's words and Ed's words was excruciating and exhausting. Could I do this? Did I want to do this whole recovery thing? Am I being forced to do it? Is recovery even possible? What if I fail – again? I went to bed that night not knowing what to do. My eyes were swollen from crying, my brain was on overload, and my heart was conflicted.

When I woke up the next morning, I went to work still not knowing what my decision would be. As day went on, the office was quiet, and I was alone. I thought about all parts of my life: Ed, my family, friends, and things I wanted to do. I took a deep breath, and, in that minute, hope showed itself to me – for a split second – I grabbed on and decided to go into treatment. On March 13, 2006, the next chapter of my life began. A chapter I said I would do, but I was scared and unsure about it. It turned out to be the most difficult decision and the best decision I've ever made. It was a chapter full of heartache, loss, fear, loneliness, doubt, grief, trust, hope, anger, and so much more. A chapter that would take everything from me that I trusted and believed and restore it to the most amazing spectacle I ever knew – me!

My Life Beyond Treatment

Finding my authentic/recovery-self took time. Recovery is not a straight line and does not happen with one or two admissions, nor does it happen in a few weeks or months. After walking through the door of Walden

Behavioral Care on March 13, 2006, my recovery journey brought me back and forth – seven admissions in one year – from numerous inpatient visits to residential to partial hospitalization, and intensive outpatient treatment, all trying to conquer this eating disorder that had been with me my entire life. Despite wanting to give up – a million times, I never did, and neither did my treatment team.

As time went on, I got stronger and stronger and began my advocacy for eating disorder recovery and sharing my story. I co-lead support groups, sat on a board related to eating disorder mentoring, was a mentor to mentees in recovery, co-facilitated recovery workshops and retreats in Tennessee with Thom Rutledge, contributed writings to various eating disorder recovery books, was a consultant, and spoke to clients, professionals, and family members. I published a book on my recovery journey called *Telling Ed No! and Other Practical Tools to Conquer Your Eating Disorder and Find Freedom*. I went back to school and obtained my Master of Social Work from Boston University, am a recipient of the Dean's Award in Leadership in Social Work, and I am a Licensed Clinical Social Worker in Massachusetts. I sit on an Ethics Committee for an eating disorder treatment facility and speak and teach about recovery at various treatment facilities, workshops, schools, and conferences.

While all my activism was happening, the rest of my life was as well. During these years, a marriage was dissolved, and I was single again until many years later, another marriage happened, where I was blessed to become a mom to twin girls. They are my greatest gift. After a short while, that marriage ended, and an extraordinary life was reborn. I speak about these difficult challenges as my life has had many ups and downs, heartache and loss, and happiness and dreams all intertwined. I have been able to feel and express every emotion, be present and mindful in each moment, and find gratitude in each day, all because of my recovery. Relapse did not happen when my life circumstances changed – for the worse or for the better. I have the ability and strength to stand in my power and not give it away to anyone or any situation. I never take my recovery for granted – ever! You also have this ability – to provide your client with the hope to stand in their power, reclaim themselves and their life. You got this!

Treatment – to Go or Not to Go

When people find out I was in treatment for an eating disorder, they are curious and ask questions like: how long were you there, where did you go, how many times were you in treatment, what did you do all day, what level or care were you in, did it work, did you have to eat the entire day? They are all valid questions based on the topic of treatment and the journey of recovery. However, rather than questions around treatment, what I would like to bring to your attention and talk about is something many individuals and providers underestimate, which is the difficult process of making the decision to get help.

The most important and difficult part of recovery is not about eating or talking about feelings, it's making the decision to get help! What happens after that decision is made is all part of the recovery journey. The decision is the foundation of the journey. You, as their therapist, have the unique and amazing opportunity to help your client strengthen their foundation. I can remember where I was, what I went through, and what I was feeling every time I made the decision to enter treatment. From my outpatient therapist suggesting I go, my family's intervention, my physician informing me my health was deteriorating, to reaching out myself to my therapist, and more. Making the decision was excruciatingly painful and the most difficult one I have ever had to make, no matter how many times I made it – which were a lot. Battling the thoughts in my head was debilitating.

Deciding to enter treatment felt like I was giving up my control, my freedom, and my security. It felt like I failed and was abandoning Ed, the one person I counted on for everything, and the one who kept me safe – or so I thought. It felt like I was leaving my entire life as I knew it and putting it in the hands of people I didn't know or trust, and starting a brand-new life that I knew nothing about or how to live. I was angry and hated myself for even thinking about entering treatment. I felt alone, afraid, and confused. I felt like my entire skin and muscles were ripped away from my body, and my tissue and bones were exposed for all to see the rawness of, and when the breeze blew over me, the pain was intolerable.

As I sit here and write, tears fill my eyes with gratitude for being alive, as I recall and feel the enormity of what I was feeling and the decisions I made despite it all. I also want you to be aware whether it's the first time or the tenth time a client has made the decision to enter treatment – no matter what level of care, it is still a difficult one. It's different, not easier. In addition, even though the client made the decision to enter treatment, they will also push back and not want it at times, and that's OK, it's normal. Your empathy, support, compassion, collaboration with other treatment providers, and being a holder of hope during this push back are a vital part of the client's successful journey.

Ways My Therapist Helped

Intertwined throughout this chapter, you will begin to see, through my experiences, the various ways my therapist helped me find my authentic self, my recovery voice, and then full recovery. Nevertheless, I would like to highlight here a few specific ways my therapist helped that you may find useful or helpful with your clients.

Being Seen

An important factor was that my therapist was interested in who I was not just what my diagnosis was, which helped me feel seen – even if I didn't want to be seen. You may be asking how did they accomplish this? Well, my therapist would ask random questions about me, not just about my eating disorder behaviors. They would follow up in later sessions by asking questions or checking in on something I spoke about in prior sessions. They made eye contact with me when they spoke and smiled, which, at times, was uncomfortable but exactly what I needed. They gently pushed me to think and talk about myself, without Ed, which was painfully hard to do as I had no idea who I was, but worth it in the end. In being consistent in doing these things, my therapist helped me be comfortable in being seen and helped me slowly find my authentic self.

Sharing

Another way they helped was that, while keeping appropriate boundaries, they shared simple things about their own life. Such as speaking about their pets, a favorite vacation they went on, a holiday they enjoy, or music they found uplifting. In addition, they weren't afraid to laugh at themselves while telling me a funny story. In doing these things, it showed me their humanness and helped me trust them and feel safe. By sharing themselves, they also provided me with the ability to visualize and hear real-life experiences from someone who was living life without an eating disorder. A real-life role model. In doing so, it provided me with excitement, imagination, and more importantly, hope!

Homework

When I thought about therapy, doing homework never entered my mind, so when my therapist gave me homework to do, I was skeptical. Well, I can say that homework became a valuable tool in my recovery. Homework provided me with the ability to think outside of the box in the most amazing, frustrating, and uncomfortable ways all at once. As I got stronger in my recovery and progressed, I was able to dive deeper into my authentic self and dream about who I was and would be without Ed. Most importantly, it helped me write a recovery narrative, which helped me uncover the real me!

A Village

Throughout my recovery journey, a treatment team was formed for me each step of the way, with each admission and outpatient. In the beginning, I was honestly annoyed by the fact that "these people" had a voice and power in what I could do, not do, and so forth. My team would be in constant contact with each other after every session I had with each of them, and I felt controlled, scared, shameful, anxious, and angry. You may be asking yourself right now, how is this a positive, Cheryl?

Well, it wasn't until my brain was nourished enough and my thoughts were becoming more of my own, versus Ed's, that I could feel the comfort, gratitude, and benefit of having an entire team on my side looking out for me and helping me step by step. The enormity of safety and support I felt was overwhelming, and the amount of gratitude I felt in knowing that because of my team working as a team, they helped save my life. Even today, I tear up knowing the outcome of my life could have been very different if it weren't for my therapist and my team! Teamwork makes recovery possible, and you are part of that amazing team – thank you!

Supportive Hope

During my therapy sessions, I cried, yelled, was silent, stubborn, rude, and most of the time, Ed spoke first. While I was expressing all these emotions and words being formulated and verbalized, my therapist was the recipient of it all. In addition, there were numerous times I called when in crisis and couldn't even formulate words.

Despite it all, my therapist(s) never left my side, were always there to text and call, and were a supportive, hopeful presence in my times of need. I would cry to them knowing I needed more help but didn't want to go, and I never felt judged. They held hope for me when I needed it and supported me in my decision(s) to seek more treatment. They were positive in their verbal messages to me, and their actions of helping me get into treatment made me feel safe, cared for, and supported. Because of their unwavering support for me and my recovery, I never felt less than or broken. I felt hopeful, strong, and brave.

A Few Tools That Helped Me Recover

Throughout my recovery journey, I utilized many therapists, tools, and avenues to help me recover. I'd like to highlight in the following pages a few real-life experiences and tools that provided me with the strength to keep going and keep fighting for my recovery and myself. These tools will give you more insight and could be utilized in your client's journey as well, if you see fit.

The Separation

In the beginning of this chapter, I explained my perspective on how I viewed my eating disorder as a destructive relationship with a person named Ed, rather than a condition, whereby using my therapist Thom's "separation metaphor" of personifying my eating disorder as a unique entity. Until I read about Thom and his therapeutic approach, I never viewed the struggle with my eating disorder in this way. To me, there was no struggle. I would be the first person to tell you that it was my voice in my head I heard; that I am the one in control, that I am making these decisions and rules, that I am not sick at all, that you are the crazy one and don't understand. All words you may hear from your clients as well, but know that those words they speak are not their own. Those words are a form of protection, so you don't see their fears, shame, anxiety, vulnerability, anger, low self-esteem, and more.

Separating and externalizing the eating disorder from myself was a turning point for me. It was life-changing in a way I never knew and provided me with the ability to breathe, find my authentic self, and empower my own (recovery) voice to be heard! Was it easy? No. Was it worth all the pain, struggle, fear, blind faith, and sacrifice? Yes!

After I read about Thom's method, I began to refer to my eating disorder as Ed; however, I still was not able to fully separate myself from him. He had been with me my entire life, and I did not know who I was without him. I could start a sentence, and Ed would finish it. It felt like he knew me better than I knew myself. I was intertwined with him in ways I still didn't fully understand.

It didn't become clear until I did the unimaginable. In July 2007, I traveled alone to a recovery workshop in Tennessee that Thom was offering. Before I made the decision, the battle in my head was intense, and Ed was relentless. He was telling me I was fine and that I didn't want or need what they were offering. He was also telling me I did not deserve to go. He told me they don't understand me like he does, and it was a waste of time and money. After numerous emails and phone calls of support from Thom and his staff, I made the decision to go. A decision that changed the trajectory of my recovery journey.

As the workshop began, Thom said, "Let's start with some role-playing." I had no idea what he was talking about and did not know what to expect. This technique was new to me as I had never done this with my therapist back home, but it soon became clear. A circle was formed around Thom and a co-facilitator, whom we will call Sarah. Thom played the role of Ed, and Sarah played the role of a person struggling with an eating disorder. The scenario playing out before my eyes was all too familiar. Ed was degrading, bossy, and so manipulative. He was trying to control Sarah, but she was fighting back and said, "I don't need you Ed, leave me alone!." Ed tried to entice her back by saying, "You need me. We are friends and I won't disappoint you, I'm here for you." But Sarah was strong and stood her ground saying, "No, I'm not listening to you anymore, Ed!"

I sat there staring at them with wide eyes at what I was seeing and hearing. It was all becoming so clear: the words, the threats, the responses, the fights all played out – live – right in front of me! The realization was overpowering. It felt like someone came running toward me, looked at me, and was screaming, "Wake up! Do you see it now?" At that precise moment, through Thom's exercise, I finally did see that I am not my eating disorder. Ed is separate from me. I was stunned, and it shook me to my core, literally. My body shook and tears filled my eyes as this realization sank into my soul, brain, and body. It was overwhelming, overpowering, and exactly what I needed and wanted.

Witnessing the battle that I fought every minute of my existence gave me a sense of identity I never had before. I knew from that moment that I was not Ed and Ed was not me. I was my own person. And now I had something and someone to fight, instead of fighting against myself.

After seeing and feeling this realization, I fought even harder for recovery. I wanted more help, and when I got back home, I reached out to Thom, who lived and practiced in Tennessee, and asked if he would accept me as a client. He did, so in addition to having a therapist in Massachusetts, I also had Thom on my team. They each practiced different modalities, so I had more ammunition to fight with. I did weekly sessions with both therapists, and then every few months I flew to Tennessee to do a week of intensive sessions with Thom that included intrapersonal exercises, role-playing, homework, support groups, and much more.

Separating and externalizing the eating disorder may be a new concept to you as you read this, but a concept you now have knowledge of and could provide your client with as a tool of strength, awareness, separation, and hope.

Transforming Ed's Rules

Throughout my entire life with Ed, he had rules for me to follow. He convinced me that if I listened to him and did as he instructed, I would be happy, successful, loved, smart, perfect, and, most of all, thin. What is interesting to note here is that these rules changed all the time, even when I was faced with the same situation. Thus, I had to listen intently as he changed the rules sometimes within seconds. It was exhausting and took all my energy and effort. I didn't want to fail. I wanted to make Ed proud, and I wanted what he promised.

One day, I was on a phone session with Thom, and I was telling him how tired and irritated I was as Ed kept changing everything quicker and more often. Thom suggested I transform Ed's rules into affirmations of recovery. He gave me an example; however, I told him I was not confident I would have the words and knowledge to transform rules that I've lived by my entire life. He told me I could do it and to take my time. He said my recovery depended on my invalidating Ed's rules.

So, one day, I sat and wrote down some of the rules Ed had for me. I stared at them and said to myself; These are the rules, this is what I know. How can they be anything else? Nevertheless, I remembered Thom's example, his advice, and his support, and decided to do it. The first one took me a very long time to transform, but as I kept going, it got a bit easier. I would like to list for you some of Ed's rules I wrote and how I reframed them into recovery statements, so you have an idea of what I, and most likely a client of yours, was/is up against. Of course, these are some of the rules Ed had for me, and your client will have their own.

Ed's rule: You must eat less than everyone else.
Reframed: I eat until I am full and satisfied.
Ed's rule: When you go out to a restaurant, only order safe foods.
Reframed: When I go out to a restaurant, I order what I want and crave.
Ed's rule: If you weigh enough to give blood, then you are fat and unlovable.
Reframed: If I weigh enough to give blood, then I am healthy enough to help people.
Ed's rule: If you eat bad food, you must restrict.
Reframed: There is no such thing as bad food.
Ed's rule: Your skinny clothes must always be too big for you.
Reframed: My clothes will fit my new body, and I will look and feel beautiful.
Ed's rule: If you have your period, it means you are too fat.
Reframed: Having my period means my body is working properly and I am healthy.
Ed's rule: If you are in recovery, you are not special or unique anymore.
Reframed: If I am in recovery, I am strong and free.

In doing this exercise with Ed's rules, I had the ability to "see" my recovery shift right before my eyes. I will be honest; it took me a very long time to believe my recovery statements. I reframed Ed's rules and read them each day, yet still followed Ed's rules. It took persistence, patience, hard work, and practice to begin to believe in my words and let go of Ed's.

As time went on, I did have the ability to hear Ed's rule (in my head) and then automatically reframe it to a recovery statement. Over time, Ed's power diminished, and I was getting stronger every day.

How You Can Help – What You Need to Know

Eating disorders are complicated and can even produce fear in a therapist treating a client who is struggling with one. In my opinion, those are both valid and true. What's also true is being fully recovered exists, and you are part of that as well. It's a gift and an honor that may not always feel that way to you, but I'm here to say: you matter, you make a difference, and because of the work you do, recovery can happen! You are an important piece of recovery!

I've mentioned a couple of tools that were pivotal in my recovery, and without them, I wouldn't be here today. I would also like to share a few things that will provide insight and help you guide your patients on their journey. Things that might seem simple to an outsider, but to a client struggling, it is anything but simple.

Permission

Entering treatment and seeking recovery is the biggest and hardest decision a person can make – whether it's your first or tenth time. That step is paralyzing. From the minute the decision is made, Ed is screaming things like "you are too fat for treatment," "they won't accept you, you are not sick enough," "they don't know you like I know you," "only I can give you what you need," and so on and so on. It is a constant battle every second, and it's exhausting.

Loved ones of a person struggling may be telling them they want them to recover, they want them to eat, and they want them to take care of themselves. However, while being told all of that, Ed is screaming saying you are not worthy, you don't deserve to eat, no one loves you like I do, and you don't have permission to do any of this recovery stuff.

Permission is the keyword here. Ed doesn't give his permission to recover, so having your client understand and hear from others that they do have permission to follow recovery is a key factor. Telling someone who is struggling with an eating disorder, "I give you permission to disobey Ed, to follow recovery and eat," is very powerful. Your client might push back with harsh words or simply say "whatever," but please remember that giving permission to your client takes the pressure off them to make that decision – a decision that is filled with fear, shame, and guilt.

During my journey, I was told once, "If you can't give yourself the permission to eat and follow recovery Cheryl, then I give you permission." That permission gave me the strength to continue to move forward. Because permission was given to me, it was easier to follow through on things. I felt less guilt and less afraid going against Ed. Being given permission felt like someone was holding my hand in support. Sure, "I" was disobeying Ed, but it wasn't just by my own hand, so it felt safer, more acceptable, and less fearful.

I will share with you a short story about how powerful giving permission is. I was speaking to clients at a treatment facility, and after my talk, I took questions and provided guidance to those struggling. A client stood up and mentioned to me that she had ordered a fear food (butter) for dinner that evening, and didn't want to eat it, and was afraid. I validated her fear and complimented her on the strength she had in ordering the fear food. I told her that ordering the butter was a recovery step and an amazing one at that – even if she didn't end up eating it. I then said to her, "I give you permission to not only eat, but enjoy, the fear food." She looked at me with wide eyes, a quiver in her voice, and said OK, I'll try.

The next day, I received an email from the client telling me she ate the butter. She told me she was able to do it because I gave her permission to do so. She also informed me she was going to have another fear food at snack – cookies. She conquered that one as well.

Choice

For someone struggling with an eating disorder, choice is something they don't believe they have. Going through life with Ed telling them what to do, what to eat, how to eat, what rules to follow, what behaviors to do, how they are to feel about themselves, what they need to look like, what they need to wear, and so on is hard and exhausting. Ed never gives them a choice to do what he says or not; he always demands they do what he says or else they will face the consequences, and they won't achieve their desires or goals, so they listen. Knowing and learning during my recovery that I had a choice was a powerful lesson. A very hard one to grasp and understand, but one that shifted my way of thinking about obeying and disobeying Ed.

The delivery and guidance of reminding someone who struggles that they do have a choice must be met with compassion, empathy, and softness. I would suggest avoiding messages that sound like: "Well, Cheryl it's your choice, do you want recovery or not"; "Cheryl, it was your choice, and you didn't do/eat it, why?" Rather, I would ask you to show your support, tell them they are strong; that you believe in them, and you are right there with them.

Choice is something that is weaved throughout recovery and helps connect the dots and makes the pieces all click together. (Re)teaching choice is powerful as you are giving your client the permission to remember, find, and use "their" voice. Choice must be taught in all aspects of life for hope to grow and strength to be felt. Teaching choice would look and sound something like this: A client walks into the room for a session, and you ask them, "Where would you like to sit today?" Providing the client with a choice of seats, rather than only one available seat, allows freedom, and subconsciously, the power of choice is planted.

Another scenario of teaching choice would be: You and your client are in the room, they are seated (and you are aware of what you/they are working on) and you say something like: "I remembered you mentioning X in a prior session and have a few things here we could utilize if you would like, which one would you prefer?" You could then show them two worksheets, offer two talking points, show them two articles to read and talk about, etc. Whatever you deem appropriate to offer based on what you and the client are working on. Providing choice here empowers the client to utilize their voice in treatment rather than talking about what the therapist thinks.

Another scenario would be: Based on the session and what was discussed, you can offer the client two choices of homework. In addition, you could also offer one choice and then ask the client if they have an idea for a homework assignment. This conversation not only allows a choice but also provides the client with an opportunity to think outside the box in terms of recovery, all while empowering their voice and choice.

It's important to note that while these scenarios of choice may seem simple and not relevant to you or me, I assure you they are not simple for the person struggling. Choice is something that must be taught by example, with understanding and care by someone like you.

Being Mindful – of Words and Actions

You, as a therapist, are part of a multidisciplinary team who get up each morning and go to work. Going to work is your normal. I am here to remind you that your normal is one of the most difficult things your client could do – it's not their normal, it's the complete opposite. No matter the level of treatment – inpatient or outpatient – your client shows up in your work environment and must eat, go against, and disobey Ed, feel, express, trust, and begin a new chapter of life that seems impossible and unreachable. So many things that are beyond difficult. A normal day for you is anything but normal for your client.

Choose your words and actions carefully. Be aware that your client hears and sees everything, even if it doesn't look like they are paying attention. They are hyperaware of other people's words, actions, expressions, and tone. They are looking for the one thing they can grab on to ... good or bad. If you are having a difficult day yourself, which we all do, try not to bring that energy to work with you by way of tone, impatience, rolling or lifting eyebrows, sighing, or speaking under your breath. Your client is vulnerable and raw from the inside out, and most likely will take the actions and words on as personal until they get stronger in their recovery and learn to deal accordingly.

Know that something that is said or done could change the direction of a client's recovery and be the thing they need to move forward or backward. To help guide you, I'd like to provide you with two words to be mindful of and some examples when working with clients who struggle with an eating disorder.

First, is the word "just." Let's say you are talking with a client about their meal plan, as you are aware it has recently changed, or the client was eating something different. You would not want to approach it by saying "Cheryl, it's just a sandwich." That sandwich could be their biggest fear food and/or could be the most calories they have consumed in one sitting for months. Instead, you could say something like: "Cheryl, I know how difficult this is to do for you. I see the strength and power within you, and I believe in you." Try to refrain from even mentioning the sandwich itself. It's not about the sandwich.

Another example would be when you are talking to a client about expressing themselves, you would not want to say "Cheryl, just say it, its ok." Expressing feelings go against everything the client believes. Usually, when they come face to face with any type of feeling or emotion, they run to Ed for help; they don't usually express it. Try saying something like "Cheryl, I know you may be feeling many emotions right now. Expressing them verbally could lessen the pain and anxiety, and we can talk about how to get through it together."

Now, I understand both examples I gave would be something anyone might say as an automatic response or statement and would roll off our tongue without even a thought, I totally get that. That's my point here though, please take a moment of thought and breath before the spoken word. Something that is an everyday occurrence for most people, such as eating a sandwich or expressing a feeling, is extremely fearful for your client, and by using the word "just", it can come off as seeming condescending, disrespectful, and showing frustration on your part, even though that isn't the intent or message. It can be received by the client as something they should just be able to do. Remember, they need to learn that they can do it without Ed.

The second word to be mindful of when it relates to treatment is the word "again." No matter whether you work on an inpatient unit, residential facility, or as an outpatient therapist, I suggest you refrain from saying to the client, "Cheryl, nice to see you again," or "Cheryl, it seems you might need a higher level of care again." Yes, it would roll off your tongue as automatic; I totally understand. However, instead, you could say something like "Hi Cheryl, nice to see you," and give a smile. For those needing a higher level of care, you could say "Cheryl, you are working hard in your recovery, let's continue to build on your strength and momentum and pursue a higher level of care."

The word "again" can be seen as a failure, leading to feelings of shame, guilt, and embarrassment. The client's internal dialog could sound like: "Yup, here I am in treatment 'again' because I failed. I am worthless and weak and even the staff and my therapist know it." It's not until the client gets stronger in their recovery that they can see returning to a higher level of care as a strength. Personally, it took the third time of being admitted to an inpatient unit (all within less than a year, along with other levels of care) until I realized and felt like I was not a failure in my recovery and could see that going back meant I was strong and still moving forward.

Now, I don't want you to be paranoid about saying or doing the wrong thing. I want you to be authentic and aware, and mindful. It takes a little bit of practice, extra effort, and energy on your part, but it is something you can do that will instill hope and strength within your client and their recovery.

Validating Feelings

I might guess you read the subheading and thought, "Of course I would validate my client's feelings Cheryl, I'm a therapist." You would be surprised by the number of times I was in treatment when my feelings were not validated, which sent me into a negative mindset that derailed me. It was all innocent and unassuming from the provider's side, but at the receiving end, it was confusing and difficult. Let me shed some light on this for you.

When a client is with Ed, feeling their feelings is something they do not do. They are on automatic every minute and go to Ed, so they don't feel. They are numb. Part of recovery is about feeling. Feeling the good, the bad, and the ugly and learning to deal with it rather than running to Ed. So, as your client is on their recovery path, please validate and respect the feelings they are having, no matter what they may be experiencing. Let me provide an example.

For instance, if you are with a client and you notice they may be experiencing feelings such as being scared, frustrated, sad, anxious, lonely or angry, please do not discount or minimize by responding "Oh Cheryl, that's silly" or "Cheryl, you shouldn't (or don't) feel that way, you're ok." Instead, try something like "Good job Cheryl in expressing (or showing) your feelings. It takes a lot of courage to do that and by feeling, that is another step forward in your recovery, awesome"! It takes a lot of strength and courage for a client to push through fear and feel something, and even more so to acknowledge when they feel it and then to follow through in a healthy and safe way. They need to feel in order to move forward. Feeling feelings is a goal your client is striving for and a step that is essential for lasting recovery, and you can help them achieve that goal!

Can't versus Won't

The last term I would like to highlight is can't versus won't. Most of us were probably taught this concept by grown-ups when we were children who were teaching and instilling in us confidence in our intelligence and strength of what we can do. I was taught that as a child, and yet with Ed, confidence in my authentic self wavered. Can't versus won't was one of the hardest lessons for me to relearn, and it integrates with choice, which I spoke of in a prior paragraph. When I was with Ed and someone suggested eating something or doing something different, my automatic response was "I can't." I felt I couldn't because I didn't know I had the choice to say no to Ed. It truly felt like I couldn't. I didn't know I was strong and power-ful enough to actually do it, and didn't understand that by saying I can't, I really meant "I won't". In the end, it's not that I couldn't eat that piece of chicken or a serving of rice, it's that I wouldn't. Some of your clients might have the same automatic "I can't" response. If so, you can gently reteach the Can't versus Won't concept in response. Below are some examples of what not to say and what to say would look like this.

If you are in session talking about behaviors, fears, or foods, etc., you would not respond by saying "Cheryl, it's not that you can't do it, it's that you won't do it, you know that." Even though you may believe that it is tough love and a logical statement of truth, it will most likely backfire and the client may follow Ed's path even more. Rather, you could say, "Cheryl, you are right – it is hard, and you are not alone in this. You are strong, have permission, and can choose recovery; I am here to help." No matter what your client's reaction, they will take the positive message in. Verbalizing to them, they are strong, they do possess the strength to disobey Ed, they do have the power of choice, they are not alone, and can do it will help remind and reteach them the difference between can't and won't.

Subtle Ways Recovery Can Show up in Your Clients

As you work with clients, there will be obvious signs of their recovery that you will notice and/or be aware of from the treatment team you are part of. For example, their weight has increased, they are attending most/all their outpatient appointments, and their mood has stabilized. Those are all wonderful signs and should be applauded; however, what I would like to underscore in this section are the subtle ways recovery shows itself that someone might miss. All these subtle things can show up in a client at any time, so it does not matter what level of care they are in, when they started their recovery, their eating disorder diagnosis, their identity, or their age – you get my point.

What is important to remember is that all recovery steps matter and should be recognized and celebrated. Below will help you identify some of the recovery steps that might go unseen to the naked eye.

Clients Sit Longer

Typical eating disorder behaviors you might come across while you are in session with a client are ones where they are pacing, jogging in place, doing squats, shaking a leg(s), marching in place, or doing toe lifts while standing. Ed prefers constant movement in any part of the body as that burns calories.

When you are in session with a client and they begin to sit down longer and have less movement in their body (even 1–2 minutes), that is recovery!

By doing that, the client is practicing being at peace in their body, and in those few minutes, they are not burning extra calories and are learning to be OK with that. In addition, in those few minutes, there is a huge battle in their head between Ed and their recovery voice, so whether it is 1 minute of no movement or ten minutes, it is to be celebrated and acknowledged.

Color

Another typical eating disorder behavior is wearing black, gray, or dark colors. Usually, the client will wear a darker color to cover themselves, hide, and hopefully not be seen – from the outside world or themselves. Also, Ed states that wearing darker colors makes you look thinner. So, the behavior can be twofold. It was in my case.

If you notice your client does this, wears darker colors, and then they come into session wearing a color on their body – whether it be a shirt, socks, bracelet or a scrunchie in their hair – that is recovery! Wearing a color for the client is them taking a risk and being vulnerable to be seen and noticed, rather than hiding and blending in.

Thank You

Usually, when a session is over with a client who is struggling with an eating disorder, their response upon leaving could go multiple ways. They could verbalize nothing and walk out. While not looking at you and walking out the door, they could say see you next week. They could say Ya, thanks (with a dismissive tone). They could be talking under their breath mumbling words you can't quite hear as they leave the office, or they could be yelling – literally – several things as they walk out the door.

When you and your client are in a session or done with a session, and the client verbalizes in a pure non-sarcastic tone, thank you – that is recovery! The thank you is your client's recovery voice, as they have heard something valuable or recognized something in the session they understand or want to think about. They may even make quick eye contact, which is also a recovery step.

Ed's voice is loud in your client's head, and if you listen close enough, you'll be able to identify Ed when he speaks. More importantly, as you listen carefully, you'll be able to hear your client's recovery voice too.

Client will Ask

As I mentioned earlier in the chapter, choice and permission are two important factors that usually need to be retaught to a client who is struggling with an eating disorder. You do that by life/therapeutic exercises, work-sheets, role playing, talk therapy, and more. This subtle recovery step folds into choice and permission as well as your need to be conscious of the scenario playing out and the context of the conversation in your session. Meaning, be mindful you aren't being the scapegoat.

The subtle recovery step I am referring to is when your client asks you for your help to decide something, or having you choose for them. An example would be – You and your client are talking about their feelings around two fear foods and their commitment to eating one of them that evening. They made the commitment with their registered dietitian, which you learned about through communicating with the RD. After hearing the patients' fears, concerns, and feelings around each fear food, they look at you and ask, "Can you choose for me"? With your client asking you that question – that is recovery!

This question is twofold in recovery based on "giving permission to re-cover" and hearing and understanding your client's "recovery voice." The question to you was asked from their recovery voice, and by answering the question and telling your client which fear food to eat, you are giving them permission to eat the fear food. In doing that, you are helping to remove the fear, guilt, and shame from them having to decide which fear food to eat, whereby it gives them the power and confidence to follow through eating it.

Remember, the choice and commitment they made with their RD before you saw them was a huge recovery step, which was most likely excruciating to decide. Keeping that recovery step in mind while you are in session, and with that, the client asking for your help is another amazing step in their recovery path, and you helped them do it!

Outward Emotion

While in session with a client or walking in the hallway/open space (if you are working in an inpatient/residential level of care), and your client shows any type of outward emotion that is out of "eating disorder character" such as a smile, a laugh, crying, anger, empathy, etc., that is recovery!

Ed thrives on your client feeling numb. Ed instructs and expects zero emotion and feelings. Usually, the client is on autopilot and hard at work listening to Ed and making sure they follow all instructions and don't break his rules. So, when your client outwardly shows or verbalizes an emotion that *is* recovery showing itself. It is very vulnerable for the client to take the risk and disobey Ed and show or verbalize anything other than what Ed says, so be attuned to what you are seeing and hearing.

When you do witness a recovery step in your client, please be mindful in your response not to utilize trigger words such as "don't" and "shouldn't." Instead, validate, acknowledge, and praise their recovery step.

I Want, I Would, I Could, I Like

When you converse with your client, you are most likely used to hearing Ed's rules, seeing the eating disorder behaviors front and center; however, hold the hope for your client, as when you (and maybe even your client) least expect it, their authentic/recovery voice will begin to emerge, so listen closely.

Your client's recovery voice will start to appear naturally as they get stronger, which your client might not be aware of. It takes a finely-tuned ear to hear the subtle ways it shows itself. Usually, it presents through phrases such as: I want, I would, I like, and I could. It would sound something like this: "My friend recently got a puppy; I think it's a Labrador. It's so cute. I would love to have a dog like that" or "Yeah, my mom got me some new fidgets. I like the way this fidget feels" or "I want to try to eat that, but I don't think I can."

All the examples above are the client's recovery voice, and the places you could take them are so exciting, hopeful, and energizing. It makes me smile and feel proud of your clients and excited for you when I think about them speaking like this and you hearing it.

Please inform your client what you hear and tell them that it *is* recovery, and you will hold their hand, and be there, every step of the way. Also, please know that when you acknowledge your client's recovery voice to them, which they may not consciously be aware of, you might be on the receiving end of Ed's nasty words, as Ed will try to jump in and hijack your client. If that happens, it's OK, you did nothing wrong and everything right! Remember, your client heard your words, you have empowered your client's recovery voice, and you have helped them take another step on their recovery path.

Hope

Hope can be hard to come by when you are struggling with an eating disorder and have little conception of what life looks like without it. It is overwhelming and feels hopeless. Hope can also be hard for you, as a therapist, if you feel like you are not helping, as you see your client struggle. The point here is to understand that there is hope everywhere, if only you know where to look.

Hope, a small word that is positively powerful – if you choose to see it that way. I do. Hope is recovery, and recovery is hope. Sometimes when the word hope is tossed around as it relates to recovery, it can feel like this enormous thing you must already have, and if you don't have it, you will never recover – that is far from the truth. Likewise, simply telling a client to have hope will not help them recover. However, giving, holding, and showing them hope – that will help them recover.

The beauty of hope is that it grows. And you do not need a large amount to start; that can be overwhelming and out of reach for most clients. At the beginning, all the hope that is needed fits on the tip of a pen. It starts small and continues to build and blossom into something magnificent and magical. You can lend it out if someone needs a boost, or give them some in order to begin. I am also a firm believer in holding onto hope for someone, especially when they feel they have none, and then giving it back to them when they're ready for it.

Hope can be seen and found in various ways in one's recovery. Most of the time, the client cannot recognize what hope looks like or feels like, so your acknowledgment to them provides the insight to see and feel hope, so it can grow even more. It also helps you hold hope for yourself.

Here are some examples of how hope shows itself: a client shows up to a group or session, a client offers a suggestion to another client, a client smiles, a clients makes eye contact with someone, a client took one bite of food, a client accepted a visit from a friend/went out with a friend, it's a clients first – or tenth time in treatment – no matter the level, a client is humming or singing a song, a client is reading a book, a client is doing schoolwork. All these things I have listed are hope in recovery, and these are recovery steps as well.

You, as a therapist, already possess hope; within yourself and for your client, no matter the circumstance. Recovery is a journey both you and your client are on together. Know that even when your client struggles, that is recovery, that is hope growing, and you are making a positive difference even if you cannot see it. Believe it for yourself and your client, and if you are unable to, know I believe and hold it for both of you!

Key Points and Takeaways

I have discussed many things within this chapter in terms of the struggle and recovery, all of which can positively impact your work and your client's journey in amazing ways. In closing, I would like to end with a few key points that are valuable insights to empower you and your knowledge to help foster continued growth for you and your clients.

First, I would like to bring you back to something I mentioned earlier in this chapter to help you see and understand the shift in Ed and why. In the tools section, Transforming Ed's Rules, I told Thom, my therapist, on a phone session that Ed was changing the rules quicker and more often. An insight for you here is that the reason Ed was changing the rules quicker and more often is because I was participating in recovery and going against him – even a slight bit. Because I was entertaining the idea of recovery and was not choosing to listen to Ed all the time, Ed was angry and became even more manipulative, controlling, and deceptive as he wanted me to be only true to him and no one or anything else.

When a client partakes in doing anything – the anything does not matter here – against their eating disorder, their eating disorder will get louder, more manipulative, and more controlling. It is frightening for you and them, certainly, but it shows such strength in your client. It shows their desire and hope for something better – even if they do not know what that something is.

It is your support, words, and guidance they will need – and not necessarily look for or ask for – to help keep them moving forward on their recovery path. When I told Thom I couldn't do the exercise, I didn't ask for his support or encouragement; he automatically gave it and said he believed in me, and he knew I could do it. By doing that, Thom was helping me write a new narrative – a recovery one!

Second, I would like to challenge you to redefine and expand the definition of progress/progressing as it relates to recovery. Seeing progress in your client is not always about what they eat or don't eat, what the number on the scale says, what their lab work results are, or what their vitals are. Yes, that is all important for numerous medical reasons in a client and can be easily defined as making or not making "progress," but that's not the whole picture. Recovery is so much more than that, and I am here to ask you to look deeper than the number on the scale or the results of lab work for yourself and for your client.

Progress can be hard to see if you are only looking at and relying on a few signs, but it is there to be witnessed if you pay attention. In paying attention, you, as a therapist, also gain hope and strength for yourself and the work you are doing. If you only look in one direction and down one path, you will miss all the seeds that were dropped along the way that will grow into a beautiful spectacle of color and form. Please, expand your view.

Third, recovery is cumulative. Recovery does not happen all at once; it occurs piece by piece, step by step, and takes time. It is important to remember all forward steps, all falls, all relapses, all plateaus … all of it is recovery. With each day, each admission, each appointment, your client is seeing, hearing, and learning about recovery and life, whether they apply it in that admission or moment or not. When they are ready, the recovery piece will show itself.

A few examples of recovery steps which can show up as cumulative over multiple admissions, few sessions or years later, are expressing any emotion, doing homework you gave them, not eating a fear food and telling you why, saying yes to something, relapsing and unpacking it with you, tattling on Ed, (re)connecting with friends or family, eating their meal plan, doing a goal sheet, remember something someone said in a support group and putting it to use in their life, ordering a fear food and not eating it, saying no to something, going into treatment, looking at a plate of food and not having a panic attack – even if they don't eat a thing off that plate, smiling and laughing. Recovery steps are everywhere if you look for them, and eve-rything is cumulative over time.

Once a step is done and accomplished, no matter what the step, it's a re-covery step and is added into and onto their path. Relapsing or going back into treatment – no matter the level – does NOT negate all the work done prior to that moment of relapse and/or needing more help. It's important to note the client does not start over in their recovery – they are already in recovery.

Your client is taking in information every minute and every day, even if you can't see it. The wisdom and guidance they receive along the way from everyone accumulates, unconsciously and subconsciously, in their mind and body, and will show itself to them as their recovery voice gets stronger. They are seeing it; they are feeling it, and they will use it.

Finally, thank you for the work you do, your dedication to your patients, and your consideration in working with the eating disorder population. I am filled with gratitude for myself and for your clients. You are an impor-tant step in the recovery journey. You are memorable and are a holder of hope. Your words and actions impact your client, their growth, and their recovery. With you, your client begins to heal, begins to eat, begins to learn, begins to trust, begins to find themselves, begins to express, begins to feel, begins to gain strength, hope, and faith to move forward. Because of you, recovery exists!

Part II

The Eating Disorder Therapist

Chapter 4

A Therapist's Perspective

Developing a Personal and Therapeutic Connection

Christina Brothers

"I don't like it, but you don't like it either." An adolescent said this to me in response to our mutual agreement to challenge her overexercising tendencies; in this case, running. This statement was striking to me because it perfectly encapsulated what the therapeutic relationship can look like, especially when working with clients with eating disorders. It involves an ask, for both therapist and client, to sit together in some degree of discomfort. You may not like an idea or recommendation, but that alone does not have to be a barrier to progress, given there is a strong relationship. What I've learned from my clients throughout the years is the value of integrating concepts like curiosity, transparency, flexibility, and vulnerability in the therapeutic relationship. I've found these strategies to be highly effective in building meaningful relationships with my clients, as they provide multiple pathways for individuals to trust in the treatment process. In this chapter, I will outline some of the concepts I've found most helpful and provide case studies to highlight these principles in practice.

Introducing Myself

The path to where I am today was not what I had envisioned for myself at an early age. I was told growing up that my only career path was to be a doctor. I intensely pursued this by completing all the required coursework for pre-med; however, in my third year of undergrad, I realized that continuing this path would only lead to my misery. Instead, I found that my actual interest was in the connection between health and psychology, for many deeply personal reasons, and I had always been genuinely curious and interested in learning about other people's lives. These were the tenants that guided me to the path that I am on today.

At 16, I found myself in a therapist's office in an attempt to repair a strained relationship with my mom, following my parents' divorce. You could say that my therapist at the time was a pivotal person in helping me to have a positive experience in therapy. I think this is often true about

DOI: 10.4324/9781003600770-6

any area of life: the positive relationships we create ultimately lead to positive experiences.

After I graduated college, I left the southern part of the United States, where I lived for most of my life, and moved to Boston. I did not know a single person in New England when I moved here, but I knew that I wanted to gain experience working with individuals with eating disorders – an interesting intersection between health and psychology. My first stop – and one that you could say was the most pivotal – was working on an inpatient eating disorder unit. The clients I worked with were incredibly generous and allowed me a glimpse into their lives and struggles. The staff were equally as generous in teaching me how to support individuals with an illness that was attempting to take over their lives. My biggest takeaway from some of those years was that if you create a truly meaningful relationship with someone, then you have the foundation to challenge them to do hard things – something that is often required in therapy and recovery.

I then pursued a Master's in Social Work while working at the inpatient unit. I continued to work there for many years, well after completing my master's degree and held various positions. Additionally, while in graduate school, I completed an internship in a community mental health center providing outpatient therapy. Upon graduation, I was offered a part-time position. It was there that I learned more broadly how mental health struggles impacted individuals in their daily lives, and how to be alongside them through these moments. These experiences were instrumental in molding me into the therapist I am today. All the individuals I met along the way, and the meaningful relationships we created, helped me to feel like I'm exactly where I should be. I feel incredibly lucky to do the work that I do day in and day out.

Today, I have my own private practice, and have for many years, while continuing to work full-time at a college counseling center. My outpatient practice consists of adolescents (individually or together with their family), college students, and adults. I tend to see a mixture of eating disorders, mood disorders, anxiety disorders, and obsessive-compulsive disorder (OCD).

My Style

Before diving too deeply, it's important to describe my style as a therapist, so you have a frame of reference as to how I approach the therapeutic relationship. Generally speaking, I try to bring a mixture of curiosity, humor, and humility to my sessions. I aim to be open and curious to an individual's experience, which I believe is an integral component to building meaningful relationships. I am genuinely interested in how others understand the world. Oftentimes, clients come to therapy only giving you a peek into their lives. Challenging them to be vulnerable requires intentional curiosity and awareness of any personal judgments you may bring into the room. There is already so much shame wrapped up in the psychology of eating disorders; adding in your pre-conceived notions or biases can quickly stifle success. Transparency is another technique I strongly subscribe to. Transparency invites trust in the relationship, and I find that even if a client doesn't like my recommendations, they may be more likely to listen and participate if they feel that I'm being open and honest with them. I will describe all of these elements in further detail throughout this chapter.

Lastly, I often find myself practicing from an Acceptance and Commitment Therapy (ACT) framework when working with eating disorders. Other modalities, such as Family-Based Treatment, Cognitive Behavioral Therapy, and Dialectical Behavior Therapy, are also helpful; however, I have found that ACT can create movement when therapy is feeling stuck. The essence of ACT is to encourage more flexibility in one's life, which is often a common goal in eating disorder treatment. Additionally, I find the ability to be flexible within therapy meets my style as a therapist. If I can get clients talking about other important areas in their life, just having that conversation in itself may challenge their eating disorder. You can fill an entire session talking about or playing out their eating disorder's obsessional thoughts and fears. And while it's important to spend time understanding, challenging, and helping clients to learn to manage these thoughts and feelings, it's also important to explore other meaningful areas of their life. By highlighting ACT themes of cognitive dissonance (e.g., the mental discomfort in conflicting beliefs or actions, for example, how the eating disorder might be negatively impacting their values in other meaningful parts of their lives) and cognitive diffusion (e.g., allowing space between thoughts and feelings, for example, observing thoughts as thoughts, not as truths), can allow for small moments of separation from the illness. This can help to challenge the common distortion that their eating disorder's thoughts and desires are their own. It is important to remind your clients that that is not true; that they are much more than their illness. It may take time and effort to fully unwrap the layers of what drives one's eating disorder behaviors, and if you face resistance, that too can provide a useful clue as to the direction of its function.

Important Characteristics of the Therapeutic Relationship

Curiosity

Most days, I'm reminded by my clients just how painful it can be to talk about emotions. The level of discomfort that clients bring to any given session may make us, as therapists, feel uncertain about how to move forward.

When in these situations, my goal is always to maintain a curious stance. It may sound simplistic, but this approach can be a powerful one for both the therapist and the client. For those in the throes of their illness, curiosity can invite opportunities for nonjudgmental interactions, which is especially meaningful for those with an eating disorder, an illness that often erodes a client's ability to be curious about, question, or try to answer why this is happening. For therapists, the value of curiosity can be somewhat overlooked, especially when the wheels of clinical diagnosis and structured treatment start turning. Allowing space in the therapeutic relationship that is free from judgment helps to foster a sense of safety for clients and gives therapists a place they can fall back to, if needed. Slowing down, asking questions, and striving for understanding also allows space for clients to feel heard. It provides moments of reprieve from judgment, which often dominates their day-to-day internal and external lives.

Curiosity can serve many purposes. It not only fosters a greater understanding of your client, but it can also provide a platform by which the therapist can model how to be curious. A foundational aspect of therapy is to encourage your clients to be more self-aware, or curious, about their thoughts, feelings, and behaviors. Eating disorders often have clients living in what I call, Reaction Land, which leaves little time for curiosity. Their eating disorder amplifies certain thoughts in an effort to increase the likelihood of a desired outcome or behavior, resulting in a protective shell of reactivity to anything or anyone that challenges those ideas. When clients are in Reaction Land, curiosity often diminishes, ultimately resulting in the eating disorder gaining more control. Therapists need to encourage moments of pause, so our clients can reflect on the *why* of a thought or behavior. These moments create opportunities to possibly challenge their eating disorder and also allow for moments of creating more depth in the relationship.

Encouraging curiosity may be met with fear by some of your clients. Curiosity may feel foreign, which can contribute to feelings of discomfort. Your ability to understand and question these fears in a manner that feels empathetic, supportive, and nonjudgmental will help your client to feel that they can trust you – and don't forget to notice what's happening in the room. Your client might not be able to articulate their discomfort as they try to be more curious, and you might have to pause if you hit an unexpected emotional trigger (or "landmine", as I tell them). Ultimately, we want to follow our clients' lead while also challenging them to create more room for uncomfortable feelings.

A recent example of this in my practice was an adolescent that I began seeing about a year ago, who came to me for help with depression and restrictive eating disorder behaviors. At baseline, this client often had difficultly questioning negative thoughts and feelings related to her eating disorder as well as more broadly in her life. Her ability to be curious about her feelings worsened when she was in a depressive episode, and if left up to her, she would rather avoid therapy during these periods because it just felt so hard. Despite this, we maintained a positive connection, but I was always aware of how difficult this process was for her, and I often acknowledged this sentiment to her verbally. When we would encounter uncomfortable thoughts and feelings, I would challenge her by saying, "Let's try and talk about this for five more minutes." This approach was contrary to my usual style, but I found providing a timeframe gave her a sense of how long the "ask" was to stay present and explore her current feelings.

Lastly, I find that remaining curious allows for more cohesion when identifying goals for treatment. Naturally, if we are aware of the specific details of our client's struggles, we are going to be better able to identify and align a realistic focus for treatment. I have found that engaging our clients in these discussions can often support increased motivation and engagement in treatment. Research has shown that treatment is more helpful for individuals with eating disorders if they perceive they have "freedom of choice" regarding their care (Mital et al., 2022). It is my perspective, as a therapist working with individuals with eating disorders, that there can often be an urge to be overly direct, or authoritative, due to the discomfort that can surface in pushing against the eating disorder. However, if you can create more depth and understanding through curiosity, you'll be able to leverage the therapeutic relationship, and your "directness" will be more in line with your clients' capabilities and feel empowering, rather than debilitating.

Transparency

When I think about transparency, I consider the ways in which to engage with clients; about who they are and what you are observing. As I dig deeper to understand more about my client as a person, their eating disorder, its impact, and goals, I try to be open about my experience of them and observations in session. I think transparency has a natural way of creating openness with clients of all ages as long as it is done with respect.

This is particularly important when trying to create an alliance when working with adolescents and families. Often, I set the stage for transparency early in treatment by letting the adolescent know my recommendations either before and/or immediately after I inform their parents. I have found that being open, or transparent, can help to foster buy-in from the adolescent, as they feel respected and included in the process. When working with adults, transparency often shows up differently and is less about secrecy. An example that comes to mind is providing clients with a thorough understanding of why you are recommending a specific challenge. Giving the client a comprehensive explanation about why you are encouraging a certain challenge can not only create more understanding but also promote trust in the relationship. This trust may be an integral feature as you start to challenge the client to act against their eating disorder. Although the client may not like the challenge itself, they will understand that you're trying to help them.

Lastly, providing direct feedback can provide clarity if there is a misunderstanding. If I notice a shift in our interpersonal dynamic or rapport, I make a point to address it directly. This allows for an opportunity to clear up points of confusion and provides a platform for repair to take place. Working through relational challenges can end up deepening the relationship by showing that you notice when something has changed in the room, that the relationship is important to you, and that you desire to understand more about what might have happened. It also shows that you can be vulnerable, which we will discuss later in this chapter.

Understanding the Role of an Eating Disorder

Much of today's formal eating disorder treatment can be overly focused on weight and behavioral patterns. While these are obviously important parts of treatment, I think it's equally important to understand what the functions of the behaviors and thoughts might be for an individual. Ultimately, the motive behind behavior will be different for each client and exploring these patterns allows for an opportunity for you to create an interpersonal connection. For example, I might work to understand how eating disorder thoughts and behaviors help the client, whereas their family members, who are watching their loved one fight a life-threatening illness, might struggle to understand how anyone could think of this illness as remotely helpful. However, as therapists, if we do not try to understand the ways in which an eating disorder might actually help our client (or the perceived need it is satisfying), and provide them with alternatives, then their weight, eating patterns, or other symptoms are likely to persist. Additionally, when treatment lacks depth, it becomes a parallel process of the client not feeling understood and treatment not working, which could result in feelings of hopelessness.

When I was a therapist on the eating disorder inpatient unit, I ran a daily group with one of my biggest mentors: Janice Blackwood. Anyone who had met Jan knew how truly special she was. She was the epitome of having the biggest heart, while also telling you your hardest reality; her empathy ran big. Having this ability is so important when working with eating disorders, and it hinges on being able to build and maintain a strong alliance. I'll talk more about my relationship with Jan later in this chapter.

In this group were folks from all walks of life. One of the things I always used to say (that I still do) is: "an eating disorder, for many, can allow them to survive when they otherwise would not have made it through something significant in their lives." That could be a traumatic experience, loss, a life transition, or any emotional experience that felt completely overwhelming. However, at some point, there must be recognition that maintaining the eating disorder begins to erode your survival, and instead of trying to save you, the eating disorder starts to turn on you.

Often in my initial few sessions, I will ask clients how their eating disorder behaviors might be helping them. Some look blankly at me, not having any idea of how to answer this question. Some are perplexed as to my phrasing, likely because they have always been told by others how terrible this illness is, or they have not allowed themselves to consider that it actually might be helping them. Posing the question in this way helps me join with the client, even if there is a lack of clarity regarding its function, by allowing them not to feel judged, which may help them to be more open in the relationship. I often cite a client's strength, such as intellect, as a way of describing how their eating disorder may be coming from a place of utility. For example, I might say, "You are clearly a very smart person and if you're eating disorder wasn't helping you in some way, then you probably wouldn't continue to use it."

There are likely many reasons why an eating disorder is serving someone well. Understanding these functions will most likely take some degree of time. However, time also gives you the ability to deepen your relationship and create a better understanding of the client's thought processes. Some of the eating disorders' functions might be obvious, but there might be others that take longer to understand. It is through your relationship with your client that will allow for other functions to become clearer.

Flexibility

Eating disorders thrive on rigidity and fear. Many individuals broadly associate eating disorders with the word "control." There's no doubt that this resonates with many with eating disorders, but I would also deepen this conceptualization by suggesting that eating disorders are also often related to the discomfort of allowing for flexibility. For many with eating disorders, there's a desire to leave uncertainty in the dust by installing faux "guard rails" of rigidity, rituals, and routine, which leaves little room for anything unexpected to arise (at least that is the hope, as unrealistic as it may be). Unfortunately, these "guard rails" can provide such immediate and overwhelming relief that it can be hard to resist, prompting life to become increasingly narrow. Over time, as clients lose more and more of what it is like to experience their emotions, fear of these feelings may reinforce the need to rely on the guardrails of the eating disorder.

As you can imagine, the major role of the therapist then becomes to challenge this inflexibility, but it is unlikely to be met with open arms. Chances are your clients have already experienced disruptions in their relationships with family and friends because they attempted to do just that. For example, while on vacation, an adolescent's family may spontaneously decide to go out to dinner instead of cooking a meal at their rented condo. The adolescent, struggling with an eating disorder, might have been able to manage deviations like this in their normal day-to-day lives; however, under unusual circumstances, like vacation, this sudden change might cause an explosion of emotion that leads to an argument with their family. Examples like this are all too common in my outpatient practice. After hearing about these instances, it puts the therapist in the difficult position of supporting the challenge that family was attempting to create, while also validating the emotional distress that your client (in this case, the adolescent) experienced. This is often another major part of the therapist's role: validating the fear your client may experience, while also empowering them to do hard things. As therapists, supporting your clients' emotional experience allows you to join with them, so they don't feel so alone. We don't want to say, "you no longer have to do the hard thing," instead, we want to say, "I'll stand next to you while you do it."

We also need to model flexibility in the therapeutic relationship and treatment broadly. It's always striking to me that the treatment of eating disorders often involves a rigid treatment plan. The very tenants that uphold the illness (i.e., rigidity), we duplicate in its treatment. Of course, there needs to be a standard of care to manage medical concerns associated with eating disorder behaviors, but it's also important to model flexibility to support the relationship and rapport. In graduate school, we are taught the importance of completing a comprehensive biopsychosocial assessment before identifying treatment goals. The same should be true here. Most likely, the medical and nutritional providers will have firm goals based on managing the medical safety of the client. Our role as therapists is to provide thoughtfulness and context to all the parts of the person: family history, cultural background, life experiences, physical and mental health, and social environment (Esbenshade & Venegas, 2024). This understanding should give you vital context for how to begin challenging the eating disorder and one's inflexibility, as you will have a better sense of the purpose flexibility serves in their life. Taking the time to dig into these areas will also allow your client to get to know you and trust you more, which will create a stronger therapeutic bond to support their treatment.

The way in which you decide to challenge your client's inflexibility is a major area to consider. Some clients will come into treatment motivated to shift their thinking and actions; for instance, perhaps their lack of flexibility is intruding on important romantic relationships or professional roles. Other clients might not know any other way to live outside of their eating disorder. If there seems to be an impasse to moving forward, I might challenge inflexibility in other, less threatening, ways. A metaphor here might be to drive a different route home or to change part of your morning routine. An eating disorder treatment example might be challenging a client's overexercising behaviors by asking them to swim or do yoga in place of intense exercise. This intervention somewhat appeases their eating disorder by involving movement, while also challenging the rituals the eating disorder has created by having them cope with the discomfort of moving their body in a different way.

In sum, the overall goal is to introduce more flexibility that might not seem as threatening to the eating disorder. It enables your client to begin to feel mildly uncomfortable and, over time, increases their ability to tolerate that discomfort. It also provides additional evidence that the client can trust you by feeling heard in the process and taking smaller, less threatening steps. This will also help as you begin to challenge the eating disorder more directly, as the client now has more familiarity with this feeling, as well as the treatment process.

Vulnerability

Vulnerability can be described and defined in several different ways; however, I believe it can best be understood when it's observed. I often know that I have hit on something important when suddenly the client goes from talking freely to struggling to share much at all. You might notice their body language shift, perhaps they start to position their body more inwardly, or they begin to blush more easily. For some clients, there might be specific areas of vulnerability that make them feel especially uncomfortable, and for others, you might find that it is difficult for them to share anything that creates an emotional pull. I often notice that for those with longstanding eating disorders there can be comfort in discussing the emotions that result from their eating disorder. However, when you challenge them to discuss the other difficult areas of their life, they struggle. An eating disorder can often serve as a superficial vessel that allows an individual to intellectually acknowledge their feelings without truly having to experience them.

Self-Concept

Poor self-concept is a predictor of relapse in those with eating disorders (Bardone et al., 2010).

In order to support our clients in a more sustained recovery, it is important to spend time and energy on identifying and improving one's self-concept. In my practice, I have seen a variety of presentations related to poor, or ill-defined, self-concept. For some, it's clear that they have always had a negative view of themselves, and for others, the eating disorder has interrupted their ability to trust themselves. Exploring the underpinnings of these challenges can have important implications for the therapeutic relationship. It can provide a more nuanced understanding as to why it might be difficult to challenge eating disorder thoughts or how body image distortions can be so convincing. How can we expect our clients to challenge these thoughts if they do not have an established internal compass – or self-concept – to guide them? And if the client is constantly unsure of themselves, then how can they feel confident challenging their eating disorder thoughts? Fortunately, one's self-concept is dynamic, meaning it can change. In the very way an eating disorder can diminish one's sense of self, therapy can help one to reestablish it. Recognizing that your client may be struggling with poor self-concept may allow you not only to target it and improve it in treatment, but also to create empathy and understanding for their lived experience.

Case Vignette: Penny

Penny came to my private practice in her junior year of college following a year abroad. After returning, Penny's parents raised concerns about her eating, and she began outpatient treatment shortly thereafter. Penny shared her parents' concerns and was motivated to feel better. By the time I met her, she had already started eating more consistently – three meals and three snacks per day. In our first session, she talked about how her disordered eating started a year and a half ago and had intensified over the last several months. She described self-imposed pressure to perform well academically as well as experiencing several aversive social situations, leading her to feel disconnected from her peers. As all of this unfolded, she noticed that she started eating less and exercising more. Then, prior to her year abroad, she remembered how fearful she felt about what she would eat in this country she had never been to before, and if she would be able to keep running. To her surprise, she found plenty of comfortable food options and still found time to run; however, despite these concerns being allayed, her eating disorder thoughts continued to encourage more restriction.

I found Penny to be quite insightful, but at the same time, emotionally guarded. This was evident from the very first session: she would often blush when answering benign questions and had difficulty elaborating on most topics. As I continued to inquire about various psychosocial parts of her life, I made a point to be aware of the tone of my voice – slower, calmer, softer – to create a sense of ease so that she felt she could be more open. I would often acknowledge to her that my questions were not easy to answer while validating her discomfort, and providing positive feedback on her ability to continue to engage with me despite her discomfort.

Throughout our work, Penny worked hard to nourish herself. She had many goals for her life and could clearly see that the eating disorder was a major obstacle to attaining those goals. We began to explore her family history and social experiences – areas she had never really thought about before. She described an upbringing in which her parents often emphasized the importance of living life in a "healthy way." She observed them from a young age, being overly careful about what they ate and incorporating rigid exercise into their daily routines. It was clear that there seemed to be a connection between these early messages and her eating disorder behaviors currently. But, instead of directly saying that to her, I asked her to be curious about her family's relationship with food and exercise. I provided education about how our environment can impact our behavior; how the messages we receive growing up can influence our actions, which was a helpful realization for Penny. She would repeatedly return to this idea over the years, particularly when she would visit her parents where those early messages were still very present.

While Penny progressed quickly in treatment, she continued to present emotionally guarded. Penny was, and always had been, a driven individual who thrived on setting and achieving goals. While this allowed for many successes in her life, it also served as a mechanism that fueled her eating disorder. I made certain to repeatedly mention that her recovery was not just another goal that she could check off her list. The emotions that were underlying her eating disorder can't simply be turned off like a light switch and ignored. This type of "white-knuckle recovery" can paradoxically create an "all or nothing" approach to treatment that can mimic the rigidity of an eating disorder. So, I started to challenge Penny to reflect on her uncomfortable internal experiences.

As we continued our work, the mechanisms behind Penny's eating disorder started to surface. Throughout her life, she struggled with perfectionistic tendencies, which seemed to contribute to her discomfort with uncertainty and emotional vulnerability. In her mind, the rigid routines she created served to protect her from those uncomfortable feelings. As our therapeutic relationship deepened, and Penny became more curious about her emotions, we found that experiencing shame would quickly evoke tears, and that she often used her academic successes to mask feelings of disappointment and inadequacy.

By the later stages of treatment, Penny learned to fuel her body intuitively and started to rebuild a more positive relationship with movement again. She understood that her parents' relationship with food and exercise did not have to be hers. She realized that much of her eating disorder was an attempt to manage uncertainty and emotional vulnerability, themes we would continue to focus on for years after. Penny learned to accept that allowing life to progress naturally also meant allowing for uncertainty, not rigidity, and that forming deep bonds with others required emotional vulnerability, not guardedness or self-judgment.

Currently, despite the eating disorder thoughts no longer being present, Penny's struggles have turned to areas that better align with her values (e.g., romantic relationships, career). She is more open about the depths of her self-critical thoughts and how quickly they can be triggered. She can name her difficulty with vulnerability in romantic relationships and challenge it directly. And yet, despite all of these improvements, my stance as her therapist hasn't changed. I remain mindful of creating a therapeutic relationship based on non-judgmental curiosity with the hope that Penny can continue to challenge herself to deepen her understanding of her emotional experiences.

Penny: Takeaways

Some of the major themes of Penny's case are perfectionism, learning to be self-curious, discomfort with uncertainty, and engaging emotional vulnerability. There were many times throughout Penny's treatment when I wasn't sure what to do. For example, she would deny that something felt bothersome, but her body language said differently, or she was unable to identify what was bothering her as she cried. When things like this occurred, I would often slow the pace of the session and attempt to explore these feelings gently. Penny provided cues (e.g., increased emotionality, visibly uncomfortable body language) that we then could return to in subsequent sessions.

Another aspect I would note about Penny is that, although being open about her emotions did not come naturally for her, she always showed up to sessions and challenged herself. Even today, there remain several areas that are hard for her to be open about, which gives a glimpse into where her vulnerabilities lie. These things were true of Penny, but not of all clients; noting the different ways that vulnerability can present is helpful to understand in our clinical work.

One of Penny's strengths, which may have allowed her to recover in a shorter timeframe, was that her eating disorder was not a part of her self-concept. We know that a less intact self-concept is a predictor of eating disorder relapse (Bardone et al., 2010), and for Penny, she knew early on that the eating disorder was taking up unhelpful space in her life and mind, and she was highly motivated to take that space back. Therefore, to support a more sustained recovery, it is important to spend time and energy in identifying and improving one's self-concept.

Boundaries

There is something intrinsic to the word boundaries that seems overly concrete, almost sterile, and lacks intuitiveness. We live in a world where therapists powered by artificial intelligence (AI) are possible, so it's important to remember that our humanness is one of our greatest assets. As therapists, we suffer, we cry, and we have bad days. The goal of this section is to give you permission to be authentic as a human being as you do this clinical work. Of course, all while maintaining your own sense of right or wrong and safe or unsafe (i.e., boundaries). In this section, we will return to many of the themes previously mentioned, as I find these aspects can both create a rich, positive therapeutic relationship or interfere with it.

Boundaries: Incorporating Curiosity

In graduate school, we are taught to hold a fairly rigid stance with what we share about ourselves to our clients, and if we choose to share something, it should be based on a rationale that is for the client's benefit. Within this lesson is encouragement to engage our curiosity. However, for new therapists, there can be an urge to balance the unpredictability that is inherent in this work with something more predictable, which creates conditions that promote rigidity. The longer I'm in this field, the more I've realized that utilizing curiosity to understand what is happening in a session can temper the urge to be rigid. It allows me to be more thoughtful and intentional in my decisions about self-disclosure. In a word, curiosity can help you to better understand why you might be choosing to share something in that moment, which may create different avenues to join with the client in ways that do not feel exposing to you.

Sheila came to me years ago for help with binge-eating behaviors. Initially, we used a structured CBT model to target her overeating behaviors; however, every time we attempted a concrete task, like a worksheet, she appeared distracted and uninterested. Instead, I started to engage more freely by using humor or incorporating small personal anecdotes, like commiserating about our favorite boy bands in the early 2000s. When doing this, I noticed that her engagement shifted instantly and significantly. What we would come to learn as treatment progressed was that she also had ADHD. Had I not shifted my stance to be more engaging, there was a high risk that she would have ended treatment prematurely, as the CBT interventions were too uninspiring for her to concentrate on. Being curious about the things that she enjoys gave me a better sense of how to join with her. Today, we even sometimes chuckle about the initial phase of our work together, yet another way to deepen our relationship.

Boundaries: Incorporating Flexibility and Vulnerability

Boundaries are often framed as binary. On the one hand, you have a lack of boundaries (which is often thought of as unprofessional), and on the other, you have rigidity and inflexibility (which can make a therapist, or any person for that matter, seem robotic or devoid of emotion). The truth is that boundaries exist on a spectrum. As Sheila taught us, curiosity can give us a better understanding of how to improve our connection with our clients by shifting where you are on that spectrum as you learn more about your clients. Being capable of oscillating from emphasizing shared human connection to more structured treatment elements is an important skill for a therapist. We need to recognize that boundaries and vulnerability are not necessarily polarized ideas – we can use them simultaneously.

I believe an important role of therapists is to model therapeutic ideals for our clients. In order to do this genuinely, there must be room to share personal details of our lives. For example, I occasionally walk across the street from my office to the local florist and put together a bouquet of flowers for myself. When I do this, I find that many of my clients will often ask about the flowers on my desk. I then tell them all the ins and outs of this hobby of mine, which helps to model a way that I take care of myself, all while never feeling personally exposed or sharing information about myself that is not appropriate for me to share.

Vulnerability involves a great deal of authenticity. Showing clients a more authentic side of ourselves, without divulging the inappropriate details of our lives, can be a powerful tool, which can help to temper the power dynamic inherent in the therapeutic relationship. It is natural for our clients to feel exposed during treatment, particularly as we strip away the protective layers of the eating disorder. It's natural for us, as therapists, to want to provide personal shared understanding to validate those feelings. But, it's a tricky to balance finding ways to show empathy while also encouraging our clients to sit in, and tolerate, their discomfort.

A great example of this is my mentor, Janice Blackwood. She had the rare quality of genuineness while never exposing a personal detail about herself. I would describe Jan as a very private person, and even though she was a dear friend of mine, there were many details about her life I never knew. The beauty of Jan was that you didn't need to know much about her personally to feel her authenticity. She accepted all the parts of who she was (the cranky, the witty, the no-nonsense), which implicitly gave permission for you to do the same. Jan was one of the funniest people I have ever known, and she never hid how she felt about something. Everyone knew when she didn't like something; it was all out there. This made her real and created a connection because there was no façade. There was no question that the underpinnings of her directness, her toughness, her expectations were because she wanted the best for you (she was consistent and persistent about that). Over the years, I have watched how others tried to duplicate her style, and it never really worked; only Jan could be Jan. Within this, there's an important lesson for all of us: identify your own style and dig into what makes you unique; staying true to who you are will most easily allow for this.

Boundaries: Incorporating Self-Concept

Poor self-concept can present as challenges with interpersonal relationships. For instance, clients may trust individuals too quickly or allow others to make decisions for them that may undermine what they need or want. For therapists, the goal is to try and create a meaningful relationship with your client that respects their perspective, voice, and opinion, while also encouraging them to go out into the world and find others that will do the same.

Case Vignette: Margot

Margot is a 15-year-old white, cisgender female, an only child of divorced parents. I started seeing her after a months-long admission to an eating disorder residential treatment setting. Prior to this, she had been admitted to a psychiatric inpatient unit following a suicide attempt. In our initial meeting, it was clear that she was experiencing many mental health challenges. As a child, she described attachment issues which led to difficulties in preschool and severe tantrums that would sometimes result in aggression toward her teachers. Regularly attending school became increasingly difficult due to these issues, so at nine years old, her mother decided to send her to a boarding school that specialized in treating "behavioral issues." Margot would go on to spend the next four years there.

She experienced many traumas of different types while away at the boarding school, mostly related to the way they attempted to correct her behaviors. Despite the many therapists at this school, she never had a positive experience with any of them. If anything, her associations with therapists, or as she would say in a sarcastic tone, "those that were there to help and protect me," were filled with punishment and abandonment.

In retrospect, it was amazing that she ever agreed to see me. From the get-go, it was clear that she was apprehensive and guarded, and understandably so. However, she also desperately yearned for connection. She began to open up about what she thought about herself, both now and historically. She struggled at a young age with significant negative self-concept and intrusive obsessive-compulsive thoughts. After months of exploration, I transparently shared my clinical opinion that she was experiencing OCD. She said that for most of her life, she just assumed that these negative thoughts existed because she was a terrible person. After being able to contextualize these intrusive, negative thoughts through OCD, it helped Margot to think differently about herself.

Margot then began to talk about her eating disorder and how she thought it started because her peers did not like her in her first year of high school. At the time, she thought if she could just change the way her body looks, then perhaps others might like her. The negative thoughts that had been around for as long as she could remember were now being weaponized by the eating disorder to perpetuate itself and its behaviors, although the real intention behind those thoughts was innocent: trying to create meaningful connections in her life and feel better about herself. Margot's early experiences with high anxiety, OCD, and the trauma she experienced at boarding school fostered conditions where it was difficult for her to create an appropriate self-concept. While I was relieved she was connecting to me early on, I was also always mindful of my boundaries.

Our relationship has gone through many iterations. For the first year of our work, she was very attached to me. I was mindful to not expose parts of myself that did not feel helpful or useful. She would often say she liked that I "kept it real." I think what she meant by this was that I was transparent with her, and if something was problematic, I would tell her and explain why. Like my mentor, Jan, I was careful to be my genuine self with Margot without compromising my sense of interpersonal safety, all the while truly wanting the best for her.

Margot: Takeaways

Throughout my work with Margot, it was important for me to be constantly aware of my boundaries. There are many clients I have worked with where I didn't need to be so thoughtful, but with Margot's early challenges with attachment, the intense negative thoughts about herself, and her traumatic experiences in boarding school, she really didn't know how to have a healthy, appropriate relationship with a therapist. For instance, at one point during our work, another therapeutic service started and abruptly ended because the new provider shared inappropriate details from her own difficult upbringing in an effort to join with Margot. I believe that being cognizant of my boundaries was an important element of Margot and I's therapeutic relationship that helped it to be an effective agent of change. Although our relationship has evolved over the years, it has landed in a healthy way, and these boundaries have helped to push Margot to try to meet her needs in other friendships and relationships.

In this field, there can often be an urge to implement rigid boundaries. By having more varied clinical experiences and a good sense of your own values as a therapist, you can gain a foundation that allows you to be more curious, flexible, and vulnerable within your own style. I often compare the therapeutic relationship to a dance: You may not always know where your partner might step; however, the more open you are to their movements, the more you will flow together. Within this dance lies the mutual trust you'll need to be able to challenge your client's eating disorder. Your openness will be important for your clients to see, allowing you to create stronger and more effective therapeutic relationships. In summary, don't let boundaries stifle you from expressing your own humanity.

References

Bardone-Cone, A. M., Schaefer, L. M., Maldonado, C. R., Fitzsimmons, E. E., Harney, M. B., Lawson, M. A., Robinson, D. P., Tosh, A., & Smith, R. (2010). Aspects of self-concept and eating disorder recovery: What does the sense of self look like when an individual recovers from an eating disorder? *Journal of Social and Clinical Psychology*, 29(7), 821–846. https://doi.org/10.1521/jscp.2010.29.7.821

Esbenshade, E. & Venegas, A. (2024.) Biopsychosocial review of eating disorders. *Open Journal of Psychiatry*, 14, 107–119. https://doi.org/10.4236/ojpsych.2024.142007

Mital, R., Hay, P., Conti, J. E., & Mannan, H. (2022). Associations between therapy experiences and perceived helpfulness of treatment for people with eating disorders. *Journal of Eating Disorders*, 10. https://doi.org/10.1186/s40337-022-00601-1

Chapter 5

Skills a Therapist Will Need

Jacquelyn "Jac" MacDougall

My name is Jac, and I am an accidental Eating Disorder specialist. I know what it's like to start out and feel as if you need to be an expert to serve people. An important mentor and friend used to tell me, "Jac, when you think you know everything, you are dangerous." His reminder that we can't possibly know everything has stuck with me over the years. I find myself reaching for that reminder when experiencing moments of imposter syndrome, which often come with the territory of doing something both hard and important. I share this as an up-front disclosure that the following chapter will include the writing of a forever-student who does not presume to know it all. A student with the knowledge that there are far more experienced professionals in this field than I. My commitment to the reader is the honest, good-faith sharing of knowledge and experience with the understanding that, as I write this, I am a human who is constantly developing my craft and regularly making mistakes. I hope this inspires confidence in your own skills and ability to help.

I started in this career by stumbling into a job. I was a twenty-something sitting in class in therapy school, and a classmate spoke about her experiences in a residential treatment facility supporting individuals recovering from eating disorders. At the time, I didn't know anything about eating disorders and thought this could be a great part-time job to earn some money while also gaining clinical experience. I was blissfully unaware of the stigma that existed within the therapy field about how "difficult" it was to treat clients with eating disorders.

I worked as a milieu therapist, the organization's form of direct care staff. I was responsible for maintaining the safety of the program's residents, upholding program policies, and helping residents to interrupt eating disorder behaviors. This ranged from assisting clients with cooking, bathroom use (I would stand outside of the bathroom to make sure they weren't using it inappropriately), meal support, and crisis intervention when all of the above moved them to their skills breakdown point.

I look back on those times with so much fondness. I loved learning about the medical complications of eating disorders and building a greater

DOI: 10.4324/9781003600770-7

understanding of the impacts of diet culture, weight stigma, and the role of body image. I was supporting clients to challenge their own deeply entrenched behaviors and beliefs, and while I was doing that, I was healing my own troubled body image as someone who had always lived in a body outside of the "thin ideal." I began to recognize societal patterns that impacted my development, and for the first time, I started to build a healthier view of my own body and self.

It's been over a decade and several job changes since that time. I love the unpredictability and intensity of the work I do. I feel connected to being able to hold hope for those who struggle to hold it for themselves. It is meaningful to me to tell my clients that recovery is non-linear, that lapses and relapses happen, and that they can still keep moving forward. This work gives me purpose and allows me to meet some of the funniest, kindest, and most creative beings I have had the pleasure of knowing. I also love helping new clinicians find what they love about this work and build their confidence in their skills and ability to help.

In working with folks across all levels of care, from inpatient to outpatient, I learned a few things. Drawing on these experiences, what I hope to give to you are some general, concrete tools that I have found helpful in my work. However, I want to stress that no skill is more important than an authentic and trusting relationship with your clients. No worksheet, website, or breathing exercise will replace the real need to first meet clients where they are as humans. Don't forget all of the great qualities about yourself that led you here, like a good sense of humor or desire to help others.

Skills Overview

Behavior is behavior and people are people at the end of the day. It is as simple, and complicated, as that. People recovering from eating disorders are looking for happiness, love, connection, purpose, well-being, security, success, autonomy, growth, and joyful experiences (in no special order). Likely, they are seeking your help because something(s) is getting in the way of them achieving these goals.

Many of the popular evidence-based practices speak the same language – just in different dialects – as they tend to be rooted in behavioral therapy. When thinking about skills use, I find that using an eclectic mix of behavioral therapies can be helpful because it allows you, as a clinician, to determine alongside your client which dialect they most connect with. In my practice, I typically don't follow any one modality to the letter. There may be therapists or researchers out there who would disagree with this approach, but there isn't enough evidence to suggest that any singular approach is superior – all have their benefits and drawbacks. In a review of treatments for eating disorders, Grilo (2024) emphasizes that current treatment options for eating disorders remain insufficient, particularly for Anorexia, and highlights the need for newer, more effective approaches.

In this section, I will begin with a brief overview of important skills-based modalities. Then, I'll walk you through some of the broader techniques I have found helpful in working with EDs, while weaving in concepts and interventions from each of the outlined modalities. For many reading this book, these concepts will be familiar. Therapists, both new and experienced, likely already possess the skills needed to treat eating disorders, and my hope is that this chapter reinforces that idea for you. I also hope that by applying these skills specifically to eating disorders, as well as reviewing important implications or considerations for common skills use in EDs, you may learn a thing or two along the way.

Please note, I would recommend further continuing education in these evidence-based practices, as this overview will not provide the full depth and breadth of modalities or their specific interventions.

Cognitive Behavioral Therapy (CBT)

In a nutshell, CBT aims to identify and challenge problematic thoughts that may be leading to maladaptive feelings or behaviors. This is done through understanding the connection between thoughts, emotions, and behaviors. Cognitive Behavioral Therapy uses various techniques to identify and restructure negative thoughts as a means to build new ways of thinking, consequently leading to different ways of feeling and interacting with the world. It emphasizes action-based approaches to change and doesn't focus too much on the why of someone's struggles. As a provider, I find CBT to be extremely helpful in illustrating the difference between thoughts, emotions, and facts. Similarly, it is full of useful tools and has a ton of empirical support behind it for successfully treating eating disorders. Christopher Fairburn (2008) created a training manual for CBT for eating disorders (CBT-E) that is a wonderful tool for a clinician to have.

Dialectical Behavioral Therapy (DBT)

Dialectical Behavior Therapy (Linehan, 2015) centers itself on acceptance and change, where individuals must first learn to accept their emotional experience in order to change their behavioral response. This modality's philosophy is based on the idea of dialectics: that two seemingly opposing ideas can both be true at the same time. It draws on mindfulness to highlight the importance of being present in the moment as a tool to increase our self-awareness which is the first step to better managing our emotions.

Dialectical Behavioral Therapy asserts that through skill use, clients can engage the best parts of both their rational and emotional minds in order to access their Wise Mind, which supports optimal decision making that will facilitate building a life worth living. DBT is intensive and traditionally involves individual and group components (Linehan, 2015). While I do not purport myself to be a strict DBT provider, my clients and colleagues know that DBT has a special place in my heart, and that DBT is what I most often reach for when looking for common-sense and concrete skills.

Acceptance and Commitment Therapy (ACT)

Acceptance and Commitment Therapy, like DBT, is a third-wave behavioral therapy, as it uses mindfulness and acceptance to increase flexibility in thought to help facilitate behavior change. In contrast to traditional CBT, ACT emphasizes accepting distressing thoughts and feelings rather than reframing them, while also committing to behaviors that align with the client's identified values. In other words, ACT supports clients in feeling their feelings, thinking their thoughts (without getting overly attached to them), and engaging in practical steps that move them in the direction of their goals and values. Core concepts include acceptance, cognitive defusion, mindfulness, values clarification, and committed action. Acceptance and Commitment Therapy emphasizes living a life guided by one's values, without allowing negative thoughts, emotions, and sensations to control their behavior (Hayes et al., 2012).

Family-Based Treatment (FBT)

If you plan to work with children or adolescents, it is important to familiarize yourself with FBT. FBT is regarded as the leading treatment for adolescents with anorexia and bulimia nervosa (although research on adolescent bulimia is limited) and has shown promise for adolescents with ARFID (Datta et al., 2023; Grilo, 2024). FBT is implemented over the course of three phases: full parental control (which focuses on weight restoration and behavior interruption), returning control (the process of returning age-appropriate independence of food and eating to adolescent), and establishing healthy identity (catching up on important milestones that may have been missed due to the ED). The therapist serves as a consultant to the family, rather than an expert, and works to shift from blaming the parents as a cause of the illness to empowering them to facilitate their child's recovery (Rienecke & Lock, 2022; Lock & La Grange, 2025). The goal of FBT is to unite the family in the fight against the eating disorder and to collaboratively work toward recovery. This approach can be particularly effective for young clients who are ambivalent or resistant to recovery, since the onus of recovery is not placed solely on the child, but is shared with the parents. However, facilitating this approach can be demanding on parents (Ganci, 2016); similarly, caregivers' emotional regulation plays an important role in treatment outcomes (Rienecke et al., 2016). A full review of FBT is outside the scope of this book. For more information, we recommend you refer to the *Treatment Manual for Anorexia Nervosa: A Family-Based Approach* (Lock & La Grange, 2025) for the full manualized approach.

Exposure and Response Prevention (ERP)

Exposure and Response Prevention is another type of behavioral therapy that has primarily been used to treat Obsessive Compulsive Disorder, though it can be effective for many anxiety disorders. The two components involved in ERP are exposure and response prevention. The client is gradually and thoughtfully exposed to feared stimuli in a controlled manner, while encouraging the client to abstain from using safety-seeking behaviors (such as ED behaviors). Doing so helps the individual confront their fears to reduce the power of the triggering stimulus over time. Perhaps more importantly, the client is taught to resist using compulsive behaviors or rituals that they typically engage in to find relief. Exposure and Response Prevention Therapy also focuses on experiencing rather than avoiding the emotional distress that triggers can cause (Foa, Yadin, & Lichner, 2012). Although there is not enough evidence to support ERP as a standalone therapy for EDs (Butler & Heimberg, 2020), its core components are commonly used in treatment. Just think about it – exposure and response prevention is occurring at every meal and snack, up to six times per day! Although this is obviously not the primary intention of meals and snacks, we are still engaging a similar mechanism of change.

Motivational Interviewing (MI)

Motivational interviewing is another client-centered counseling approach designed to help individuals resolve ambivalence and increase motivation for change. Several key features of MI lend well to working with clients of all needs. MI emphasizes collaboration, seeing the therapist as a partner rather than an expert, by creating a level playing field and promoting a non-judgmental and respectful relationship. Viewing the relationship as collaborative allows the client to identify their reasons for change by exploring their values, desires, and motivations. The therapist's role in MI is to center the client's autonomy and agency for change, rather than forcing change upon them (Miller & Rollnick, 2013). Similar to ERP, MI is not intended to be used as a standalone approach; however, it can serve as an effective supplement to other treatment approaches.

How Skills Support ED Therapy

Established practice involves individualizing care to the specific needs of the client. The following section of this chapter highlights how skills and concepts from the above modalities can support your work with clients working toward recovery. Of note, these are big picture concepts, and you should view them as such. Some skills will apply better than others, so you will become used to identifying when more practice is needed and when it's just time to try something else. Special considerations and adjustments must be made for specific client needs, such as cognitive diversity or sensory sensitivities.

Supporting Curiosity

Curiosity is an essential ingredient to the therapeutic process. Marsha Linehan (2015), the creator of DBT, writes that engaging curiosity to objectively observe one's inner self and outer surroundings, without judgment, is an essential ingredient to change. The core of this process is simply mindfulness. Before anything can be different, we must first see a situation for what it is. Curiosity can help our clients slow down and observe their experiences, rather than pushing painful thoughts or feelings away. Instead of immediately jumping to "I can't do this," a client may instead think, "What's making me uncomfortable right now?" "When else have I felt this way?" "What did I do to get through then?" or "What other skills can I try to help myself?" I have found that awareness, cultivated by curiosity, can support skill use for anyone, regardless of eating disorder status.

The Power of Knowledge

I was surprised, early in my outpatient career, when I took the time to explain some very basic neurology to a teenage client. She would go on to reference that conversation over and over again throughout our work together. I find that clients respond well to general education about how their biology affects their emotions; teaching things like the limbic system and prefrontal cortex as well as how neurotransmitters and hormones impact our emotional experience. Understanding some basic neurobiology can help clients demystify and validate their emotional experiences, reducing feelings like shame and self-blame. That said, there's no need to hold a full-blown neurology lesson; just start with something simple, like the window of tolerance.

As you may already know, the window of tolerance (Siegel, 2010) is the optimal level of arousal when distressed while remaining present in the moment – not shutting down or becoming emotionally dysregulated. Within the window, one can remain relatively in control and interact with others, despite experiencing an emotional or physical stress response. When outside of their window of tolerance, they may experience hyperarousal (e.g., overwhelming emotions, challenging cognitions, hypervigilance) or hypoarousal (e.g., dissociation, disconnection, numbness). A person within their window of tolerance may still feel uncomfortable, but they can think logically, problem-solve, and interact with their emotions in effective ways. A person with an ED outside of their window of tolerance may engage in behaviors like restriction, purging, compulsive exercise, or others that help them to cope with their distress in the moment.

A goal of therapeutic interventions (of all kinds) is to support the expansion of one's window of tolerance by approaching (not avoiding!) challenges. To do this, we might first help clients become aware of their limits. How do they stay grounded and connected when distressed (DBT)? How can they better tolerate to challenging situations (ERP)? How can they build a toolbox of emotional regulation skills (CBT/DBT)? Things like objectively identifying or labeling emotions, deep/diaphragmatic breathing, progressive muscle relaxation, body-based practices (e.g., yoga, tai chi, etc.), self-soothing skills by using their senses, grounding techniques (such as calm, safe exercises), sleep hygiene, balanced nutrition, and appropriate movement can all help to support one's window of tolerance.

When we ask clients to approach their fears while regulating their nervous system responses, we build their window of tolerance and reinforce the message that they have all the resources they need to tackle the obstacles they are facing. While we, as people, may have the very human urge to avoid the things that make us uncomfortable, that temporary relief typically only serves to reinforce unhelpful avoidance in the long run. This is an important reminder for both therapists and clients alike.

Supporting Trauma Recovery

Experiencing trauma is common among those with eating disorders (Convertino et al., 2022). I often hear well-meaning providers say that we need to "treat the eating disorder first" before attempting to resolve underlying trauma. However, I have found that avoiding trauma in this way just ends up prolonging the recovery process. I think their advice is well intended, meant to ensure that clients are stable enough to tolerate the difficult work of processing trauma, or possibly out of fear of making the eating disorder symptoms worse. While it is important to establish a foundation of medical and emotional stability (e.g., skills and grounding training or developing an emotional support plan that involves loved ones) before beginning trauma work, it is also generally the case that clients with EDs in outpatient treatment are stable enough to engage in this kind of work. Out of an abundance of caution, I would recommend discussing the prospect of trauma work with the entire outpatient team before active interventions.

The Gift of Ambivalence

I often hear providers say, "they [the client] are not ready for recovery" – I hate hearing this. It usually comes from a place of frustration, such as feeling like the client has taken a step backward, or in response to feelings of inadequacy as we cope with our perception that we failed to help our clients. But know this: if we allow our discomfort to distract us, we get caught in the trap of rejecting the gift that is ambivalence.

In ED treatment, ambivalence is the space between hope and fear (of change). I have met very few people who were "fully ready" for recovery at the start of their journey. By design, recovery is not a straightforward path and often involves glimmers of motivation and bouts of self-doubt. Alternatively, I have yet to meet a client who wants everything to stay the same. An underlying assumption of DBT is that for those experiencing severe mental health crises, life is painful as it is currently being lived (Linehan, 2015). I find this is particularly true for eating disorders.

I often liken recovery to repeatedly touching a hot stove – over and over and over again. I ask clients to trust that the pain will eventually stop, but I am unable to tell them precisely when that will be; only that I have hope that it will. When a client contemplates challenging their eating disorder, that is an inherently difficult and brave act. Just like touching the hot stove, every fiber within them is telling them not to challenge the ED, but in order to overcome it, they will likely have to do the exact opposite of what their body and mind are telling them to do. And in the face of adversity, we all, as humans, will have moments of hesitation, fear, doubt, or ambivalence. As a therapist, demonstrating the ability to embrace ambivalence by acknowledging the very real and valid reasons our clients are engaging in their eating disorder behaviors can promote acceptance. And like DBT suggests, it is through acceptance that we can cultivate change (Linehan, 2015). In ED treatment, it's not only important to talk the talk, but also walk the walk.

Case Vignette: Maya

Maya is a young adult I saw in my outpatient practice, "because the rest of my team thinks I need a therapist." At first, she wasn't interested in therapy, "I don't understand it," she would say, and she wasn't convinced she wanted anything to do with recovery. She had seen a number of therapists before me and had reasons why they didn't work out after only one or two sessions. While she was always kind and respectful, she was clear that she wasn't "all in" on recovery.

A year into our work together, therapy had been focused on harm reduction as we discussed areas of her life that she did want to improve. The bulk of our work involved relationship building and motivational interviewing, along with elements from CBT, DBT, active listening, and empowering her to assume responsibility for her recovery. I did this by reflecting to her that she was the only one in control of how therapy (and her life) would go.

In addition to developing new hobbies, she was able to identify the unhelpful ways she was thinking about herself, which made her feel badly. She also named where those core beliefs came from and agreed to incorporate trauma work into her treatment plan. As it turns out, she also realized along the way that it's a lot easier to improve other areas of her life when she was nourished. Today, we talk very little about food, and she sometimes jokes that we don't even work on her eating disorder (but we do, though). My once skeptical client, who didn't believe in therapy, now cites many positive changes in her life. I believe this progress was made because we both prioritized building a therapeutic relationship as we looked for the motivation for change that she did have, and worked indirectly from there, instead of me trying to convincing her to engage in recovery head-on.

Skills to Promote Cognitive Flexibility

Many clients use rigidity, black and white, or all-or-nothing thinking to cope with uncomfortable emotional experiences. Similarly, they may follow rules to help them reduce emotional discomfort or adopt rules that have been reinforced by their environment. With eating disorders, the particular rigidities and rules just so happen to involve food and bodies. Clients may have varying degrees of insight about how rigidity does and does not serve them in their day-to-day lives. As with everything else in this chapter, once the therapeutic relationship is solid (e.g., maintaining a nonjudgmental stance, using open-ended questions to uncover your client's goals), there are a few skills I rely on when it comes to promoting flexibility in thought.

Invariably, we have all experienced an automatic reaction to a problem. The intensity of a situation might impact the way we think about it and lead us to the belief that we have limited choices in approaching or solving it. This can either keep us stuck or drive us to react impulsively based on old patterns of thinking, feeling, or behaving. Dialectical Behavioral Therapy offers a simple way of approaching a problem by outlining the various ways you can tackle it – or SCREW it (Linehan, 2015). SCREW is an acronym that stands for: Solve it, Change your perspective on it, Rationally accept it, Engage in misery, or make it Worse.

In my work with eating disorders, I find that identifying the option of "staying miserable" can be mobilizing for clients who would otherwise choose to do nothing (i.e., stay miserable) had it not been so explicitly clear. I will always remember the day that I invited Maya to contemplate changing nothing in her life. She vocalized that this idea, and inevitably staying miserable, felt like "giving up" – and she wasn't interested in that. The following week, she came to her appointment citing measurable changes in her behavior throughout the previous week. Outlining one's options, even less than ideal ones, can lead to creative and flexible ways of thinking about the problem.

Walking the middle path (Linehan, 2015) is a DBT module that engages dialectics. It encourages clients to embrace more accepting (e.g., both/and) thinking, instead of polarized (e.g., either/or) thinking, to support a more balanced and flexible view of the world. With many clients who are struggling with eating disorders, specific foods may be labeled as "good" or "bad," "healthy" or "unhealthy." Dietitians, therapists, and other ED professionals are often dispelling the myth that food functions as "good" or "bad," rather than being the mechanism through which we fuel our bodies or connect with others. Encourage clients to think in broader strokes that support a healthier and fuller relationship with food and their bodies. Recognizing extreme beliefs and challenging them can apply to many populations beyond EDs.

Another DBT concept, willingness vs. willfulness (Linehan, 2015), can also help to embrace flexibility. DBT defines willingness as being open to experiences or situations that may help clients reach their goals, even if it means being uncomfortable in the process. Willfulness, on the other hand, refers to rejecting reality (e.g., not being open to new ideas or situations), which ultimately leads to suffering (Linehan, 2015). When a client is struggling to accept something that they (logically) know will help them in their recovery, I will often revisit this concept. Recently, I used willingness vs. willfulness with a client who was feeling stuck. With weight restoration being a central part of her treatment plan, she reached a point in her recovery where some of her pants were getting tight, making her feel uncomfortable about her body. We would then go on to uncover that she has previously created a rule for herself: no matter what, she would not buy new pants. When we took a hard look at the areas where she was being willing and willful, she realized that this rule was willful – it rejected the reality that weight restoration needed to happen in order for her to recover. Despite having the time and resources to buy a new pair of pants that fit her body comfortably, it was this rule that kept her from wearing comfortable pants. Even though buying new pants brought up uncomfortable thoughts and emotions in the moment, once she embraced willingness, it led to more comfort in the long run. Working with folks to sort out where willingness can support their recovery process can be a positive and collaborative intervention.

Acceptance and Commitment Therapy (Hayes et al., 2012) is another way to address rigid thinking. Cognitive defusion is a skill that involves encouraging clients to label their thought as something separate from themselves; in other words, "I am not my thought." A thought is also not a fact, truth, or command. By separating oneself from their thoughts, we hope to reduce the power and influence that uncomfortable or unpleasant thoughts have on their emotional and behavioral responses. This separation may allow clients the space to identify behaviors that align with their values and goals, rather than reacting automatically to whatever the thought says. Humor is one of my absolute favorite ways to employ this skill: encourage clients to say their thoughts in a funny voice out loud, or sing their thoughts, or picture their thoughts being shared by a cartoon villain that makes them laugh, to reduce their power. An even simpler example of cognitive defusion is when someone says, "I am an idiot." Instead, we may encourage them to reframe, "I am having the thought that I am an idiot." Practicing this separation can allow clients to detach from their thoughts as absolute truth.

"Checking the facts" is another tool that can further assist work with unhelpful thoughts. Checking the facts involves examining the evidence to support or disprove a thought or belief to assess whether one's interpretation of a situation is accurate. Many eating disorder clients have a distorted sense of how others see them. You might ask your client, "Is there concrete evidence for this thought?" or "What do you actually know about how others are perceiving you right now?" By challenging these assumptions, clients can reduce the power of false beliefs and gain a more realistic, balanced perspective by shifting from automatic reactions to more evidence-based thinking.

Make Time for Emotional Literacy

We all have varying degrees of awareness about our emotions as well as varying emotional experiences. We are biologically wired to feel, but it is largely an individual endeavor based on our genetics and lived experience. One way we can support our clients is by helping them build an understanding of their own emotional experience and how to work with – and not against – it.

First and foremost, I like to start by gaining an understanding of how clients relate to their emotions. I have heard everything from "I love to deeply feel my feelings" to "I wish I didn't have feelings at all." One of my long-term clients regularly jokes that I continually disappoint her because I won't give her a lobotomy. But instead of taking away emotions from those that I work with (like my client would want me to do), I try to help them understand that emotions are crucially important and valid, but they are not always aligned with the facts of a situation. Sometimes, the intensity with which we feel may be ineffective, and other times, complete avoidance of our emotional experience may lead to our lives shrinking in ways that don't serve us either. As you can see, these challenges reach far beyond the specific population of folks with eating disorders.

Regarding concrete skills, I rely heavily on DBT. Distress tolerance skills like TIPP, distract with wise mind ACCEPTS, Riding the Wave, Self-Soothe, and Radical Acceptance help clients to tolerate the acute moments of distress, or life's toughest moments, without resorting to ED behaviors. Emotion regulation skills (e.g., ABC PLEASE; Linehan 2015) support clients in getting back to basics – reducing emotional vulnerabilities and their associated impulses. All of these skills are attributed to Marsha Linehan (2015), and chances are you already have her manual at your fingertips.

Ultimately, we don't need to overcomplicate our approach. Emotion regulation, distress tolerance, and understanding and validating one's emotional experience can benefit clients with eating disorders, just as it would all human beings. One caveat to this is that with every skill, we need to use common sense to determine if it is the right fit for your client. For example, someone who is compulsively exercising will likely not benefit from the "intense physical activity" component of the TIPP skill. If you're ever unsure about whether a skill will be helpful or not, seek supervision to talk it out. With time and practice, these skills support clients in reducing emotional suffering and building a balanced and self-compassionate approach to their own experiences, without needing to resort to unhealthy coping mechanisms.

Walk the Walk

As previously noted, I believe that collaboration is an essential part of the therapeutic process. It's important to recognize the difference between collaboration – meeting our clients where they are – and enabling their eating disorders. As clients uncover how their experiences impact their illness, part of the job of a therapist is to reflect the client's initial goals back to them and call them to action to take reasonable steps toward their goals. This sometimes sounds like, "and what do you want to do with this information?" or "I've heard you talk about challenging bingeing, when and how can we plan for you to start?" Sometimes, it just means compassionately calling them out with good humor and not allowing my own fear, discomfort, or anxiety to make me hesitant to challenge them.

For instance, it might be unrealistic to expect a client who engages in purging to stop "cold turkey." The individual is not to blame for developing their eating disorder, and simultaneously, they are the only person responsible for resolving it. In this case, DBT might suggest using the "delay" skill, which involves pausing before acting on an urge that is in opposition to a client's goals (in this case, the urge to purge), engaging in self-soothing techniques, and then evaluating the impulse after some time has passed. Even if the client engages in the behavior anyway, they are still practicing how to manage an impulse and potentially widening their window of tolerance to give them time to use another skill.

When treating eating disorders, having an awareness of the various behaviors and how they may present is certainly helpful, but I want to remind the reader that most behaviors can be broken down. Ask yourself (and your client): "What purpose is this behavior serving?" When we collaborate with our client to source something else that is helpful, adaptive, or more aligned with their values and goals, we are supporting action toward change. This is a clear instance where collaboration with an eating disorder-specialized dietitian and physician can be invaluable. Often, our teammates are already doing amazing work to break down ED behaviors and set measurable goals and exposures. When this work is already happening, our role shifts to supporting those goals and collaborating with our teammates, cheering on our client when they take steps in the recovery's direction, and being compassionate when they struggle.

Connection

Eating disorders are isolating disorders. Fears of judgment or social events that revolve around food may lead clients to miss out on experiences that may or may not include eating. The act of breaking bread is a central part of many cultures around the globe. In the West, there are countless ways that we casually refer to food, whether it be directly or indirectly – it's literally baked into our society (see what I did there?). Think back to your last holiday gathering and contemplate the remarks you heard as everyone gathered around the table. Chances are you heard things like, "I'm being so bad today [for eating this type or quantity of food]," or "calories don't count on holidays," or "good thing we're going to walk all this off later!" among many more. Now think about how one might react to those comments as they are in the throes of an eating disorder. It is no wonder these situations are often avoided (and just think about how many parties you go to that don't include food, probably not many).

Studies have shown that isolation and loneliness are correlated with more severe eating disorder behaviors (Cortés-García et al., 2022). When a client's support network is aware of the eating disorder, they can provide accountability and safe spaces for recovery. There is evidence showing improved treatment outcomes from having involved family for both adults (Fleming et. al, 2022) and adolescents (Rienecke, 2017). You'll find that some clients are ready to involve their support system from the outset of treatment, while others may take years to get to that point. Including in treatment the important people in a client's life also opens the door for interpersonal effectiveness skills (e.g., DBT), like building and maintaining personal relationships, ending destructive ones, and boundary setting. These are key topics in any therapeutic relationship and can help strengthen a client's relationship by considering their own needs and self-respect.

Values – Not Just Something You Find at Walmart

Human beings are inherently meaning-making creatures. We seem to constantly be looking for identity and purpose. For some, eating disorders may temporarily serve as a coping mechanism, providing an outlet from pain that feels unmanageable. However, while the behaviors may offer short-term relief, over time, they ultimately end up interfering with one's ability to engage in their day-to-day life. They can also get in the way of their relationships, workplaces, hobbies, and more. This conflict between the eating disorder's short-term benefits and its long-term damage creates a cycle that can be difficult to break. However, with the right support, people can begin to rebuild their connection to life and find healthier and more sustainable ways to cope.

When people hear that I am an eating disorder therapist, they assume that I spend most of my days talking about food and bodies. On the contrary, I spend a great deal of time digging into what makes my clients' lives full of meaning. Are there creative pursuits that bring them joy? Do they have career aspirations? Are they seeking to further their relationships, their education? No matter what, supporting clients in building the lives they would like to be living is helpful for their mood and motivation. When there are meaningful factors that drive clients to be connected to their lives (without the barriers that an eating disorder can bring), well then, that gives us one more tool in our toolbox to aid in recovery. Talking about meaningful activities is another great opportunity to explore what sparks joy for our clients, support them in processing emotions, or enhance their ability to self-monitor their recovery process. I have several clients who find journaling, poetry, and art beneficial for personal expression. The more we can support our clients in making their lives full and robust, the less room there is for thoughts like, "without my eating disorder, who am I?" At times, clients may feel as though they've lost everything to their illness, but even the smallest step can be a significant move toward recovery.

Depression and eating disorders go hand-in-hand, with some studies finding depression as the most common comorbid diagnosis with EDs (Herzog et al., 1992; Kaye et al., 2008). And when a client's mood impedes their motivation to engage in meaningful activities, it can be challenging to know how best to support them. Alongside other skills we've reviewed, I often provide psychoeducation on CBT's behavioral activation, which is a tool that can be used to break the cycle of depressed mood. For clients who resonate with DBT, I introduce opposite action to shift their emotional and behavioral responses. While both approaches share the goal of increasing engagement, they have slight differences.

Behavioral activation encourages clients to engage in positive activities that interrupt inactivity and isolation, which often reinforces depression. Opposite action (Linehan, 2015), on the other hand, goes a step further by asking clients to do the opposite of emotion-driven impulses, offering them an opportunity to feel a different emotion. For example, a client feeling anxious may have the urge to avoid a social situation. By practicing opposite action, they might instead choose to attend the event despite their fear, ultimately allowing them to experience the emotion shifting after the task is completed. Both approaches encourage clients to experience their discomfort rather than avoid it, allowing them to challenge their emotions with practical and intentional action. By offering both methods, clients can choose the approach that best fits their needs and preferences at the time.

Case Vignette: Erica

I met Erica as a young adult when I was working on a psychiatric inpatient unit. For the first time, she was actively engaging in treatment of her own accord; however, she was short on hope, actively using ED behaviors, and struggling with trauma symptoms that were, in part, due to the restrictive, locked nature of the inpatient unit. She struggled to regulate her emotions and trust her providers. At times, she felt angry and anxious around staff, while also feeling lonely, but yearned for connection. We tried several traditional grounding skills to establish safety and connection, but they didn't take. While all of this was happening, Erica was also grieving the loss of her identity as a circus performer, and at the time, needed to take a step back from her passion to work on her eating disorder recovery. Together, we sought permission for her to have access to her juggling materials on the unit, which wouldn't typically be allowed. Erica was able to use juggling as a mindfulness technique – rhythmic and monotonous, up and down, up and down – which helped her through the discomfort of challenging her eating disorder behaviors. I don't think there was anything magical about juggling, but meeting her where she was at was the starting point to her feeling safe and connected to someone who was trying to understand her experience.

Erica and I worked together for several years when she needed "tune-ups" in higher levels of care. We built a relationship that was trusting and mutually respectful, a dynamic that was born out of a simple and creative approach to a DBT skill that she still uses to this day. Although we haven't worked together in quite some time, she still generously emails me updates on her life. She and her outpatient team have focused on building her "life worth living," and she has returned to performing for the first time in years. Included in this life are her beautiful cats and a solid community of friends.

She is an advocate for raising awareness and reducing stigma for those living with mental illness. Recently, she invited me to a public forum where she spoke about her recovery and shared that juggling is still one of her favorite distress tolerance skills.

Relapse Prevention

Like all good therapy, we are tasked with helping our clients be prepared to do this work without us – because let's face it, we won't always be there when they need us. In ED therapy, like many other forms of treatment, an important way we do this is through relapse prevention: identifying potential triggers, emotional or psychological warning signs, how to cope, and people to call. Here again, there is no magic. Trust your wisdom and intuition as a helper. Teach your clients the difference between a lapse (e.g., a return to ED behaviors for a short time) and a relapse (e.g., full regression into ED behaviors for a sustained period of time). As you gain more experience, you'll get better at recognizing red flags. And relapse isn't always overt. Even for those who seem all-in on recovery may find that they have fallen backward into a relapse; "I didn't think my exercise was that bad, it used to be way worse!"

At the end of the day, our goal isn't to have all the answers or create the perfect plan that anticipates every possible challenge. What matters is to have a plan. One that supports your client as they build confidence in accessing the tools and resources they might need when difficult situations come up. By encouraging them to rely on their skills and support network, we empower them to navigate the ups and downs of their recovery journey.

Case Vignette: Holly

I started seeing Holly when she was 17 years old, deep in the throes of anorexia. She was painfully shy and reserved, with blunted affect throughout all of our sessions. Holly's breakthrough came when she realized that her desire to be thin (and resulting body image distress) was related to her severe social anxiety. Her social anxiety manifested as feelings of self-doubt and obsessive worry about whether her friends actually liked her or not. Through a combination of hard work, nutrition, and family support, she developed a coping skill plan that really worked for her, allowing her to progress through treatment and stay connected to the important things in her life. Holly is now 21 and a student in college. She still experiences challenges with her body image, which could be points of vulnerability – or potential relapse – for her eating disorder. She has gotten used to bringing these examples to our sessions to process, all the while not giving in to eating disorder urges, despite their temptation. She uses skills like journaling and poetry to process her emotions as well as DBT's Self-Soothe and TIPP skills to manage physical symptoms of distress – all of which are part of her relapse prevention plan.

ED's Do Not Discriminate

When you've met someone with an eating disorder, you've met a person who happens to have an eating disorder. This may not be earth-shattering information, but it can easily be forgotten in the pursuit of stringent treatment modalities, evidence-based practices, and empirical research. While it's true that best practices result from using research to inform clinical care, we need to remember that our clients are multidimensional people with unique needs. Research methods that "control" for important factors, like gender, race, and age, to show statistically significant associations reduce our clients to merely an average. Similarly, automatic assumptions or one-size-fits-all approaches don't work for everyone. Regardless of the therapeutic approach, collaboration and partnership are the secret ingredients to effective therapy.

That being said, special consideration must be paid to neurodivergent clients, in particular. According to Cobbaert et al. (2024), neurodivergent people experience eating disorder symptoms over a longer period and experience poorer treatment outcomes when compared to neurotypical people with eating disorders. Those with Autism Spectrum Disorder (ASD) or Attention Deficit Hyperactivity Disorder (ADHD), along with an eating disorder, may experience difficulties with sensory processing, executive functioning, social communication, or emotional processing, along with a higher likelihood of chronic illnesses and systemic discrimination (Cobbaert et al., 2024). A good example of this is those with Avoidant Restrictive Food Intake Disorder (ARFID). This diagnosis can involve sensory processing differences and a need for consistency that severely limits food variety. A typical approach to treatment may be to gradually expose the client to a variety of textures, tastes, temperatures, etc., to expand their tolerance for acceptable foods, thereby increasing variety. It may also be helpful to enlist the help of providers with specialized training. For example, collaboration with an ASD-specialized Occupational Therapist may help to tease apart legitimate sensory needs from eating disorder fears.

Understanding Important Context: Weight Stigma, Diet Culture, and Other Considerations

In general, we live in a world that celebrates certain body types and devalues others. Entering the eating disorder field without being aware of this would be like conducting surgery without first going to medical school.

Undoubtedly, as a therapist, you have already learned the importance of the therapeutic relationship as an agent of change. In most cases, the therapist is no longer the "blank slate" that Freud originally envisioned. Gender identity, race, ethnicity, culture, socioeconomic status, and other intersections of identity are all important factors in therapy. Despite Freud and his disciples' best attempts, you just can't take the therapist out of the room. I think Taylor (2018) said it well, "Our beliefs about bodies disproportionately impact those whose race, gender, sexual orientation, ability, and age deviate from our default notions. The further from the default, the greater the impact. We are all affected - but not equally" (p. 51).

In the interest of time, I will operate on the assumption that we agree these factors are important and have a profound impact on the therapeutic relationship. I will never forget being a new therapist, sitting with a client in distress. They lived in a larger body and struggled significantly with shame and a sense of "otherness." Through tears, she stated, "Jac, you don't understand. You're fat, but you're beautiful. You walk around so confident, and you have great style. I will never have that because I'm just fat." At that moment, I could feel my face become hot and flushed, and I started to feel other physiological cues of anxiety as I reacted to my body being so blatantly judged. I remember feeling how important that moment was for my client, but at the time, I didn't know what to say. I now know, years later, that there really weren't the "exact right" words in that moment.

This interaction, among many others over the years, taught me an important lesson: how clients perceive my body helps me understand how they view bodies generally. To some clients, I am a therapist who lives in a body they fear. To others, I carry the privilege of being able to shop wherever I want and find clothing that fits off the rack. I hold the privilege of air travel without needing to be concerned whether I will fit in the seat or must pay for two tickets as well as the gift of mobility and joy-based movement without pain. It is important that you're aware of your privilege and take it into account in the therapeutic relationship.

My body has been an important tool to me, since I'm a therapist who lives in a larger body and routinely does things like eat, dance (never well, but joyfully, nonetheless), wear clothing that fits, and have meaningful relationships. My experience is in stark contrast to common ED distortions of living in a larger body. And I appreciate being able to model the alternative.

It is important to examine and unpack the assumptions we have acquired from our own cultures and upbringings due to the simple fact that we are entering into a relationship that is a human one. An example of this would be asking the same diagnostic and evaluative questions to a fat client as you would to a thin one. Don't make the mistake of assuming that a client who lives in a larger body is presenting for binge-eating treatment. Similarly, don't assume that a client in a thin body is restricting. There is little information to be had by observing only their body. A good starting point is Ramos and Goodwin's (2024) questions for providers to ponder and work through before beginning body image work with their clients:

- How do I feel about my own body?
- Are there any unhelpful ideals/beliefs that I have about bodies?
- What further work do I need to do for myself regarding body image?
- What are my areas of privilege to be aware of with clients when doing this work?

I have found that it helps no one to avoid the thought that clients are observing my body. In fact, Rance and colleagues (2014) found that in addition to reacting to our bodies, clients "not only observed, speculated, and made assumptions about their therapist's body but also that their assumptions and speculations had the potential to influence both their beliefs about the therapist's ability to help them and their willingness to engage in therapy" (p. 2). Sometimes, when a client seems hesitant to discuss their body image fears, I ask how they perceive my body might be affecting their willingness to be forthcoming. It is rare for a client to want to make someone else experience the discomfort they feel about their own body, leading them to hold back from disclosing beliefs about their body for fear of hurting my feelings. Having open, honest conversations about body differences and how they might show up in the room allows us to demonstrate acceptance and hopefully reduce any fears that could be getting in the way of progress. This might sound like the following:

> By now, you've realized I live in a larger body. I am wondering if how you see my body ever impacts your ability to process your fears about (weight gain, being fat, living in a larger body, etc.—you will want to use language your client is comfortable with here, not everyone is comfortable with reclaiming the word fat).

Opening the door to these ideas and normalizing honest dialogue is essential in navigating any potential barriers that may interfere with our client's process. As therapists, it is so important to acknowledge the privilege that we carry into the therapy space. We need to be aware and acknowledge the ways inequities have impacted our clients. For instance, awareness of thin privilege can help prevent microaggressions and minimize the risk of unintentionally invalidating our clients' experiences.

It is crucial that we help our clients differentiate between eating disorder distortions and valid concerns shaped by societal experiences. I've found that a surefire way to lose a client's trust is to deny the reality that the world is often harder for people who live in larger bodies, whether we do so purposefully or not. I have several clients who experience real fear about whether they can fit into airplane seats. It would be potentially damaging for me to challenge that as a distortion. Instead, I would choose to acknowledge the very real barriers that people face every day when they live in bodies outside of the thin ideal. I would, of course, offer support in reframing actual distorted thoughts; for example, the belief that eating a slice of pizza will inevitably lead to significant weight gain. By holding both the external realities and the internal distortions, we as therapists can provide validation, build trust, and support change simultaneously.

Conclusion

Thank you for investing the time to start to learn how to support clients working toward eating disorder recovery. While foundational knowledge is, of course, important to eating disorder therapy, I hope this chapter has boosted your confidence and reinforced what's most important. We are here to build authentic relationships with our clients that are trusting, understanding, and meaningful. When the therapeutic relationship is strong, we can get curious and collaborate directly with our clients to seek out which skills will help them. We can sit with them in the beautiful and scary place that is ambivalence, and we can support them in working toward their goals, on their timeline.

References

Butler, R. M., & Heimberg, R. G. (2020). Exposure therapy for eating disorders: A systematic review. *Clinical Psychology Review*, 78, 101851.

Cobbaert, L., Millichamp, A.R., Elwyn, R. et al. (2024). Neurodivergence, intersectionality, and eating disorders: A lived experience-led narrative review. *Journal of Eating Disorders*, 12, 187. https://doi.org/10.1186/s40337-024-01126-5.

Convertino, A. D., Morland, L. A., & Blashill, A. J. (2022). Trauma exposure and eating disorders: results from a United States nationally representative sample. *International Journal of Eating Disorders*, 55(8), 1079–1089.

Cortés-García, L., Rodríguez-Cano, R., & von Soest, T. (2022). Prospective associations between loneliness and disordered eating from early adolescence to adulthood. *The International Journal of Eating Disorders*, 55(12), 1678–1689.

Datta, N., Matheson, B. E., Citron, K., Van Wye, E. M., & Lock, J. D. (2023). Evidence based update on psychosocial treatments for eating disorders in children and adolescents. *Journal of Clinical Child & Adolescent Psychology*, 52(2), 159–170. https://doi.org/10.1080/15374416.2022.2109650

Fairburn, C. G. (2008). Cognitive behavior therapy and eating disorders. The Guilford Press.

Fleming, C., Byrne, J., Healy, K., & Le Brocque, R. (2022). Working with families of adults affected by eating disorders: Uptake, key themes, and participant experiences of family involvement in outpatient treatment-as-usual. *Journal of Eating Disorders*, 10(1), 88. https://doi.org/10.1186/s40337-022-00611-z.

Foa, E.B., Yadin, E., & Lichner, T.B. (2012). Exposure and response (ritual) prevention for obsessive-compulsive disorder (2nd ed.). Therapist guide.

Ganci, M. (2016). Survive FBT: Skills manual for parents undertaking family based treatment (FBT) for child and adolescent anorexia nervosa. LMD Publishing.

Grilo, C. M. (2024). Treatment of eating disorders: Current status, challenges, and future directions. *Annual Review of Clinical Psychology*, 20, 97–116. https://doi.org/10.1146/annurev-clinpsy-080822-043256

Hayes, S. C., Strosahl, K. D., & Wilson, K. G. (2012). Acceptance and commitment therapy: The process and practice of mindful change (2nd ed.). The Guilford Press.

Herzog, D. B., Keller, M. B., Sacks, N. R., Yeh, C. J., & Lavori, P. W. (1992). Psychiatric comorbidity in treatment-seeking anorexics and bulimics. *Journal of the American Academy of Child & Adolescent Psychiatry*, 31(5), 810–818. https://doi.org/10.1097/00004583-199209000-00006

Kaye, W. (2008). Neurobiology of anorexia and bulimia nervosa. *Physiology & behavior*, 94(1), 121–135. https://doi.org/10.1016/j.physbeh.2007.11.037

Linehan, M. M. (2015). DBT skills training manual (2nd ed.). Guilford Press.

Lock, J., & Le Grange, D. (2025). Treatment manual for anorexia nervosa (3rd ed.). Guilford Press.

Miller, W. R., & Rollnick, S. (2013). Motivational interviewing: Helping people change (3rd ed.). Guilford Press.

Ramos, K. & Goodwin, N. (2024, August). *Embracing YOU: Effective strategies for treating body image concerns* [Conference Presentation]. Eating Recovery Center Virtual Conference 2024. United States.

Rance, Nicola M.; Clarke, Victoria & Moller, Naomi P. (2014). "If I see somebody …. Therapist or anything, I'll immediately scope them out": Anorexia Nervosa clients' perceptions of their therapist's body. *Eating Disorders: The Journal of Treatment and Prevention*, 22(2), 111–120.

Rienecke, R. D., & Le Grange, D. (2022). The five tenets of family-based treatment for adolescent eating disorders. *Journal of Eating Disorders*, 10(1), 60.

Rienecke, R. D. (2017). Family-based treatment of eating disorders in adolescents: Current insights. *Adolescent Health, Medicine and Therapeutics*, 69–79. https://doi.org/10.2147/AHMT.S115775

Rienecke, R. D., Accurso, E. C., Lock, J., & Le Grange, D. (2016). Expressed emotion, family functioning, and treatment outcome for adolescents with anorexia nervosa. *European Eating Disorders Review*, 24(1), 43–51. https://doi.org/10.1002/erv.2389

Siegel, D. J. (2010). The mindful therapist: A clinician's guide to mindsight and neural integration. W. W. Norton & Company.

Taylor, S. R. (2018). The body is not an apology: The power of radical self-love. Berrett-Koehler Publishers.

Chapter 6

Working with Families

Stuart L. Koman

My name is Stu Koman and I've spent my career as a builder of healthcare systems and as a practicing psychologist with a specialty in working with families. I learned early on that if you really wanted to work with adolescents, you simply had to work with their families, and that was at a time when families were often seen as the primary problem, not the solution. I began my career about forty years ago at Charles River Hospital, a small psychiatric hospital in Wellesley, Massachusetts, which opened one of the first psychiatric units in the state dedicated to the treatment of adolescents. It's hard to imagine that today we've come such a long way, but back then, if you needed acute psychiatric care, adolescents and adults were treated together on the same unit.

During my time there, I learned that most families were desperately trying to figure out how to help their children, and most of the system seemed to want to affix blame and separate them. I felt so strongly about what I was learning that I wrote a book with a colleague entitled *Handbook of Adolescents and Family Therapy*, edited by myself and Marsha Pravder Mirkin, PhD. Over time, my career moved into more administrative roles, but throughout my entire career, I have remained a family therapist. It's who I am and what I value.

More recently, I was the founder of Walden Behavioral Care, a comprehensive system of care devoted to the treatment of eating disorders. Walden has grown over the years and is now a part of a large system of care that covers the entire country. I look back at my years working in eating disorders and again marvel at how far we've come. My value, working with families, became a core tenet of treatment at Walden. In fact, throughout my years at Walden, I insisted that families be an integral part of every treatment and worked to educate our staff on the distinct needs of families that have a member who is struggling with an eating disorder. I was often brought in for family consultations and remember one case which seemed to harken back to the days at Charles River, though this time, it was not the system that was against the family; it was the blame and shame the family put on

DOI: 10.4324/9781003600770-8

themselves. In parents' minds, they had failed in adequately providing nutrition to their child.

Why Are Families Important?

Many eating disorder therapists can give you a long list of reasons, or more often excuses, for not working with families. In truth, families can be frightening. For a therapist, it feels like you have to keep track of ten things at once and manage a three-ring circus all with very little training. And there is a complication with eating disorders as many individuals (and their families) prefer to think of the diagnosed illness as a "one person" problem – the "identified patient." Add to that, many individuals struggling with an eating disorder believe strongly that they are the cause of the illness and hence feel that they must manage the illness by themselves. But it's not that simple. There is no such thing as a case that doesn't involve a "family." Rather, I encourage you to think of the family as an important component of the full picture of any case you encounter. And this is true even if there is a problem in engaging the family (they might be resistant, or tired) or if the patient is reluctant or refuses to allow the family to participate, or even if the members of the family are deceased or unavailable. These are certainly barriers to overcome, but should not constitute a valid reason to eliminate a family from consideration in treatment.

My advice is that as a therapist, it might be a good idea to stay away from even calling your work with a family "family therapy." I offer this because of the level of vulnerability a family feels during the crisis of an eating disorder, and given our history of blame in mental health, I would use language that offers support to a family rather than "treatment." Of note, this chapter had originally been planned as the "Family Therapy" chapter, and I elected to rename it "Working with Families." My intent is to encourage you to create an invitation to assist a family knowing full well that most families expect, at least on some level, to be blamed for the problem.

A fairly recent practice in behavioral health has been to think of the family as the "root" of the problem, and effective treatment often resulted in the "parentectomy" in which the parents were blamed and removed from the life of the identified patient. I worry that we run the risk of continuing this kind of thinking in eating disorder treatment and want to be clear that the current thinking about the development of an eating disorder points to a convergence of factors – genetic, biochemical, and environmental, all of which result in a complex symptom configuration with disordered behaviors around food. While the family environment can certainly contribute to the development of the disorder and, in some cases appears quite related, as in a family in which other members have an eating disorder or where there is a strong "diet" culture or other peculiarities around food, there are also many situations where a link between family and an eating disorder appears to be very remote.

There is a famous case (and training video) of Salvador Minuchin, a psychiatrist, who is generally thought of as one of the "fathers" of family therapy, specifically the brand known as Structural Family Therapy. Dr Minuchin works with a family with the presenting problem of anorexia in a daughter. We watch over a few sessions as Minuchin, the family therapist, works to re-empower the parents to feed the daughter appropriately and address the communication patterns within the family. After several sessions over a couple of months, we witness the abatement of anorexic patterns.

While it's never said, one logical conclusion that the trainees watching the video could make is that the family patterns led to the development of the eating disorder, instead of the idea that treating the family may be the most efficient way to address the issues that have arisen from the development of the eating disorder. The problem with this questionable viewpoint is the lingering attribute that families are to blame for eating disorders, a belief that many families hold, often silently, when an eating disorder is discovered. As a side note, the same attribute about families and causation was popular in the literature on schizophrenia, and this has now been rejected as well.

The "good news" is that we've come full circle in accepting the importance of including the family in the treatment of an eating disorder. The family consumer movement, such as Families Empowered and Supporting Treatment of Eating Disorders (FEAST) and others, that has worked to dispel the notion that families cause eating disorders has embraced Maudsley Family Therapy and Family-Based Treatment (FBT) as the treatment of choice for adolescents with eating disorders. A deep exploration of each is beyond the scope of this chapter, but I would encourage the reader to learn more about each as both of these approaches are conceptually based in a structural family therapy approach and the work of Minuchin and others.

Before moving on, I am gratified by the formal position adopted by the Academy of Eating Disorders in 2009. In it, the Academy says that "While family factors can play a role in the genesis and maintenance of an eating disorder, current knowledge refutes the idea that they are either the exclusive or even primary mechanisms that underlie risk." The Academy of Eating Disorders, "stands firmly against any etiological model of eating disorders in which family influences are seen as the primary cause, and condemns generalizing statements that imply that families are to blame for their child's illness."

In summary, we work with families in the treatment of eating disorders because to not do so is to deny a major possible avenue for assistance. As therapists, I think we all agree that a life worth living takes place in a social context, and most people develop their most critical living skills in the context of a family. In treatment for an eating disorder, families are critical in all phases of therapy and must be engaged.

That being said, despite a client's reluctance and a family's struggle with blame, everyone needs support on their road to recovery, and while the degree of support may vary with the length of the road, family members are most often the first line of support. Part of moving away from the language of "Family Therapy" is an awareness that working with families can take different forms or approaches. It is not really even necessary to think of family treatment in more conventional terms.

What to Do?

Working with families really comes through two very different approaches, one that feeds into the other, and both of which are useful to a family. I refer to the first approach as family counseling and the second, family therapy. Both are different ways to approach working with families, and they are not mutually exclusive. In practice, I often find that family counseling blends into family therapy.

Family Counseling

Family counseling involves assisting the family by providing information and direction aimed at understanding an eating disorder and the implications of the illness for themselves and for their family members with an eating disorder. While the primary goal is to align the family behind the person with the eating disorder and to engage all family members in the recovery process, it begins with providing a good deal of education, including access to written information and other sources of knowledge (videos, blogs, etc.) and possibly connection to other families who have been through this before or are experiencing a similar situation (i.e., Support Groups). I often refer to family counseling as family psychoeducation, but I like the less stigmatizing phrasing of referring to it as simply "providing education."

With eating disorders, families rarely come through the door with a lot of information and have a tremendous thirst for knowledge. Eating disorders are mystifying, and all families appreciate the value of having a therapist who can provide basic education about what this experience is like for an individual and, more broadly, for an entire family. Of course, providing education in the context of family counseling does require a specific skill set. It is imperative that the therapist be respectful, meaning they can join with the family in what they do know and help the family fill in the gaps of what they don't know. And it is important that the therapist be compassionate and certainly a good communicator. And the payoff can be great. Providing education to a family about an eating disorder greatly decreases their anxiety and helps the family to better understand the experience of the member who is struggling with an eating disorder as well as their own reactions to the illness. It also allows the family to assess the therapist, particularly the therapist's ability to be nonjudgmental. Good education encompasses providing support, imparting knowledge about each specific disorder, and building relationships.

Whenever I begin teaching a family about eating disorders, I am always struck by how the discussion opens and the volume of questions that follow. Interestingly, the questions often lead to important information about how the family has reacted to the family member who is struggling and give a window into how they communicate and what they currently understand about eating disorders in general. Of note, I never allow an educational discussion like this to pass without offering local and national organizations as a resource. They are abundant, and I particularly direct parents to support groups, often part of these organizations, in which parents and loved ones can share their experiences, specifically what has helped and what has not, with other families. I have found time and time again that the support that comes from other families can sustain a struggling family over time. There is a common bond that is helpful among families that have shared such an experience as an eating disorder, just as there is a bond among individuals and families facing other health challenges.

In short, education and connections decrease the sense of isolation and shame for both the person with an eating disorder and for the family itself. At times, I have engaged a family in a discussion that compares the experience to a family in which a member has been diagnosed with a different medical illness, such as cancer. With a shift in view, there is often a relief of the stigma and blame that are such a part of eating disorders. Education frequently results in improved understanding and support for the individual with an eating disorder.

What Is Family Therapy?

Often, when working with a family, a shift occurs from family counseling to more formal family therapy. It's not a sudden change but occurs slowly, and once the family has assessed the therapist, they feel a sense of confidence and trust, and a lack of blame or judgment. It is a signal that the family has bought into the idea that working together can make a real difference in the treatment and the probability of recovery. Unlike family counseling, family therapy requires that the therapist develop a systemic understanding of how the family operates and then works to use that understanding to promote change in existing familial patterns. There is often a focus on achieving specific goals, for instance, structural, communication, and behavioral.

As a treatment modality, family therapy is valuable to a family as it creates an understanding of many aspects or patterns in the family environment, which can impact the member struggling with an eating disorder. Importantly, it offers the opportunity for the family to explore and potentially make actual changes in their environment. At a minimum, family therapy can make it clear to the person with an eating disorder which family patterns have been problematic for them, and then offer the opportunity to relieve that influence.

Like family counseling, providing family therapy requires a specific skill set on the part of the therapist. These include respect, compassion, and, of course, good communication skills. But somewhat different, it also requires a degree of competence in providing family therapy. A family therapist must have a certain skill level to engage in the process of assessing and intervening in family patterns of communication and behavior that are found to be obstacles to the process of recovery. These patterns can be the product of years of family interactions and may have a basis in patterns that date back many generations or can be relatively new patterns that have developed as the result of or in response to other family stressors, including the developing eating disorder itself. As a therapist, the challenge is to engage all pertinent family members in a positive effort to openly discuss patterns within a family and then to make changes in support of the recovery process. The art of family therapy is in creating an environment in which family members may very well believe it will be easier and ultimately more effective for multiple members to make changes rather than to rely solely on the person with the eating disorder to make all the changes or "just get over it."

Goals of Family Therapy

There is no set number of goals to begin family therapy, but I'd encourage you, in discussion with the family, to set two or three at the onset. Once some are established, additional goals can easily emerge while working with a family. I like these areas in which to engage a family as examples, as each provides a way to think about the work ahead:

1 Family therapy teaches family members about how families function in general and, in particular, how their own family functions
  One of the first great interventions I've found is in creating the understanding that there are no "perfect" families, that there are commonalities among all families, and especially the understanding that everyone in a family affects everyone else in the family. It reduces blame, and as trust develops and the fear of criticism dissipates, discussion will inevitably open up. With each, there becomes an opportunity for all members of the family to participate and shift the focus from "every family" to "our family."

2 Family therapy helps the family focus less on the member who has been identified as ill and more on the family as a whole

It is very common when I begin with a family, to have a family member who is clearly identified as the "patient." In fact, were it not for this member, no one else from the family would even be in the room. With eating disorders, this is always the case. One person in the family is struggling while others seem to be living healthy lives. The rest of the family is often struggling with a lack of understanding, even trying to accept why someone would restrict or engage in any food-oriented behaviors. A skilled family therapist can artfully shift the focus away from the individual with the eating disorder (to their great relief), and to the larger challenge of trying to understand the relationships, strengths, alliances, and boundaries that are part of the lives of every family member. Any progress in family therapy comes not from changing the behaviors of the one identified patient, but from garnering the collective strength and support of the family against an eating disorder.

3 Family therapy assists in identifying conflicts and anxieties within the family unit, and, most importantly, can help a family develop strategies to resolve them.

While certainly a lofty goal and not one that happens right away, it is ultimately what we want to happen and almost always begins with the processes of educating families about how families work in general and then strengthening all family members so they can truly work on their problems together. When this does occur, a family is really working as a unit. They are more receptive to opportunities to learn new ways to handle long-standing conflicts and to make changes to the patterns that have lingered within the family system. Implied in this work is a realization that sometimes the way family members handle problems makes them more likely to develop symptoms. This is because family dysfunction creates "stuckness" in the system and limits the ability of members to adapt and grow. Over time, a lot of energy within the family becomes habitual or mechanical and is unwittingly devoted to maintaining the "stuckness"; we think of this as, perhaps, protecting the family from getting worse. This "resistance to change (the expected consequence of a stuck system)" is to be expected and becomes the primary target of successful family therapy.

The Potential for Positive Change

Recovering from an eating disorder can be a long and, at times, very winding road. On that road, there are times when steps forward feel like great progress, only to be seemingly undone by a step backwards and a reemergence of symptomatic behaviors. During those tumultuous times, families are a powerful resource as holders of hope and perseverance. I have found that the family as a unit is a powerful force for keeping all its members as part of an intact family. It is the family that decreases the sense of isolation that clients struggle with after a setback, reinforcing the message that the person struggling is seen, cared about, and worthy of their assistance. It is quite profound and comforting when a family can communicate that "we're all in this together" and "we will support you through this journey."

Second, families are a source of motivation for the client and can provide needed support at times when the client is either too entrenched in their eating disorder thoughts or simply too exhausted. I always encourage families to speak directly to motivation and support, and tend to use very concrete language. It is quite positive when a parent, for instance, can take up my suggestion and say directly to their son or daughter, "I will carry the load for a while."

The same thing occurs with the message of hope. I have found hope to be one of the most powerful tools in eating disorder treatment, especially as clients struggle with periods in which they feel no hope. At times when the client cannot even imagine getting past their eating disorder thoughts to a future in which food is normal again and activities with food are not loaded with crippling anxiety, I call on family members to "hold the hope."

Lastly, families can be instrumental in creating change through their willingness to make personal changes themselves. Family members can model positive changes in treatment through recognizing some of their own behaviors or patterns and resolving to change them. The message in a family session that we are all in this together is wonderfully compassionate as well as therapeutic. In the end, nothing is more compelling to the client than seeing and experiencing real change in other family members.

Beginning Family Therapy: Critical Messages to Parents/Caretakers When Working with Eating Disorders

I find it helpful in the first session to lay the groundwork for what will happen in our family sessions, and frankly, what will not. I anticipate in this first meeting that the family coming through the door is likely very stressed and urgently wanting to make this problem "go away." They crave a return to normal, and they feel terribly blamed. I remind myself often of the many messages they have likely received, both intended and unintended, in which they are seen as the cause of their child's eating disorder. Because of this, I always make a clear statement to all in the room that "You didn't cause this." In truth, most don't believe me at first, as they feel quite guilty and shameful, but verbalizing this message is important, and I believe it must be spoken because forward movement cannot occur without it. I also repeat this message again and again in the following sessions, using language like "no one wanted this to happen" and "no one caused this to happen." I find that over time, a greater understanding of the disorder can be helpful in relieving the family of self-blame and leads to more effective means of support for the person with the eating disorder.

It is very hard to anticipate anything with great consistency in family therapy, but in the case of eating disorders, the family often arrives with a spectrum of feelings about the disorder and the identified patient. It is not uncommon to encounter a strong sense of "family versus the member," and as a family therapist, your challenge becomes allowing space for the negative feelings to be openly discussed while creating the idea that it is possible to hold two views at the same time including the possibility that they can both be true.

Particularly in the early sessions, it is important to challenge the family with the question of "who is responsible for recovery?" This line of questioning and the discussion it provokes begins a shift from the identified patient being solely responsible to a shared awareness of the illness and the potential role that can be played by multiple members of the family. Of course, none of this can happen if you, as a family therapist, are not able to join with the family. It is your ticket for admission. For that to occur, a family will be asking themselves a few important questions, whether spoken or not. They will first want to know "do you understand our dilemma?" and from there, "do you understand our family?" If, as a family therapist, you are able to convey a sense of empathy for the family and a willingness to work with them around the struggle they all find themselves in, then the final question, also unspoken, is "can you offer us hope?"

I am also very clear with the family that this is serious (deadly) stuff. I state what we know in terms of the lethality of the illness with the intention of keeping the serious of this work front and center. This is very important as the client begins to improve, as there is a tendency for the family to breathe a sigh of relief and hope that this terrible problem has passed. They run the risk of falling away and moving on to other things in life prematurely. Keeping the seriousness of the illness front and center helps keep everyone engaged.

And I dispel the myth that there is a quick fix here, sometimes using the analogy that eating disorders are not like a light switch. There is no instant on or off, and it will take time and hard work to change. I try to prepare the family that recovery will take time, and I ask all members of the family to commit to the journey. My message is always one of hope – that total recovery from an eating disorder is possible, though the road to recovery may be long and winding. It is never linear.

Last, I always make the point of giving permission for members of the family to take care of themselves. Eating disorder treatment takes a long time, and often, by the time a family gets into family therapy, they have likely been dealing with the eating disorder in a crisis mode for quite a while. Most likely, they are exhausted. It is important that they hear from me that, in order to take care of their family member, they must also take care of themselves. In fact, it is often useful to have a very direct talk with members of the family about how they will take care of themselves. This is particularly important for parents, as they have likely been solely focused on their child with the eating disorder and will need to adjust their lifestyles going forward in order to make treatment work.

Assessment

Because eating disorders are complicated, I generally find that the more people I involve in an assessment, the easier it is to get a full understanding of the life experience of a client. Input from extended family members like grandparents or family friends and teachers can greatly enhance this effort as it provides a critical "other view" to what is "reality" from those who live with them. For a client struggling with an eating disorder, this can also provide the opportunity to gain information and a perspective on the client's life prior to the onset of the illness.

Early in the assessment, I try to create a sense of hope by providing an opportunity for the family to talk about the client's strengths, personal interests, and life aspirations. To bring this side of a client to the forefront, I often try to externalize the eating disorder. That means I talk about it as if it were its own entity as if the eating disorder has taken up residence in the client's head and blocked out much of the client's true nature. I once introduced this way of thinking about an eating disorder to a family in a session and the client jumped right in describing their eating disorder as "the worse boss I could ever imagine." They saw their eating disorder as always critical and never satisfied. With that orientation, my job, as the family therapist, was to gather the full support of the family in helping my client battle against that mean boss. In these situations, it is always the positive things I learn from a family about the strengths and aspirations of their loved one that really help win the battle. I join with the family in keeping that true self front and center.

Some Good Questions

Most times I've worked with families, the initial point of engagement was as an informational resource and can be thought of as a time for the family to assess whether or not they are willing to speak more directly to the workings of their family. In essence, for this to happen, they have to feel that you, as their family therapist, are working in their best interest and are nonjudgmental. I am often aware of a shift that occurs when a family is willing to move from meeting to learn about eating disorders to one in which they are working in what I would call family therapy. When that shift happens, I have a short list of "go to" questions, each of which can broaden the discussion on a more personal level. As the therapist, your role is to ask the question and then listen. Most assuredly, discussion will follow.

My first question is "What is your theory about why this is happening to your family?" Despite the simplicity of the question, I have always found that families hold many theories about why this is happening, and specifically why this is happening now. In fact, there may be as many theories as there are people in the room, and each comes with its own perspective and value. It's important for the group to hear each one and thoughtfully consider it. And, from my perspective, the great thing about theories is that they are just theories. The discussion they engender becomes a window into how each member of the family thinks about the eating disorder and the role it plays.

The second and third questions often go together. I first ask, "What would your family be doing in life now if this hadn't occurred?" and then follow up with "(If this hadn't happened) Would anyone in your family be doing worse?" Both are powerful questions as they bring the eating disorder into the family as something that impacts them directly (not just the client) and introduce the idea that maybe others (aside from the identified client) may also be struggling. One of the most important things that the therapist must do in their approach is to effectively "join" with all members of the family. This requires that the therapist truly embrace the idea that each member is doing their best in life given what they must deal with, and then help them commit to engaging in the process with the best of intentions.

My next questions are generic family therapy questions, but set the stage for a shift from talking about eating disorders to a more intimate discussion about what is happening within the family. I ask, "Have you ever been in serious family therapy before? How did it go? What seemed to work for you; what seemed to backfire?" I find that it is always a good idea to get a read on what has happened before in a family. If they have prior experience with family therapy and it went well, I want to know specifically what was useful to them. I want to build on what worked as much as possible. And conversely, if a prior experience has gone poorly, I want to know the specifics and work as deliberately as possible to avoid any past mistakes. In this situation, I want to make a concerted effort to commend the family for their willingness to try family therapy again.

And last, I like this question, "Understanding that there is no magic wand, what are you hoping we can do for you?" This creates the floor for treatment and sets the beginning of expectations for treatment. Importantly, it also signals the shift from the identified patient with an eating disorder to a family focus with an outcome that all members are hopefully willing to work toward.

Issues Often Seen in Families with ED

In every session, I work to understand the interplay between individual development and the family life cycle as they are intertwined. As an important part of gaining this understanding, I've found it useful to commit an entire session to building a family genogram (i.e., a visual diagram that outlines family relationships and notable medical or psychological history to identify patterns or issues within the family system) to learn what has happened in the family across multiple generations and more specifically what have been the family's challenges through time. This often leads to a discussion around where we (the family) are currently stuck, including an understanding of when and why this occurred. This allows for a shared awareness of the "problem(s)" facing the family and the beginning of a plan for how to address them.

Invariably, this leads to a structural analysis in a family, most often focused on boundaries and enmeshment, alliances, and triangulation. I try to understand how communication happens and, when focused more on specific events that occurred, look for behavior chains to illustrate the complexity of some family problems and potential areas for change. I think of this as the "action" of the therapy hour and where themes emerge.

If you've studied family therapy or had the experience of providing some family therapy, you are probably aware that with careful observation and thoughtful questioning, themes within the family will emerge. Some of these themes are shared across many families, not just among families with someone struggling with an eating disorder, and while relatively common, they can create and even support some of the challenges facing a family. A very common one is overprotectiveness. This is a generalized family style in which parents convey a high sense of fear or trepidation with the world. Their caution can create a belief among younger family members that the world is a fearful place; for a young person, that worldview can be quite limiting. That is not to discount the parent's fear; in fact, in many cases there is a legitimate reason from a valid life experience of one or both parent(s). Out of their own best intentions, this worldview is passed on, often unintentionally.

Also common is rigidity or control within a family. While all families do have their own rules or expectations, heightened rigidity and a sense of overcontrol can be present and limiting in some. This can become a treatment issue when it is how a family responds to the status quo in the face of change. Consider, for instance, the developmental stages a child goes through as a part of normal development and the monumental challenges each developmental phase brings. If these challenges are managed within the family by becoming increasingly rigid or controlling, the opportunity for the child to successfully negotiate a developmental change with a sense of success or failure is lost. We see this for some individuals with an eating disorder, during transition points in life; for instance, moving from middle school to high school, or the transition from high school into college (an environment often away from the childhood home). Similarly, in some families, there is a sense of perfectionism, the notion that appearance and performance are everything. With the additional messaging from our beauty- and youth-focused culture, such a theme in the home can be overwhelming and ultimately challenge a child's understanding of those around them, and especially of themselves.

In addition to these themes, it is important for the therapist to be aware of the structure within a family and any changes in structure. These usually present as boundary changes and can include a growing enmeshment between one parent and a child they may overly identify with, to clear hierarchy changes, as when a divorce occurs within a family. In both cases, developing the ability to speak directly to these can create a shift in a family and ultimately increase the support for a family member who is struggling.

Traps

As with most therapeutic relationships, there are times when things seem to go awry, and in my experience, it may be due to a stuck point, or, sometimes more accurately, a "trap" that the therapist has unwittingly fallen into. It makes sense to be aware of a few of these and always to assess realistically the successes or challenges of each session. The first of these traps is communicating a negative attitude or blaming someone in the family (often for the eating disorder). This generally derives from over-identification with either the parents or the child, and if unchecked, it can erode the forward momentum of a family by limiting honest discussion.

Related to this is the ongoing challenge for you, as the therapist, to contain or manage your own anxiety. Although easier said than done, it is not helpful when the therapist is as anxious as the family. Although we all experience some degree of anxiety (even with years of experience), I have found it helpful to try to relieve myself of the burden of making the meeting "successful." To do this, I see my role more as a facilitator of discussion, and in that light, my goal is to keep discussion going and, when needed, to objectively and kindly challenge what is happening in the room, often by asking for clarification when the session gets heated or off track.

And a final trap, which I do see as a trap, is the positive task of recognizing change when you see it. Although this may seem simple, it is often a challenge for the therapist, especially when working with an eating disorder. For a family in which a member is struggling with an eating disorder, small steps are often enormous strides. It is critical to notice them and then to educate members of the family on the brave work or shift that has taken place. For instance, learning in a session that the adolescent daughter had gone out with her friends for pizza this week may be a huge success. It required the daughter to challenge herself with food and friends, something which may be very much out of her comfort zone. Such effort may be lost on a family who do not see why something so "normal" is cause for celebration. It is often the job of the therapist to identify these small steps forward and use each to educate the rest of the family while acknowledging the hard work of a family member pushing back against an eating disorder.

Aftercare and Follow through

As family treatment advances, families are a critical part of facilitating a home setting that supports health and recovery. This usually comes in the form of ongoing awareness of the support that is needed for the individual struggling with an eating disorder. I always make a clear statement of the need for ongoing support. For many families, when the signs and symptoms of the illness begin to lessen, there is a tendency to move on from the recovery effort. It is almost as if the signs of recovery signal that the crisis is over. It is not so. Many clients will confide in me that one of their fears about beginning to recover is that their family will decrease their support efforts and will think (and perhaps wish) that they are all better and no longer struggling. And while an individual may be improving, the struggle often remains internal and private. It is during this time that the client's family must be vigilant to follow through with an aftercare plan. It is not the time to think that everyone is "safely out of the woods." Eating disorders are crafty, and the effort against them must remain strong even when the road to recovery seems underfoot.

Similarly, I always anticipate with families about the risk of relapsing, especially during times of transition. A common example is a young adult who is leaving home to go away to college. Although a wonderful life milestone, for some individuals, this time of transition in life can be a time of great stress. Being away from home without daily support and structures, coupled with a whole new way of getting nutrition, including new foods, large dining halls, and people one has never met before, can bring eating disorder thoughts and behaviors roaring back. It is essential to anticipate these life changes and the potential risks involved and to proactively plan additional check-ins and support.

A Case Study

This case study examines the treatment journey of Stacy, a 14-year-old girl, who has battled anorexia for over 2 years. She has been in and out of various treatment programs, but without significant progress. Stacy was recently admitted to a private psychiatric hospital by her mother, Helene, who is the primary caregiver. The hospital staff, unable to assist in her refeeding, sought the expertise of an experienced family therapist to intervene before recommending a transfer to the state hospital.

Helene arrives first for the initial family meeting with the new family therapist and is escorted to the meeting room on the psychiatric unit, where the sessions take place. She is dressed casually and appears calm and familiar with her surroundings and the way things operate in this setting. She has done some research to gather information about the therapist and understands the connection between the therapist and the program. Helene is an intelligent woman with a background in social work who currently teaches in a religious school. The mother is very involved in her daughter's care, her only child from a previous relationship, with no current involvement from the father. Helene states that she had initially refused treatment for Stacy in this program and has brought her daughter to numerous other places without any significant improvement in her condition. The fact that they have now come here for help is worrisome as she had viewed this as a last resort. She is aware that the treatment team is talking about referral to the state hospital, but, surprisingly, does not seem panicked or overly distressed.

After a few minutes, Stacy arrives, escorted by nursing staff and trailing an IV pole apparatus that houses nutrition in liquid form for nasogastric tube feedings. She is dressed in a hospital johnnie, avoids eye contact with the therapist, appears listless and ashen, and responds to the therapist's attempt to shake hands with a shrug. Helene greets her daughter and enquires about her condition and activities. Stacy engages with Mom with unexpected energy. It appears that Stacy and Helene are close confidants. Though she is not overtly rebellious, Stacy is initially difficult to engage. She states that eating makes her anxious and is refusing to eat on her own. She is depressed, she says, because she doesn't want to be in the hospital; she does not admit to any significant body dysmorphia or negative self-image. She says she doesn't know why; she just doesn't want to eat.

Both Mom and daughter date the onset of the girl's anorexia back several years, coinciding with her transition from a highly supportive school environment to a public middle school. Helene also reveals that it was a particularly difficult time for the family as they were confronted with a major health crisis of her mother's partner, a father figure named Bobby, who then died of Cancer. Neither mother nor daughter thinks that this loss has anything to do with Stacy's illness.

Therapeutic Observations

Early in the therapy, it was observed that the patient had become a "professional patient" over the past two years, essentially a "hollow ghost" of her former self, showing no interest in her previous activities and active social life. She has become dependent on nasogastric tube feeding for nutrition and shows little interest in engaging in the therapeutic program. However, she continues to do her schoolwork and, when asked, says that she believes she will go to college. Stacy states that although she has lost contact with friends and is anxious about how they would respond to her, she, nevertheless, would like to talk to her closest friends and see them if possible. Similarly, the mother has become entirely consumed by her daughter's care, neglecting her own wellbeing and social connections. She is able to continue at her part-time job and keep up the home, but otherwise has no time for friends and family, even though she is close to her elderly parents. Neither Stacy nor Helene has any interest in the daughter being sent for custodial care to the state hospital, which is the only remaining level of care.

Developing a Treatment Plan

A comprehensive plan was developed with the involvement of Helene and Stacy that centered around reconnecting them to their previous lives. Given how close they are, it is reasoned and discussed openly that they would have to move forward together. The primary motivator for Stacy is the possibility of getting out of the hospital, but she is also motivated by the idea of alleviating her mother's deep concern for her. Helene's motivation is simply "getting my daughter back," but she also admits to feeling extremely fatigued and having a sense of hopelessness about the future that is uncomfortable and unusual for her. Both feel some relief that the treatment will proceed in a new direction with one caveat: how to deal with Stacy's inability or refusal to eat. We agree that while we can go slow and provide Stacy with support, she will need to move toward eating on her own, starting with weaning her from the NG tube over a period of a couple of weeks. At the same time, we agree that Helene will undergo intensive training in Family-Based Therapy (FBT) to prepare her for Stacy's eventual return home. While FBT has been tried before without much success, this effort has the benefit of agreement between Helene and Stacy. The plan to reconnect them to their previous lives and to new activities also takes shape. Stacy develops a short list of friends to reach out to as a first step, and other activities, such as shopping and ice skating, that she would like to do when she is out of the hospital. Mom prioritizes caring for her elderly parents as a first step, and then seeing friends and looking for a new job as things she wants to do in the near future. Both agree to begin immediately.

Another key aspect of this recovery process, the "planned re-admission" is developed with hospital administration and staff. All parties agree that Stacy is not benefiting from the traditional hospital program and will regain weight slowly, if at all. The idea of her being discharged for short and then longer periods of time to re-engage in life and increase her motivation to move beyond the eating disorder seems logical and worth a try if the proper health safeguards are in place. These include frequent meetings and on-call access to an outpatient therapist who can assist Stacy and Helene to follow through with the feeding schedule, access on an urgent basis to her primary care physician, and rapid re-entry to the hospital if absolutely needed. Once these safeguards are in place, we agree to "discharge" Stacy for one week after two weeks in the hospital, successfully enacting the first steps of the plan. There is increased energy by all parties involved to work toward the outlined goals. Most importantly, Stacy begins to eat on her own, nibbling at first and then eating some fuller meals, and gets to the point where the NG tube can be removed making the first discharge possible. Over the two-week period, Stacy also reaches out to a couple of friends who are thrilled to hear from her. We begin to see a glimpse of the "old" Stacy, a smile here and there, and a wry sense of humor often directed at the therapist. Helene participates as well, and with encouragement, is "forbidden" to come to the hospital every day as she's been doing.

The plan proceeds over the next several months with Stacy being discharged and readmitted four times. Each discharge is planned for a longer time at home. The path is rocky at first with Stacy refusing to eat according to plan and calling the nursing staff at the hospital for support. She barely gets through the first week, and she and her mother are initially relieved when she returns to the hospital. However, this doesn't last long because she has experienced a taste of life as she knew it. As hoped, while she was at home, she reconnected with her teachers and had friends over and was even able to go shopping for a short time. She chafes at the rules and lack of freedom in the hospital, and this trend continues to build on each successive discharge and re-admission. Throughout the process, the most difficult part is following the nutrition plan, but Helene is steadfast in executing her responsibilities under the FBT feeding process, and they make slow progress with the steady assistance of their talented outpatient therapist.

Each time Stacy is discharged and readmitted, the family therapy takes on additional issues, most importantly, concerns about Helene. We discuss the observation that with all of the anxiety and attention to Stacy's condition and needs, there could not be much time or energy for Helene to "have a life." We all agree that this is something that would be good for both mother and daughter. We further learn that Helene's life took a major blow when she lost Bobby. As before, neither Helene nor Stacy makes any connection between this sad event and Stacy developing anorexia, but the timing is certainly suspect, and there does not appear to be any recognition or "working through" of the traumatic impact of this event. As we discuss Bobby's passing, we also learn that Helene has not been to the cemetery for quite some time and that Stacy's only time there was the funeral itself. With significant coaxing, we develop a plan for Helene and Stacy to visit the grave during the next discharge period. At the next meeting upon returning to the hospital the third time, I inquire about how the cemetery visit went, and they look at each other, and Helene says, "we were so busy; we just didn't have time." Eventually, the visit does take place, and both report that it was "sad," but they were glad to have done it. Helene further states that she was relieved to be able to tell Bobby that Stacy was doing better and "was going to be ok." For her part, Stacy says that she was happy to be there to support her mom this time in a way that was not possible when she was younger.

Postscript

Approximately ten years have passed since Stacy was in the hospital. She stays in touch, writes notes, and sends pictures periodically. She no longer has anorexia, though she feels anxious around food occasionally, mainly when there is some big transition in her life. She continued in outpatient therapy for several years and returns when she feels the need. Stacy graduated high school, attended prom with her boyfriend, went to college, graduated from college and nursing school, and now works in pediatrics. Helene and Stacy remain very close, though both are busy in their respective lives. They feel deep gratitude for the help they received.

References

Klump, K.L., Bulik, C.M., Kaye, W.H., Treasure, J. & Tyson, E.P. (2009). Academy for eating disorders position paper: eating disorders are serious mental illnesses. *The International Journal of Eating Disorders*, 42(2), 97–103.

Part III

The Multidisciplinary Team

Chapter 7

The Therapist as Collaborator and Connector

Amy Mayer

When my outpatient colleagues learn that I work with eating disorders, they often respond with:

"That sounds so stressful"
"I don't have enough experience to work with this population"
"Does anyone get better?"
"I don't have what it takes to work with people who are starving themselves, bingeing, or purging"

However, the same colleagues work with people dealing with equally challenging conditions, such as substance use, acute trauma, mood disorders, and psychosis. In this chapter, my goal is to demystify the eating disorder field and demonstrate how a multidisciplinary treatment team approach provides better care for our clients, while making this work more manageable for outpatient therapists. Throughout, I will present, and talk through, sample scripts for establishing and communicating with a treatment team.

Whether you are new to the mental health field or an established therapist interested in developing a clinical specialty in eating disorders, this chapter is relevant for both. For newer clinicians, maybe someone who recently completed a graduate program and has an interest in developing a specialty with this population, this chapter will provide you with the "how-to" of providing treatment and communicating within the context of a multidisciplinary team. On the other hand, if you are an experienced therapist with robust clinical expertise but have limited or no experience treating eating disorders, this chapter will orient you to the deeply satisfying work of treating eating disorders as part of a team.

Throughout this chapter, I will take you through a step-by-step process showing you how to create an outpatient treatment team and demonstrate how to work with other professionals to provide compassionate, evidence-based care.

DOI: 10.4324/9781003600770-10

Who I Am and How I Landed Here

In the mid-1980s, with a newly minted undergraduate degree in Sociology, I moved to Boston with the vague idea that I wanted to be a psychologist. At the time, I was happy to get any job that would provide me with experience in a mental health setting. It was by a stroke of luck that the director of an inpatient psychiatric unit that specialized in treating eating disorders, Dr. M. Villapiano, needed a milieu therapist to work on the unit with adolescents and adults.

As you can imagine, in the '80s, an inpatient eating disorder program was a novel idea, and the unit at Hahnemann Hospital in Brighton, MA, was a cutting-edge program. Client meals were prescribed by eating disorder specialized dietitians and supervised by milieu therapists, like me. Throughout the day, clients participated in a range of group therapies, such as Cognitive Behavioral Therapy, Art Therapy, and Nutrition Education. Each day, they would have individual therapy with their assigned staff psychotherapist (yes, individual therapy was offered five times per week) and met with their dietitian multiple times throughout the week for nutrition counseling. While many of the clients had already spent a tremendous amount of time reading and thinking about food, they harbored misconceptions about how to properly nourish themselves that were addressed in weekly nutrition groups. Family therapy sessions with parents, siblings, or spouses were provided by the clinical staff, and psychiatrists provided medication management. On the weekends, clients would go out on passes into the community to practice eating meals outside of the hospital. Most inpatient admissions ranged from four to six weeks.

I vividly remember a client from this time referring to the milieu therapists as the food police, which was actually kind of true. For instance, we followed a very specific protocol for mealtimes. When the meals arrived, we first checked that each tray matched the dietitian's prescribed meal plan. Then we gathered everyone into the dining room, seated them at their assigned spots, placed their meal on the table in front of them, and then started a timer – 30 minutes (that's how long clients had to complete their meal). We periodically checked the clock and reminded clients how much time they had left. There were also rules about what was allowed to be discussed at the table; food, weight, and body image were strictly off-limits. New clients, in particular, were often highly anxious, tearful, and angry as they pushed themselves to eat as much of their meals and snacks as they could tolerate.

As I became more experienced, I learned how to offer gentle encouragement while setting rigid boundaries when a client insisted that something was wrong with their meal or protested that they had been given too much food. I also became really good at bringing up non-food-related topics, such as stories about pets, recent movies, TV programs, or even the weather – anything that helped cut through the fear and anger that was often present at the table. At the end of the allotted time, I would record the amount they had eaten. When someone did not complete their entire meal, they were asked to drink a high-calorie protein shake. For an hour after the meal ended, I would supervise the clients to make sure no one went back to their rooms to engage in maladaptive behaviors, such as exercise, purge, or self-harm.

Looking back, those years were my orientation to working with eating disorders. Through supervision by licensed staff as well as collaboration with more experienced milieu therapists, I learned the important skills of providing comfort, structure, validation, and limit setting. I also learned a great deal from all the clients I encountered; and one way I can think to thank them is by encouraging other professionals to join me in providing empathic, understanding, and compassionate care to those with eating disorders.

Below are my "Eight Lessons from a Former Milieu Therapist" and their relevance to outpatient eating disorder treatment:

1 People who have been restricting or bingeing and purging are at risk of serious medical consequences. A major objective of an inpatient eating disorder program is refeeding (i.e., restoring nutritional and medical stability). Many of the inpatient clients were relearning how to eat enough food to maintain a healthy medical status. Eating was also important in helping them to engage in therapy and recovery.

2 Many with eating disorders feel hopeless that anyone will understand what their world is like. In the throes of their illness, it's difficult for clients to imagine getting better and leading a "normal" life. They often felt terribly guilty about the impact their behaviors had on their family, friends, and co-workers. A good team of professionals (both inpatient and outpatient) helps clients to hold on to hope throughout the recovery process.

3 People without any advanced training can play a significant role in a client's recovery. The milieu therapists of the inpatient unit spent the most amount of time with clients, and we were often the first to know when a patient was having a particularly hard day. We were also the first to know when they started to get better, such as noticing when a client was completing meals with less anxiety. Occasionally, some clients would even acknowledge that they were looking forward to a snack or dessert. Because of my experience as a milieu therapist, I am always interested in learning from the people who spend the most time with our clients. For example, a cafeteria monitor might notice that a student is tossing their lunch into the trash, or the coach of the softball team may know that a student is stressed about an upcoming test, which is impacting their performance. Those on the frontlines can provide invaluable insight.

4 With good treatment, most clients make progress. Improvement is non-linear; recovery can take a long time involving all sorts of twists and turns, and some days may be easier than others. While eating disorders have among the highest mortality rates of all psychological illnesses, keep in mind that for some, treatment can take years. Similarly, a subset of individuals will live with chronic eating disorder symptoms and require the help of an outpatient team to support living with, and managing, their symptoms.

5 Every discipline is equally important. Daily rounds on the inpatient unit allowed me to listen to trained dietitians, psychiatric nurses, psychiatrists, and group therapists as they discussed each client's progress in the program. Providers from different fields would learn from each other, and clients ultimately benefited from those exchanges.

6 Eating disorders often begin during a life transition, such as entering high school, starting college, a year abroad, the breakup of a relationship, or the loss of a job. What usually begins as an attempt at "healthy eating" or "losing a couple of pounds" takes on a life of its own.

7 As clients become better nourished, they start to regain their complexity and humanity, with all kinds of interesting beliefs and goals. Each person is truly unique. In other words, symptomatic behaviors can infringe on one's individuality and emotionality, while intensive psychological and medical treatment allows patients to recapture these vital and unique characteristics.

8 Clients were not cured when they left the hospital, but many were medically stable (e.g., better nourished) and had made progress in terms of understanding how to cope more adaptively.

The next – and longest – step in my inpatient clients' journey was to begin in outpatient therapy.

The Multidisciplinary Team Approach

After I finished my post-doctoral training and obtained a professional license, I decided to supplement my full-time job with a small private practice that included several people with eating disorders. In addition to providing individual therapy, I often assumed the role of building the outpatient team, which consisted of assessing clients' needs and providing referrals to professionals who could meet those needs. My approach to building this team is hardly rocket science. My basic philosophy, consistent for over twenty-five years, is that clients benefit from ongoing communication between their providers. While it takes a village of both professionals and non-professionals to support an individual's recovery, that same village needs to be held together; we do that through communication. A brief, concise email written at the end of a session can easily be sent to a group of outpatient providers, which helps to keep us informed and engaged in our shared effort.

Technology has made it much easier for multiple providers to communicate, such as calls, emails, text messages, video chats – there are many ways to stay informed. I recommend keeping communication brief and to the point. Medical providers do this well, leaving a short and precise message. A good example of this is Dr. G, a busy internist whom I collaborate with often. Immediately after a client's medical appointment, Dr. G writes a two-sentence email (most of which is in the subject line) describing the salient parts of their outpatient visit. For example (with abbreviations),

"Pt's wt. is down 0.5lb. Vitals WNL. Did blood work, next meeting in 2 wk."

Do pay attention to the content of what you share with providers and the way it is written. Some communications are too sensitive or nuanced for a quick email. In these instances, let your colleague know that a phone call is necessary. And remember that technology can be harmful when it's shared with people who don't have permission to read it, so be careful with this powerful tool.

Now, you might be thinking, "This sounds way too hard. I barely have time to complete my paperwork. I can't imagine finding the time to call other members of an outpatient team." These are valid concerns. In my experience, the most work (and the part that tends to take the longest) is setting up the team at the beginning of the treatment, but once it's established – I assure you – it will save you time.

It is important to assess the elements of a client's outpatient team in the very first session. Many times, clients already have an established team of providers making the process as easy as getting releases to speak to their physician, outpatient dietitian, and prescriber. Other times, you will be the first person they seek for help. In these cases, I assist clients by providing referrals and inquiring with the referred providers about their availability. Clients appreciate this kind of outpatient model because it relieves them from having to continuously, and repeatedly, update each provider about what happened in their various appointments. Likewise, I often hear comments that an outpatient team helps them feel like they are being taken seriously.

The Parts of the Team

Whether you're working with a person with Bulimia Nervosa, Binge Eating Disorder, Anorexia Nervosa, or AFRID, all can benefit from a multidisciplinary team. The team consists of an individual therapist, a registered dietitian, and a medical physician. The exact make-up of the team depends less on the disorder and more on the client's needs and goals for treatment, and while team configurations will vary, below is what I regard as the "primary disciplines" needed for a complete multidisciplinary outpatient team. Of course, someone who has access to insurance and financial resources may be able to create a team with four or five different providers, but not all will require this level of support.

Individual Therapist

Mental health providers, such as licensed psychologists, social workers, and professional counselors, typically have two intertwined roles of individual therapist and team coordinator. The first, and most obvious, job of the individual outpatient therapist is to provide therapy. The therapist should evaluate the client, provide an initial psychiatric diagnosis, and develop treatment plan goals. Additionally, the individual therapist functions as the outpatient team coordinator, meaning they hold the responsibility of setting up the interdisciplinary team (if there isn't one already in place), educating the client about the multidisciplinary team approach, and coordinating initial contact with team members. If, in the course of your global assessment, you find that the client is lacking important elements of the multidisciplinary treatment team, then it is your responsibility to make the appropriate referrals for those services. Of course, it is also true that all team members share the role of "team coordinator" as other disciplines have the same duty to make referrals to appropriate providers, should they identify a gap in the client's treatment team. When meeting with clients who already have established teams, I would advise reaching out to the other team members and asking to be integrated into their preexisting communication system. If a streamlined way of communicating does not yet exist, then work to establish one (see more about this process, including examples, in the sections below).

Primary Care Physician

Primary Care Physicians (PCPs), who often consist of medical doctors, family nurse practitioners, or physician assistants, monitor the client's medical stability. The PCP is responsible for the overall medical health of our clients. The frequency of PCP meetings is typically determined by the client's medical stability. For example, if the client is regularly losing weight or experiencing unstable vital signs, the PCP may want to see the client weekly or as often as necessary. In those whose treatment plans require weight restoration, PCPs and dietitians often work together to establish an appropriate weight range and track the client's weight progression. It is not always the case that clients will see what they weigh when taken at medical appointments. Some clients will have blind weights, which means they do not see or know their weight at all; whereas others may have informed weights, where they do not see the number on the scale, but are told what they weigh afterward, usually during a one-on-one meeting. For those who want to return to exercise or sports, the PCP is the person who decides whether they can be cleared to participate.

In addition, some clients will have a psychiatric provider who prescribes and monitors psychiatric medications. These providers are often a part of the multidisciplinary team, although not all clients with eating disorders will require psychotropic medications for successful treatment. Psychiatric prescribers consist of psychiatrists and nurse practitioners with specialized training in psychiatry. They assess for co-occurring disorders and whether initiating a psychiatric medication is warranted. If medications are started, prescribers typically meet with clients on a monthly or bi-monthly basis to monitor for efficacy and side-effects and make adjustments as needed. Psychiatric prescribers work closely with the team and can be particularly helpful for clients whose symptoms do not improve with behavioral interventions, like psychotherapy, alone.

Registered Dietitians

Registered Dietitians (RDs) are trained and licensed in the science of nutrition and dietetics. They work with clients to provide guidance on adequate nutrition. Dietitians play an integral role in the eating disorder treatment team. They determine the client's nutritional needs, outline their eating regimen, provide nutritional counselling, and challenge clients to incorporate fear foods (i.e., foods that were once liked but now make the client fearful). Alongside the PCP, dietitians help establish a biologically appropriate weight range for each client. Dietitians, like therapists, typically meet with clients weekly, and I've found that clients deeply value the work of their RD.

Possible Additions to the Team

Depending on the client's need and – frankly – their access to resources, the following disciplines may also be incorporated as additional elements of the team:

Family Therapist

Eating disorders are family disorders. When one family member has an eating disorder, it impacts the entire family system, often changing the dynamics of the family in significant ways. I strongly believe that parents play an important role in their child's recovery. Family therapy can be a powerful tool to provide support, education, and a safe place for families to address complex issues that arise over the course of an eating disorder. Unlike individual therapy, a family therapist interacts with the family as a whole. Conflict, as described by the client in individual therapy, may sound completely different when viewed through the perspectives of other family members. An individual therapist can learn a tremendous amount through collaboration with a family therapist, which can then be used to help the client in their individual therapy.

Couple's Therapist

Eating disorders thrive on secrecy. I've worked with clients who hid their eating disorder symptoms from their loved ones for years. Couples therapy can be helpful in creating a safe space to talk about the eating disorder, treatment, and ways in which their partner can support them. Although couples work begins with talking about the eating disorder, it often ends up exploring deeper issues, such as intimacy and communication, in their relationship. A couple's therapist typically collaborates with the individual therapist but may also benefit from communication with the larger team.

Group Therapist

Group therapy can serve many purposes in the treatment of eating disorders. Some groups can focus on support, while others take a more didactic approach in developing specific skills, like Cognitive Behavioral Therapy (CBT), Dialectical Behavioral Therapy (DBT), or Acceptance and Commitment Therapy (ACT). These groups are usually time-limited, so it is useful for the outpatient team to know that the client is participating in a group. Contact with the group leader at the beginning and end of their group work can provide information about what the client worked on, the quality of interactions with the other group members, and their investment in the group experience.

School Counselor (for Adolescents)

Some parents and legal guardians do not want any information shared about a child's eating disorder treatment with school administration. They worry that school staff will not keep this information private or that it will impact the child's school performance or college references. I always find it useful to spend time understanding their concerns and ask them to thoroughly weigh the pros and cons of including school-based supports in the outpatient treatment team. Adolescent clients who attend high school spend approximately 30 hours a week there, and if the school doesn't have information about their symptoms, there will be little opportunity for pertinent information from school to make its way back to the parents or the treatment team. I find most schools tend to be very helpful. For example, I have had schools offer staff to help monitor lunch and snacks, or prepare a private space where a parent can go into the school to personally supervise their child's meal.

A Word about Virtual Treatment

Virtual treatment has expanded access to specialized care, particularly for those in rural areas, where there is little support to be found for eating disorder treatment. While virtual treatment isn't for everyone, in many cases, it increases access to treatment and allows for a wider selection of providers across a larger geography. In the US, since mental health clinicians are licensed by state, it is now possible to create an outpatient multidisciplinary team across great distances. For example, I work with dietitians and psychiatrists who live over one hundred miles away from me, and their virtual contribution to treatment is invaluable.

Beginning Treatment with New Clients: The Evaluation Process

When I start with a new client, we embark on an intake process that typically takes between two to four sessions. For the very first session, I set aside 75 minutes in order to listen carefully to their story. Building rapport starts from the very beginning, and my primary goal for the first session is to make sure the client is willing to return for a second session. I remind myself, and the client, that the strength of our connection is crucial for successful treatment. Understandably, clients usually feel anxious and exposed as they describe what brings them to my office. Throughout this process, I am listening carefully for clues about the diagnosis.

At the beginning of my career, I remember a wise and experienced colleague saying, "Eating disorders don't exist by themselves." My colleague was referring to the likelihood of other symptoms, or comorbidities, that exist alongside the classic signs and symptoms of an eating disorder. By the end of the evaluation period, I try to provide the client or their family with realistic, yet hopeful information about treatment. It's important to note that my approach to this conversation may differ depending on who I'm seeing. For example, if the client is an older adolescent or young adult, I may emphasize the negative consequences of untreated symptoms of restrictive eating, purging, or overexercising. For parents who are often exhausted, worried, and angry at their symptomatic child, I listen and validate their concerns while offering the message that if we work together, they can be the key to their child's recovery – this is an especially important message for parents who so often blame themselves for their child's eating disorder.

To introduce the idea of a multidisciplinary team, I start by saying that I only provide individual therapy, and it's likely I will need to refer them to a medical specialist and dietitian with specialized training in eating disorders. I also say that as I get to know them more, we might also discuss other referrals for specialized care that I cannot provide but feel may help them. For instance, this may include a prescriber for a psychopharmacology consult or a family therapist. I validate that this kind of comprehensive treatment style is a big undertaking. It may be difficult to juggle the various demands in their lives – work, children, spouses, friends – as well as the added costs that come with attending more appointments – transportation, copays, time off from work. I also give them a sense of what treatment might look like over the long term. Although initially a client might require weekly meetings with me as their therapist and every-other-week meetings with their medical provider or dietitian, over time, the frequency of these appointments will change and is likely to decrease as their symptoms improve. But in the event of a relapse or resurgence of symptoms, appointments may need to increase.

It is also during the first few sessions that I assess barriers to treatment; chief among them is financial. A multidisciplinary outpatient team includes at least two (or more) professionals, and insurance may not cover them all. While some clients and their families are fortunate to be able to pay for treatment out-of-pocket, that is certainly not true for all. When considering the make-up of a client's outpatient team, this should be considered. It is important to be realistic about what elements are essential to providing adequate treatment. Similarly, individuals with marginalized identities may also experience barriers to treatment, including working with teams of largely white, cisgender clinicians. It is important to acknowledge these disparities and work to build a diverse, inclusive team that reflects and affirms the identities of our clients, whenever possible.

Lastly, I spend time discussing the contours of privacy and confidentiality as well as reviewing my Informed Consent for Treatment form. I do not assume that a new client is knowledgeable about confidentiality in outpatient therapy, as some may never have been in therapy before. An important caveat to privacy and confidentiality is the multidisciplinary team. Sharing important details of your client's life may be pertinent and necessary for other team members to know. As such, you will need to use your clinical judgment as to what information is necessary to share with the team and what is not.

Building an Outpatient Treatment Team

Some patients begin therapy with preexisting relationships with other providers. In these cases, the first step to building the team is obtaining permission to contact other established providers on their team. However, if you are providing referrals for new services, it is important to know that it is not always a quick process – it can take weeks or even months to pull together all the elements of a team – and I suggest first focusing on the medical provider and registered dietitian. It is at the end of the initial evaluation period that I send an introductory email to all clinicians involved and share pertinent information. Notably, enlisting the team at the beginning phases of treatment will make communicating easier and will be more helpful to your clients.

You might be thinking, what if my client objects to me collaborating with other providers? If a new client expresses unease with the multidisciplinary team model, I take time to understand the nature of their discomfort. I have found that typically, their concern is related to the limits of confidentiality. I try to allay this concern by making it clear that there are limits to what is shared, even between providers. For example, a PCP does not need to know intimate details of everything that is discussed in our therapy sessions; that is, unless it has implications for the client's physical health. I remain cognizant that clients may have had past experiences where their privacy was violated, and I make sure to validate these concerns. I also provide education about the value and importance of the multidisciplinary team approach, which is the gold standard for eating disorder treatment according to the American Psychological Association (Crone et al., 2023). Furthermore, it would be unwise to treat an eating disorder as a solo practitioner due to the likelihood of medical complications that therapists, like me, are not qualified to treat. If the client remains adamant that they do not want to engage in this treatment style, and we have discussed their apprehension at length over the course of several sessions, I might compromise and agree to see them with only a PCP on the team. If they also object to that, then I tell them that I am not willing to provide treatment for an eating disorder without being able to collaborate with a medical professional. We can talk about limitations in terms of what gets shared, but we cannot eliminate that member of the team.

Sample Scripts: How Do I Approach Other Team Members?

When contacting a medical provider for the first time, I always use email. I address the provider using their formal name and credentials. Some examples include:

Dr. Smith or Ronald Smith, MD
Jan Block, RNCS

Be sure to provide your name and credentials in your signature. Examples:

Dr. A. Mayer, Licensed Psychologist
or Amy Mayer, PsyD
Dan Green, LICSW
Dana Green, LMHC

One of the most important parts of this initial contact is figuring out how you will handle future contacts. Some prefer email, others prefer texting. I often text to set up a phone call or get another provider's contact information, but never to discuss treatment issues. Also, I never identify the client's full name, or other personal details, when using electronic communication. When exchanging identifiable details, I prefer to speak by phone. If I don't have a provider's email address, I will mail a paper copy of my completed release of information, including my contact information, email, and cell phone number.

Email sample:

Subject: Our mutual client NR (see attached release of info)
Hello Dr. Lam. My name is Amy Mayer, PsyD, a psychologist practicing in Boston, MA. I can be reached at 123-456-7899. Your patient, NR, was recently referred to me with symptoms of disordered eating. She has not seen you since her yearly physical last May. I'm asking her to make an appointment with you to make sure that she's medically stable to pursue outpatient treatment. My evaluation will take two to three sessions, and I just saw her for an initial appointment. I am scheduled to see her again on 5/2. I am looking forward to collaborating with you.

Script for the front desk or when leaving a voicemail:

This is Katherine Kane, LICSW. My number is 123-456-7899. This is a message for Dr. Payne regarding patient Nina Smith, DOB 12-12-2001. I have a signed release and I'm calling to speak with Nina's primary care physician. I can be reached at the following times (list two options), or I can call back if you can give me good times to speak with Dr. Payne.

If you are not accustomed to speaking to physicians, the initial contact may seem intimidating. I can assure you that most medical doctors are grateful to know that their patient is being evaluated by a mental health provider and are often more than happy to take a few minutes to exchange information.

Script for reaching out to a registered dietitian:

Hi, I'm Amy Mayer, a psychologist in private practice. I received your name from our colleague Beth P and from the Eating Disorder Association listserv. I'm in the process of evaluating a client who has a recent history of depression and restrictive eating. The client has a PCP and she's made the decision to work with me in my private practice. Please let me know if you have time to collaborate care. I'm available to speak on the phone at a time of your convenience. You can reach me at amymayerpsyd@gmail.com or 123-456-7899.

Case Vignettes

Outpatient treatment teams are not one-size-fits-all. It requires that the needs of the client are at the center of treatment, and it is also important to remember that the multidisciplinary team works in the service of their mutual client. Below are some examples of themes that may arise in treatment.

Vignette 1: Diana

Diana is a 24-year-old, single, biracial, cisgender female who was referred to me by her former therapist from her college's counselling center. Upon graduation, she moved to Boston and continued to stay in touch with her college therapist by phone. Six months after her move, Diana began bingeing and purging, which resulted in her fainting as she exercised at a gym with some friends. She was rushed to the emergency department, evaluated, and released the same day. She then attended a local residential eating disorder program and stepped down to a local Intensive Outpatient Program (IOP) for a one-month course of treatment.

By the time we started working together in outpatient therapy, she was medically stable and had not binged or purged for one month. She had a PCP with experience working with eating disorders and started on antidepressant medication. She also started meeting with a registered dietitian named Sandy.

Diana was fortunate to have insurance and a financial safety net from her parents. One of the major obstacles early on was scheduling therapy appointments, as Diana worked 50 (or more) hours per week as a teacher's aid. She was hesitant to ask for time off for her appointments, and although I was able to offer after-work timeslots, she found it stressful to leave work with enough time to get to our appointment. She agreed to sign a release for me to speak to her PCP. I then sent the below email to both her PCP and RD to introduce myself and request that we share pertinent information as her multidisciplinary team.

From: A, Mayer, ind. therapist
  Re: new client DH
  To: Primary Care Physician, Registered Dietitian
  Hello. This is Amy Mayer, a psychologist and the individual therapist for your client DH. In this email, I am including DH's PCP (Dr. S) and her dietitian (Sandy) in the hope we can collaborate. Below is my most recent update and I would welcome getting brief updates following your meetings.
  DH presents with a diagnosis of Bulimia. She just completed a residential treatment program and has abstained from bingeing and purging for one month. She presents as more anxious this week, due to work stress and office talk about possible layoffs. DH works 50 plus hours a week and scheduling regular appts is challenging.

This week's goals:

1 Eat at least two out of three meals per day and one snack. Eat with roommate when possible.
2 Review basic concepts of CBT from info received in Residential program and identify irrational thoughts about food and weight.
3 Set up an appointment with RD.

My questions:

Sandy, have you heard from DH yet?

Dr. S: DH told me that you have some concerns about her low/normal heart rate. How often will you be seeing her? Will you also be getting weights?

The best way to reach me is through email. For the first few weeks, I'll send a summary following my sessions with her. Looking forward to collaborating.

ASM

My email to team after our second session:

Hi All,

Discussed transition from IOP to regular outpatient treatment with this team. Nervous about having to be responsible for all her meals, but excited to finally finish intensive treatment. Says parents are supportive and Mom has offered to drop off some meals to her apartment. DH is in a relatively new relationship with a partner, but they haven't talked very much about ED history.

Her PCP responded with a two-sentence email following their appointment, and so did her dietitian. This would continue throughout the first year of outpatient treatment.

Diana was invested in therapy and made slow but steady progress over the course of five years. By the end of the second year, she was no longer bingeing and purging, and her weight was in a healthy range. Though she continued to struggle with a good deal of anxiety regarding normal eating, especially if it involved socializing with friends, she also continued to struggle with her body image. Diana went to graduate school during the third and fourth years of treatment. She and her husband started to meet with a couple's therapist and eventually married at the beginning of her fifth year in treatment.

Diana's symptoms are much better now. She is a valued colleague in her first professional job and has been at an appropriate weight range for several years. She describes herself as having a much better relationship with food and is beginning to address longstanding body image issues. For example, she now wears short-sleeve shirts and sleeveless dresses when it's hot outside and even wore a bathing suit on a recent vacation. She told me she spent time swimming in the ocean for the first time in a decade. In reflecting on this recent victory, Diana said, "As my team would say, I wore a bathing suit, and I lived to tell the tale." Diana continues to see her couple's therapist, whom I keep in touch with every other month, as well as her dietitian and PCP, although we no longer need to collaborate.

Vignette 2: Amira

Amira is a 20-year-old, non-binary college student who was referred to me from their PCP after recently experiencing significant weight loss. They live with their mother and younger sibling, working part-time at a restaurant while attending community college. Amira reported a history of "picky eat-ing" and, as a child, was evaluated for ARFID at Boston Children's Hospital, though they remember very little about that period of their life, saying, "I met with a social worker a few times and also another person who helped me eat different kinds of food." Over the past three months, Amira reports that they have lost 20 pounds by cutting out all animal-based proteins, limiting carbohydrates, and eating only one meal and a small snack each day. In addi-tion, they were working out daily for at least an hour and experiencing intense body image distress. Amira is a hard-working student with the goal of finish-ing their second year of junior college and transferring to a four-year college.

Amira worried about their family's finances and their mother's stress who juggled multiple jobs and family responsibilities. Amira's mother's full-time job was as a nursing care assistant on the night shift in a hospital. It was a stressful job that provided stable income and good health insurance bene-fits, which made it possible for Amira to have the comprehensive outpatient treatment team they needed. I agreed to see Amira for a reduced fee due to these financial hardships.

This is my introductory note:

From: A. Mayer, Individual Therapist
  To: PCP and RD.
  A is a twenty-year-old, who uses they/them pronouns with a diagnosis of Anorexia Nervosa. Client has a history of AFRID but currently meets criteria for Anorexia Nervosa. Reports "pretty good" relationship with mother, who is worried about them and wants to be supportive. Mother prepares dinner for A most nights before she leaves for her job.
  In therapy, we focused on how to identify irrational thoughts related to eating and body size. Mood is moderately depressed with intermit-tent Anxiety. Sent a release to Children's Hospital to get records about AFRID dx.

This is a note following an individual therapy session

From: A. Mayer, Individual Therapist
　To: PCP and RD
　Met with A. and discussed current mental status. They report increased difficulty following the meal plan and difficulty getting out of bed on non-school days. "I'm not sure that my anti-depressant is helping." No reported suicidal ideation but experiencing increased depressive symptoms. They continue to be preoccupied by schoolwork and making enough money at job as server.

A brief email follow-up from A's RD provides more info about her food intake.

From: RD
　To: Ind Tx, PCP
　Client's food log indicates that they are completing a full breakfast and dinner, but lunch is less consistent and typically closer to a snack in volume. Goal this week to include more food at lunch and add an evening snack.

Response from PCP:

From: PCP
　To: Ind Tx, RD
　Vital signs WNL. Weight unchanged from last visit. Patient tearful when discussing weight range. Motivated to transfer to four-year college in the fall.

I responded with the following brief follow-up questions:

Question for PCP:
　Please provide guidance about how much exercise is safe at this point. Do you have info about the client's report of taking an anti-depressant?
　Question for RD:
　How much do you think the client is eating?

RD response back to outpatient team:

I'm still working on getting a good history. Current intake is not nearly enough to maintain weight. Their weight history suggests that current weight is too low and will need to restore at least ten pounds. I am confirming that the team is aware that client has a history of taking laxatives, most recently as the week after discharge from the hospital. A has agreed to dispose of them or bring them to our next session. I'm concerned about them as a restaurant server. Amy, is that something you will discuss with them?

My response back to the outpatient team:

No, I am NOT aware of A's recent laxative use. Thank you for that information. Will discuss at next meeting. I totally agree with you about the restaurant server job, but it's also a very good source of income, so I doubt that quitting is in the cards. Maybe we can all talk to them about finding ways of snacking during quiet moments at work or eating a full meal before the shift begins. The restaurant does not provide food for the staff.

You might be asking yourself: How does this exchange help? I'm letting the team know that Amira is ambivalent about recovery, minimizing the severity of their symptoms, and that they are prioritizing school and exercise instead of eating disorder treatment. Amira doesn't buy in to the idea that they need more nourishment to be healthy, and I'm guessing that they may not be telling the RD how they feel about the meal plan. Perhaps my note gives the RD a heads-up that this is something they can continue to discuss. Likewise, the information about laxatives is important and something I can follow up on in my next session.

Vignette 3: Sarah

Sarah is a 30-year-old single, cisgender woman with a diagnosis of Binge Eating Disorder. She was referred by a work friend who was concerned about her health after she gained 20 pounds over the past year. Up until college, Sarah reported that she ate "normally"; however, after graduation, she moved into a studio apartment in Boston – her first time living alone without roommates – and over the course of a year, started engaging in binge eating behaviors three to four times per week, typically late at night after a stressful day of work. For Sarah, a binge episode usually began by eating an entire bag of vegan snacks, followed by a pint of ice cream, and several microwave containers of Mac and Cheese. She described eating very quickly, feeling completely out of control, and that it always happened in the privacy of her apartment. Afterward, she experienced intense feelings of disgust with herself, which led to highly self-critical thoughts for her "lack of discipline." In the days following these episodes, Sarah would try to follow a strict vegan diet, often skipping breakfast, eating a "healthy" lunch at her desk, and getting take-out for dinner. She would walk two miles back and forth to work and attended a workout class on the weekends. Sarah was clearly quite distressed by her binge-eating episodes. She had never been in therapy before and was open to the concept of a multidisciplinary outpatient team, which consisted of a therapist, dietitian, and PCP.

My first note to the PCP and dietitian:

> Individual therapy with Sarah will focus on CBT, particularly using mindfulness to address the bingeing episodes. Sarah says she misses her tight-knit group of college friends, most of whom live in the Midwest. She comes from a large, close family and has no relatives here in the city. She works at least fifty hours per week. I'm hoping that an emphasis on Interpersonal Therapy will help Sarah focus on increasing her social support network here in Boston to decrease her feelings of loneliness and isolation. A voracious reader of diet-culture books and blogs about "healthy eating", Sarah has many misconceptions about food and nourishment, which may be helpful to address in sessions with the dietitian.

Vignette 4: Kendra

Kendra is a 38-year-old, married, African American woman. We met in 2010, when she was 19, after she was required to take a medical leave from college. She had just completed the first of what would go on to be ten hospitalizations and other intensive treatment programs for Anorexia Nervosa, as well as OCD and PTSD. Kendra spent our first session expressing frustration about her inpatient experience and the inpatient team's recommendation that she delay her return to college; "I worked so hard to get into this school and it's the only thing I really care about." Her anger was palpable and mostly directed at the hospital staff and her parents.

Like many young adult clients in the early stages of treatment, Kendra was deeply ambivalent, or uncertain, about her willingness to recover from her eating disorder. After consulting with her inpatient therapist, her parents told her that they were not willing to pay for college until she had an outpatient team she would see regularly, and that her outpatient team would have to agree that she was healthy enough to return to college. With that, Kendra reluctantly agreed.

From the get-go, I knew that Kendra needed an experienced, no-nonsense PCP, but before I had time to make a referral, Kendra's heart rate dropped to a dangerous level and she needed to be hospitalized. During her hospitalization, I made a referral to Dr. L whose direct approach would be a good fit. Dr. L was undaunted by the ups and downs of Kendra's early outpatient treatment. She could easily tolerate Kendra being on the cusp of requiring more intensive treatment, and did not hesitate to hospitalize her when necessary. To Kendra's credit, she always respected Dr. L (I think partly because she was intimidated by her), but had Kendra not been willing to abide by

Dr. L's recommendations, it would have been impossible for me to treat her in my practice.

Seemingly, the biggest barrier to her improvement was her ambivalence, which resulted in a belief that she would not benefit from treatment. However, she was motivated to get back to college, so despite her seeming lack of investment to get better, she would have to meet the basic requirements of wellbeing that her parents and treatment team outlined in order to return.

Kendra spent the first two years of our treatment cycling in and out of various levels of care. She was unhappily living with her parents and eventually started taking college classes at a community college, even though she desperately wanted to return to her prestigious one. Unfortunately, she was unable to remain out of the hospital long enough for that to happen; however, she did apply to a local university in their honors program. Kendra rolled her eyes when she shared that she was accepted, making a self-deprecating comment: "I'm not proud of this, any idiot could get into this program."

In her late 20s, Kendra started attending a weekly therapy group that focused on helping her to better engage and understand her peer relationships. She attended it faithfully for a year. During that time, I connected with the group therapist every several months. I was pleased to learn that she was kind and attentive to the other clients and considered a valued member of the group.

Over the past 15 years, Kendra has been in some form of outpatient treatment for her various diagnoses; Dr. L and I have been constant throughout that time. The rest of the outpatient team has ebbed and flowed for various reasons. These changes resulted in Kendra working with several dietitians, two prescribers, and being disconnected from Dr. L for a while due to her medical needs. For the first five years, Dr. L managed Kendra's psychiatric medications; however, we decided to make a referral to a psychiatrist for a psychopharmacological assessment and medication management. She has been established with the current iteration of her treatment team for over ten years, but it has not been without difficulty. There have been office location changes, scheduling challenges, and trouble using public transit to get to appointments. This all changed after the pandemic, when virtual meetings have greatly improved her access, particularly with her prescriber and individual therapy appointments – only meetings with Dr. L continue to be in person.

Today, Kendra is medically stable, although her weight never made it into her target range. Despite this, her last hospitalization was nine years ago, and she has moved out of her parents' home. Reluctantly, she gave up on her dream of attending a highly ranked university, instead graduating from a local university. After graduation, she got a job at an accounting firm as an administrative assistant and transitioned to a more satisfying role within the company, which has allowed her to have good health benefits and financial independence. The focus of Kendra's treatment has shifted away from managing eating disorder symptoms to working through trauma and anxiety. She has been on multiple medication trials with limited success, saying she might explore other kinds of treatment, like transcranial-magnetic stimulation or ketamine. While the multidisciplinary outpatient team began as a response to her struggle with anorexia nervosa, the therapeutic focus has changed to include more supportive work to supplement the meaningful life she built for herself.

Final Thoughts

Our clients often struggle with the belief that they are alone in the world. We know, as therapists, that we need other people to help us through life's journey. We model this concept for our clients when we work to establish a team of multidisciplinary providers who are devoted to helping them. When clients struggle to hold on to hope, we are there to provide perspective and remind them of all the small steps that accumulate during recovery.

Our clients are keen observers of the people around them; the treatment team is no different. A healthy outpatient treatment team assists each other in managing our own stress related to providing exceptional care to individuals who are at risk of serious medical and psychiatric consequences from eating disorders. As clinicians, we learn from each other and lean on each other when we are unsure of how to respond to a crisis or a treatment impasse.

At different points in treatment, our clients may struggle with different parts of the recovery process. Sometimes it may be maintaining a medically appropriate weight, other times it may be working through underlying emotional issues, such as family conflict or resolving past trauma. By creating a supportive network of knowledgeable and caring providers, we increase the likelihood that clients can turn to someone on the team for support or feedback without feeling judged or hopeless. Each member of the team has different expertise, but I find that we're particularly helpful when we frame ourselves as a group of providers with a common cause: supporting our clients.

Reference

Crone, C., Fochtmann, L. J., Attia, E., Boland, R., Escobar, J., Fornari, V., Golden, N., Guarda, A., Jackson-Triche, M., Manzo, L., Mascolo, M., Pierce, K., Riddle, M., Seritan, A., Uniacke, B., Zucker, N., Yager, J., Craig, T., Hong, S.H. & Medicus, J. (2023). The American Psychiatric Association practice guideline for the treatment of patients with eating disorders. *American Journal of Psychiatry*, 180(2), 167–171. https://doi.org/10.1176/appi.ajp.23180001

Chapter 8

The Role of an RD in Treatment

What a Therapist Needs to Know

Caroline Mendes and Marcia Herrin

Nutrition – the process by which the body takes in and uses food – is both simple and complex. Eating is a fundamental human behavior; we are born with the innate ability to seek nutrients and energy for survival. One's relationship with food, however, extends beyond physical needs and intertwines with emotions, beliefs, social interactions, and cultural influences. In modern times, for many with and without eating disorders, nourishing themselves is anything but easy. Widespread nutrition misinformation, the abundance of food choices, weight-focused culture, and health care in which higher body sizes are equated with poor health all contribute to the challenges many face in nourishing themselves with ease. Nutrition counseling for eating disorders reflects this same duality: simple in its goal – helping individuals eat what their bodies need – but complex in its execution.

Nutrition misinformation is a significant public health concern with approximately 50% of the nutrition information that's available online being assessed as "inaccurate" (Denniss et al., 2023; Diekman et al., 2023; Kreft et al., 2023). Thanks to social media, our clients are exposed to false or misleading information about food even when they are not actively seeking it out, and those who struggle with high weight concerns are especially susceptible to these messages (Georgiou et al., 2025).

Registered Dietitians (RDs) use nutrition counseling to guide clients to nourish themselves, reduce disordered eating behaviors, and challenge deep-seated beliefs about food and body that are barriers to normal eating. Proper nutrition can restore brain function, emotional regulation, and cognitive clarity that facilitates more effective therapy. When clients are adequately nourished, they are better equipped to engage in therapeutic work, process emotions, and challenge disordered thoughts.

The goal of the nutrition information provided in this chapter is to equip therapists to collaborate effectively with the RD on the multidisciplinary team, while also giving you a basic knowledge of nutrition, so as not to perpetuate the unhelpful information often found in unregulated sources. It's

DOI: 10.4324/9781003600770-11

important to note that therapists are not expected to provide clients with nutrition education or address clients' misconceptions, instead directing clients to consult with an RD.

What Is a Registered Dietitian?

An RD is a nutrition expert with specialized education in food science and dietary factors that influence health. In the US, registered dietitians may use either the "RD" credential or "RDN" (Registered Dietitian Nutritionist) credential. For the purposes of this chapter, we'll be using RD for simplicity. Anyone in the US, regardless of educational background, can legally call themselves a "nutritionist" because the term is not regulated by the federal or (most) state governments. This is in contrast to "registered dietitian nutritionist" or more simply "registered dietitian" which are protected, regulated titles requiring specific education, supervised practice, passing a national exam, and ongoing continuing education. Given the unregulated title of "nutritionist," it is best to refer clients with eating disorders to an RD. However, not every RD has experience in treating eating disorders, and those not knowledgeable about eating disorders can cause more harm than good.

Nutrition Counseling

Nutrition counseling, also referred to as nutrition therapy, is a collaborative process in which RDs provide psychoeducation and guide clients in making behavior changes to support wellbeing. Similar to therapists, RDs use counseling skills in sessions with clients, although the topics in session are directed toward food, eating, exercise, health, and body concerns. Because eating and body are central to eating disorder pathology, nutrition counseling and psychotherapy often overlap. The RD's main focus in eating disorder treatment is to support clients in normalizing their eating and weight. Psychotherapists, on the other hand, focus on food and body issues in exploring how related behaviors and beliefs impact emotional wellbeing.

Many people with eating disorders have deeply ingrained fears and misconceptions about food, such as labeling foods as "good" or "bad" or fearing certain food groups. Nutrition-focused psychoeducation provides accurate information to help unlearn these beliefs, challenge diet culture, and reduce fear-based thinking. It promotes the idea that all foods can fit into a healthy diet and that nourishment is about more than just calories. Many eating disorder distortions begin with a kernel of truth: take sugar as an example. It is clear that eating excessive amounts of sugar is correlated with chronic disease and weight gain. It is not unusual for someone with an eating disorder to become aware of these health risks and develop an intense fear of eating sugar (even small amounts of it), or to feel substantial shame and guilt after eating foods that are high in sugar. When working to help clients establish normal eating habits amid the growing trend of labeling foods as "good" or "bad," it's important for all clinicians involved in their care to be mindful not to over-emphasize the most recent developments in nutrition science – particularly during the early stages of treatment. Knowledge is (eventually) power and can provide some reassurance and new ways to reframe thinking patterns. However, because eating disorders have strong genetic roots, simply providing information or raising awareness is usually not enough to eliminate symptoms or change the underlying pathology – despite what many clients, providers, or family members might hope.

Eating in ways that are aligned with recovery can be extremely anxiety provoking, but necessary for recovery. Given the genetic roots of eating disorders and how eating disorder behaviors impact brain function, clients often need to engage in recovery-focused eating behaviors before their thinking patterns and anxieties change. To facilitate this, RDs may use food-based exposure interventions during sessions, such as eating a fear-inducing meal or snack with the client. Other types of experiential interventions may include collaborating with the client as they create meal plans or grocery lists. More direct examples of experiential exposures could include grocery shopping, ordering groceries online, or preparing a meal. For families engaging in Family-Based Treatment (FBT), it may involve having a family meal during a session so caregivers can receive guidance about plating appropriate meals and supporting a child who is struggling to eat.

To be able to break cyclical patterns of disordered eating, RDs often help clients discover how these patterns relate to other parts of life, such as childhood eating experiences, self-compassion, trauma, emotions, or lifestyle factors (just to be clear, the RD's role is not to address trauma or other psychological conditions, rather it is to guide clients in building bridges between their eating behavior and personal circumstances or experiences). For example, a client with binge-eating disorder who struggles to stop eating when they are full may come to understand that this behavior was reinforced by their parents in childhood by forcing them to eat everything on their plate. Or a client who has experienced sexual trauma may come to recognize that their desire to maintain a very thin body by restricting food may stem from a wish to be less visible or sexually attractive. In these types of cases, such insights may arise in sessions with the RD, who will then collaborate with the therapist to further address this in psychotherapy.

Nutrition: The Nuts and Bolts

In this section, we'll review basic information about nutrition. To effectively treat eating disorders, therapists benefit from having a basic understanding of frequently used nutrition terminology and what normal eating looks like. Most individuals start off knowing what eating well is, but lose confidence in feeding themselves, often due to a cultural hyperfocus on nutrition alongside confusing and conflicting messages about what is "good" or "bad" to eat.

Calories, one of the most recognizable concepts we'll talk about, are simply a measurement of energy. When RDs talk about calories in food, we're simply referring to the estimated energy that food provides after being broken down by the body. *Metabolism* is the chemical processes that convert food into energy and essential molecules necessary for life and health. Metabolic rate is the pace at which the body burns calories over time. Interestingly, smart devices, apps, wearables, and websites purporting to estimate metabolism are not proven to be accurate.

Macronutrients are nutrients that the body needs in significant quantities to provide energy and are necessary for growth and maintenance of organs, bone, and muscles. There are three main types: carbohydrates, fats, and proteins. All three play important roles in maintaining health, and if any of these macronutrients are deficient, it often leads to negative health impacts.

Carbohydrates are the body's primary source of energy and play a crucial role in fueling essential bodily functions, including brain activity, heart muscle contractions, and metabolism. We require more carbohydrates than any other macronutrient. Sources of carbohydrates include grains, cereals, breads, starchy veggies (like potatoes), fruits, dairy products, and sugars. *Proteins* provide structural components essential for growth, repair, and the production of important chemical compounds. Their primary role is to build and maintain body tissues, including organs, muscles, hormones, immune system, and neurotransmitters. Despite common misconceptions, the body cannot directly use protein for fuel. The body actually requires less protein than carbohydrates or fats – only about 20% of food intake needs to come from protein. *Fats* are an important source of energy and a key component of various body structures. When the body is at rest, fatty acids (what fats are broken down into) provide most of the energy needed (and are essential for the absorption of the essential fat-soluble vitamins A, D, E, and K).

Micronutrients are essential nutrients the body needs in small amounts. The two main types of micronutrients are *vitamins* (compounds produced by plants and animals) and *minerals* (found in soil and absorbed by plants and animals). As micronutrients are found in all types of foods, normal eating usually provides adequate amounts.

Nutrition and Eating Disorders

What Is "Normal Eating"?

In this chapter, the term normal eating is used to describe a pattern of eating that is balanced in macronutrients while providing the essential micronutrients (and calories) to maintain a normal weight. Most people meet their nutrient needs by eating three meals a day that contain the basic food groups: carbohydrates, fat, protein, dairy foods, fruits, and/or vegetables. Younger people, and those needing to gain weight, need snacks as well to meet higher energy needs for growth and weight restoration. We believe that normal eating also regularly includes foods that we eat for pleasure, which is why we recommend desserts with lunch and dinner.

Undereating and Overeating

Eating disorders disrupt normal eating. Observed disruptions in normal eating vary greatly but can be broken into two main categories: undereating and overeating (with or without compensatory behaviors). *Undereating* is when clients do not provide themselves with enough calories or nutrients, it is more often the case that they're also lacking in macronutrients. Conversely, *overeating* is consuming more calories than the body needs. Both undereating and overeating occasionally occur in mild forms in normal eating. However, in eating disorders, when we talk about under- and overeating, we are referring to patterns that can cause significant health problems, not simply missing a snack or leaving a restaurant uncomfortably full.

Undereating occurs most frequently in restrictive eating disorders such as anorexia nervosa (AN) and avoidant restrictive food intake disorder (ARFID); however, it can occur across all eating disorder diagnoses. For instance, undereating is believed to be at the root of binge eating disorder behaviors, and we can see undereating in clients of any body shape and size. A client may be eating three meals and snacks daily and still be undereating if those meals and snacks are too small. Conversely, some clients may be eating a substantial dinner but skipping other meals or avoiding particular food groups, such as carbohydrates or fat intake.

Overeating is most often found in binge eating behaviors and bulimia nervosa; however, similar to undereating, it can occur in all types of eating disorders. Overeating, or binge eating behaviors, typically occur in association with foods that are "forbidden," such as sweets or snack foods; however, it can happen with any food and is often dependent on what food is available.

Recovering physically and psychologically from an eating disorder involves returning to regular and normal eating patterns. Nutrition and eating disorders are so intricately connected that genetic research has indicated that undereating can activate genes that are associated with eating disorders and that normalized eating and restoring to one's biologically appropriate weight shuts off these genes (Käver et al., 2024). In sum, normal eating is essential to recovery.

Evolution and Genetics in Eating Disorders

From an evolutionary perspective, eating disorder behaviors are theorized to be adaptations that promoted survival. For example, certain behavioral responses to calorie deprivation may have helped protect humans from starvation. Binge-eating may have ensured individuals ate larger amounts of food when it was available after food scarcity. Common features of anorexia, such as restriction, excessive movement, a perception that the body is bigger than it is (body dysmorphia), could have made it possible for individuals to migrate, traveling long distances, with very little food, to find new food sources (Guisinger, 2003). Neophobia of novel foods, described as fear, disgust, or gagging when presented with unfamiliar foods characteristic of ARFID, protected humans from consuming poisonous foods (Białek-Dratwa et al., 2022; Tybur et al., 2013). Thus, it is possible that eating disorder behaviors had utility in primitive times. However, in modern times, the evolutionary adaptations described above become problematic when these behaviors occur when access to safe food is bountiful.

A substantial body of research exists that supports the role of genetics in determining susceptibility to eating disorders, including which specific disorder might develop. Biological traits like perfectionism, harm-avoidance, and/or anxiety can contribute to the development of restrictive eating behaviors. Conversely, those who possess traits of novelty seeking and impulsivity are at higher risk of developing binge eating or bulimic behaviors (Hill, 2024). Research suggests that epigenetic alterations in AN are at least partially reversible with weight restoration (Steiger et al., 2019; Hübel et al., 2019).

This phenomenon was first documented in research in the Minnesota Starvation Experiment, published by Ancel Keyes in 1950 (Kalm & Semba, 2005). Conscientious objectors to World War II participated in the study designed to induce semi-starvation followed by a re-nourishment period, in hopes of learning how to refeed those liberated from Nazi concentration camps. As participants were underfed, they developed symptoms indicative of an eating disorder – obsession with food, ritualistic eating, body image discomfort, declines in physical and mental health. After a period of re-nourishment, eating disorder symptoms resolved. The Minnesota Starvation Experiment serves as an early example of how food intake and weight loss alone can trigger eating disorder symptoms without any initial concerns with body shape and size.

In our work with clients with eating disorders and their families, highlighting the biological nature of eating disorders can help them shift focus away from self-blame for the emergence of their eating disorder. That is, a client did not choose an eating disorder, and parents did not cause their child's disorder. Furthermore, the type of eating disorder one develops is determined largely by genetics. The understanding that food deprivation and weight loss are catalysts for an eating disorder can instill hope that normalizing eating and weight leads to recovery.

Nutritional Consequences of Eating Disorders

Eating disorders severely disrupt normal eating leading to serious nutritional consequences. Changes in one's metabolism, oral and gastrointestinal health, delayed gastric emptying, and constipation are all common issues that those with eating disorders face.

Undereating forces the body to conserve energy by prioritizing the most critical functions, like keeping the heart beating, while slowing down less essential processes such as maintaining body temperature, hair growth, and digestion. In other words, metabolism decreases as energy intake is decreased, eventually allowing some to maintain weight with very little intake. Low metabolic rates in response to undereating occur across all body shapes and sizes, not only in low-weight individuals. Because of the reduction in metabolic rate that accompanies undereating, clients often voice, "I am afraid I have ruined my metabolism"; however, there is no evidence that metabolism does not return to normal with regular eating (Most & Redman, 2020; Reed et al., 2024).

Digestive health is affected by eating disordered behaviors (i.e., restriction, binging, and purging) causing uncomfortable and often painful symptoms. Early fullness or bloating, known as delayed gastric emptying, even after eating small amounts of food in the refeeding phase, is important as it is the result of malnutrition. This sensation is often described by clients as my stomach is "shrinking" (though the stomach itself doesn't actually shrink). This phase, when delayed gastric emptying is most pronounced, makes the common advice to "Eat when you are hungry and stop when you are full" not very helpful.

Constipation is described as bowel movements that are infrequent (less than three per week), hard or bumpy, require straining or discomfort when passing, or a sensation that not all stool has passed (Włodarczyk et al., 2021). In anorexia, constipation is the most frequently described gastrointestinal symptom, and high rates are also reported in bulimia and likely ARFID (Lin et al., 2021; Atkins et al., 2023). Constipation can cause pain, bloating, and a sensation of fullness, which can impact clients' motivation to eat adequately. The cause of constipation in eating disorders is multifactorial and relates directly to eating disorder behaviors like restriction, purging, and laxative abuse that alter how the gut functions. Psychological distress is also a likely contributor to constipation. As common nutritional treatment for constipation, such as dietary fiber or fluid intake, can decrease appetite and interfere with increasing calorie intake, polyethylene glycol (Miralax) is often used under the supervision of the RD or medical provider. Treating constipation in eating disorders is essential to decrease barriers to normal eating. Caution should be taken in the use of stimulant laxatives, as laxative abuse can lead to dehydration and severe medical complications.

Acid reflux, or stomach acid entering the esophagus creating a burning sensation and uncomfortable pressure, is another frequent digestive complaint most commonly associated with purging behaviors, but can also accompany delayed gastric emptying. Dietary modifications exist to reduce acid reflux such as decreasing consumption of foods associated with increased risk of acid reflux such as tomato sauce, orange juice, chocolate, and high-fat foods. Eating smaller meals and relying more on snacks is also recommended. Caution is advised with these dietary strategies to reduce acid reflux they can inhibit weight restoration or increase the risk of binge eating if meals are less satisfying.

Dental erosion is up to five times higher for clients with eating disorders than for normal eaters (Lin et al., 2021). Those engaging in self-induced vomiting sustain the most damage to their teeth due to frequent exposure to stomach acid and then brushing immediately after vomiting. Poor oral health for whatever reason can cause pain and discomfort with eating, leading to a lowered desire to eat in anorexia and ARFID. Oral pain can also impact the types of foods clients eat by limiting them to focus more on semi-soft, easy to chew foods. This dynamic is further complicated in those engaging in purging, as these types of foods (semi-soft, easy to chew) are frequently relied on during binges due to their ease in regurgitating. Purging via vomiting can also cause enlarged salivary glands leading to facial swelling around the jaw, creating body dissatisfaction and a perception of weight gain. Nutrition psychoeducation regarding the ineffectiveness of purging to counteract calories consumed can be helpful at motivating clients to interrupt purging behaviors (Kaye et al, 1993).

Chronic metabolic conditions such as diabetes, high cholesterol, non-alcoholic fatty liver, and "obesity" frequently co-occur in our clients struggling with binge eating. Dietary intervention for these conditions that instructs the restriction of certain foods, such as avoiding foods high in saturated fat to manage high cholesterol, limiting refined carbohydrates to treat diabetes, or reducing calories for weight loss, should be avoided while clients are actively engaging in eating disordered behaviors. Restriction of foods, even for health reasons, can interfere with normal eating and trigger eating disorder behaviors. Permission to eat all foods and generous meals that include dessert is necessary for recovery. Of note, high cholesterol levels are also common in AN and normalize with weight gain (Ohwada et al, 2006).

Problematic Dietary Patterns in Eating Disorders

In addition to undereating or overeating, clients can be eating the appropriate amount of calories and while engaging in eating patterns that are detrimental to health and promote eating disordered behaviors. For example, fasting for 15 hours, then eating adequate calories may increase the risk of binge eating; likewise, severely reducing carbohydrates can impair brain function.

Reduced Carbohydrate Diets

The popularity of reduced-carbohydrate diets dates back to the 1860s. Today, low-carbohydrate diets, or "low-carb," are marketed for their efficacy in promoting fast weight loss – an attractive prospect to many eating disorder clients concerned with body shape and size. The reason for initial rapid weight loss when carbohydrates are limited is due to fluid loss, not fat loss. When carbohydrates are reintroduced, fluid levels are normalized, and weight goes up.

Carbohydrates are recommended to be about 50% of one's diet; thus low-carbohydrate diets can lead to health consequences. The brain depends solely on carbohydrates for energy, making carbohydrates essential for optimal cognitive function and emotional stability. Unlike other organs, which can use fatty acids for energy, the brain runs on glucose (which is a carbohydrate) alone. When glucose is limited, the body adapts to maintain brain function by converting muscle protein into glucose. For our clients who typically want to maintain muscle, understanding how insufficient dietary intake of carbohydrates may lead to muscle loss can help increase carbohydrate intake. Although the body cannot use fats to create glucose, what it can do is produce ketones from fat as an emergency energy source; however, this process can only provide up to 70% of the brain's energy needs. Prolonged low-carbohydrate diets and use of ketones can create "keto fog," which can present as forgetfulness, poor attention, and deficits in executive functioning (Afzal & Salzman, 2024). Reincorporating carbohydrates can improve brain function, which can be a source of motivation for some clients.

Furthermore, reduced carbohydrate diets have health consequences throughout the body, not only the brain. Frequent side effects of inadequate carbohydrate intake include gastrointestinal upset, headache, and fatigue. Longer-term consequences of low-carbohydrate diets include bad breath (also known as "keto" breath due to increased ketone production, see above), constipation, insomnia, dehydration, high cholesterol, kidney stones, and low bone density, which could lead to increased risk of bone fracture (Maguire & Youngson, 2022). Despite the documented health consequences of low-carbohydrate diets, they continue to be prevalent, and even recommended, by medical professionals.

Anti-fat bias, where fatness is blamed for chronic health conditions and prioritizes weight loss above risks of diets, is a significant public health concern. Carbohydrates are often inappropriately blamed for the existence of health conditions such as diabetes and obesity. For instance, it is a common misconception that excessive carbohydrate intake, in particular high intake of sugar, causes diabetes; however, only when dietary intake of carbohydrates significantly exceeds recommendations are there associations between carbohydrate intake and diabetes (Hosseini et al., 2022).

Additionally, there is a bias regarding chronic health conditions in that they are caused by lifestyle factors, such as a poor diet, wherein the individual is blamed for the development of the disease. Dietary intake alone cannot cause chronic disease and contributes a small percentage of risk. Consequently, many clients reduce or eliminate carbohydrates in a misguided effort to lose weight or improve health. This is a major concern, especially for clients with binge eating, since eating carbohydrates reduces appetite and promotes a feeling of satiety (i.e., fullness), so when carbohydrates are eliminated, hunger cues increase. For example, when clients eat meals without carbohydrates, such as a salad with grilled chicken, they might feel fullness in their stomach while also experiencing an urge to continue to eat. This simultaneous sensation of fullness and hunger can trigger binge eating and lead clients to distrust their bodies (Hosseini et al., 2022).

High Protein Diets

In Western society, there is a pervasive over-promotion of consuming protein, which is evident not only among bodybuilders and gym-goers, but also in popular diet culture and mainstream health messaging. Protein is viewed as the "good macronutrient" for its role in muscle building and ability to promote satiety. Protein curbs hunger because it takes longer to digest than other macronutrients as well as impacting the hormones that decrease hunger. Because protein is a slow and inefficient energy source, when the body uses it for energy, nitrogenous waste (mainly urea) is produced, which can stress the kidneys. Higher than recommended protein intake can slow digestion leading to gastrointestinal complications such as early fullness, constipation, and bloating, which complicate the relationship between food and eating.

Foods that do not traditionally contain protein are being manufactured with added proteins such as frozen waffles, cereal, and cookies. Our clients, who are vulnerable to these messages, often find protein-rich foods to be "safe foods" and over-consume them, despite the body requiring less protein when compared to carbohydrates and fat. This is especially common in men with eating disorders, where building muscle is a primary concern rather than being thin, where high protein intakes displace other foods that provide essential nutrients such as fruits, starches, and fats.

Low Fat Diet

Fat is essential for the absorption of fat-soluble vitamins, such as vitamins A, D, E, and K. Since fat is higher in calories per gram (9-per-gram versus the 4-per-gram found in carbohydrates and protein), many clients with eating disorders tend to avoid eating fats to reduce caloric intake. Additionally, the overlap in terminology between *dietary* fat and *body* fat can lead clients to assume that fat intake directly translates to fat accumulation in the body. Insufficient intake of fat can lead to health issues, including menstrual abnormalities (such as amenorrhea), fertility problems, and decreased sex drive. Common signs of fat deficiency include irregular menstrual cycles, dry skin and hair, sleep problems, difficulty concentrating, excessive thirst, and poor wound healing.

Vegetarian and Vegan Diets

Vegetarian and vegan diets are increasing in popularity. Eating less meat purports to support health, the environment, weight loss, and animal rights. This is particularly tempting for clients with restrictive eating disorders, who benefit from being able to avoid foods in socially acceptable ways. For example, clients may facilitate restriction by reporting they are vegan, instead of citing their true intent to facilitate eating avoidance; likewise, clients struggling with ARFID, where meat is frequently avoided, might state they are vegetarian, so they are not pushed into eating these feared foods (Salvia et al., 2025).

Traditional vegetarian diets restrict meat, poultry, and seafood, or all living animals, but many vegetarians eat animal products such as dairy and eggs. Vegan diets rely only on plant-based sources to meet nutrient needs. Clients who follow these diets are at increased risk of nutrient deficiencies, such as low protein, iron, calcium (if excluding dairy), B12 (vegans), zinc, as these nutrients are found in higher concentrations and more easily digestible forms in animal products and meats. Inadequate intake of protein can reduce satiety, which can increase the risk of binge eating, and lead to increased anxiety and depression as the brain does not receive adequate building blocks to produce neurotransmitters (Gauthier et al., 2015; Haleem, 2012; Terry et al., 2022). Low intakes of calcium are associated with impaired bone health, which can exacerbate impacts of undereating on bone density. Clients who follow vegan diets are at risk for B12 deficiency, which can cause fatigue, which impacts client motivation for recovery or ability to make dietary changes.

"Clean Eating" or Excessively Healthy Diets

In response to research on the negative health effects of processed foods and their association with "obesity," *clean eating*, or a focus on eating whole, unprocessed foods, has become a societal focus. Those with eating disorders are vulnerable to these messages, which can lead to an extreme avoidance of processed foods. However, "processed foods" are not clearly defined; they simply refer to any food that is changed from its original source. For example, most people think about Twinkies or Oreos as "processed foods," however, freshly cut apples bought at the grocery store also meet the definition of a "processed food" since they are altered from their original source (i.e., peeled and cut).

An over-reliance on whole foods such as fruits, vegetables, whole grains, plain meats, nuts, and oils, while avoiding most packaged foods is problematic. This style of eating can make it challenging to meet energy requirements, as not eating foods with added sugars or preservatives eliminates large categories of foods that are part of normal eating. Also, avoiding these enjoyable foods can contribute to social isolation as clients feel unable to participate in social activities, like traditional cookouts, ice cream socials, or pizza parties.

Weight and Eating Disorders

Eating disorders occur in all body shapes and sizes. The size of a client does not determine the severity of the eating disorder. However, a person's current weight in relation to their weight history is an important factor in eating disorder treatment. Significant and rapid changes in weight can signal a higher risk of medical complications and more severe eating disorder behaviors. Rapid weight gain can be indicative of more severe binge eating behavior, where clients are consuming consistently excessive amounts of calories. In bulimia, if rapid weight gain occurs after a client interrupts more severe purging, it could be a sign of fluid shifts as the body retains fluid as it works to adjust hormones that regulate hydration (Nitsch et al., 2021).

Greater weight loss over shorter amounts of time can signal more severe restrictive eating, which increases the risk of medical complications, such as bradycardia (low heart rate), hypoglycemia (low blood sugar), and refeeding syndrome (a dangerous shift in electrolytes that can occur when food intake is rapidly increased). Assessing if someone is underweight is crucial for setting nutrition counseling goals and supporting eating disorder recovery. When body weight falls outside of a person's biologically appropriate range – the genetically determined weight range where their body functions best – body functions and mental health can be impaired – it's nearly impossible to fully recover while underweight.

Traditionally, underweight status has been defined using body mass index (BMI) in adults. BMI is a ratio of height to weight, where lower numbers signal underweight and higher values show overweight and obesity. In 1998, the National Institute of Health (NIH) lowered the BMI categories to match the World Health Organization (WHO) criteria, which was lower to account for lower BMI genetically found in Asians born in Asia. Therefore, expectations for what is a healthy weight are skewed in non-Asian populations, with non-Asian clients with lower BMIs (that are technically in the "normal" range) being miscategorized as "healthy." Although BMI can provide some insight into health outcomes, it is not an accurate measure of nutritional status and health, particularly in the context of eating disorders. Despite its limitations, BMI remains a tool used in medical settings, including insurance authorization and eating disorder treatment.

To better assess whether someone is underweight, it is important to consider their weight history. A client's weight history is not just a discussion about recent weights, but rather, a recollection of weights throughout life beginning in childhood, continuing through adolescence, and ending with noteworthy adult weights. Special attention is paid to weights that correlate with eating disorder pathology onset and other important environmental factors, such as use of psychiatric medications, illnesses, or major life events. Family history of weight is also included in weight history, given that weight is in large part determined by genetics. Based on weight history, current physical and mental health status, and eating disorder behaviors, RDs determine a biologically appropriate weight (BAW), which is a five-pound range a client can easily maintain without the use of eating disorder behaviors. BAW is continuously re-assessed throughout treatment and can change as more information is gathered. It is important to highlight that BAW is a weight range, not a specific weight, and setting strict weight targets for patients can be harmful. For example, if a patient is told their "goal weight" is 140 pounds, and they see their weight go above that number, they may try to lose weight through the use of eating disorder behaviors or experience feelings of failure. In cases where a "goal weight" is set, it's better to think of it as a "minimum safe weight" rather than a goal weight.

In the case of children and adolescents, a BAW is more accurately assessed using growth charts, typically found in their pediatrician's medical records. Children's growth is tracked over time using three charts: weight-for-age, height-for-age, and BMI-for-age. These charts use percentiles ranging from the 5th to the 99.9th percentile, based on data from national studies. Recently, the CDC added growth percentiles above the 99th percentile called Extended BMI-for-age Growth Charts (Centers for Disease Control and Prevention [CDC], 2025; see the resources section for more information). However, it is important to note that growth charts are based on data from the 1970s, which doesn't account for the fact that Americans have increased in size; therefore, those in higher BMI percentiles may be more normative than they appear. Recent research examining the accuracy of BMI-for-age charts found that almost 66% of children that the BMI charts identified as "overweight" had normal fat levels, and that they overestimated the prevalence of overweight while underestimating the prevalence of underweight children (Agbaje, 2025).

Standard practice in assessing weight in children and adolescents is to maintain growth on a consistent growth curve staying within a few percentiles as the child matures. When a child with an eating disorder has lost weight, the goal is to help them return to their pre-eating disorder growth percentile, while factoring in increases in age if necessary. Children and adolescents presenting with BMI percentiles above the normal range despite significant weight loss, as seen in atypical anorexia, are at risk of the same severity of medical complications as those presenting with abnormally low BMI percentiles. Previously, target goal weights were based on achieving 50% of BMI percentile for age (mBMI). The Society for Adolescent Health and Medicine (SAHM) now recommends in its Medical Management of Restrictive Eating Disorders in Adolescents and Young Adults (2022) that target goal weights consider premorbid trajectory for height, weight, and BMI; age at pubertal onset; current sexual maturity rating; as well as parental heights. Jary et al. (2024) found that historical BMI percentile for age better predicted physical and psychological recovery than did mBMI-based weight goals in those with typical and atypical AN. For children and adolescents recovering from binge eating disorder, gradual weight loss that naturally occurs as the binge eating stops – without restricting intake considerably – is acceptable, as long as it doesn't trigger further binge urges or affect their growth and development. Weight loss at any stage of recovery can trigger eating disorder behaviors and should only be considered with a careful, multidisciplinary approach.

For adults with eating disorders who are not determined to be underweight, normalizing eating is the primary focus of treatment. Undereating and disordered eating can occur without significant weight loss or gain. The body may change weight as it adjusts to regular, balanced eating. This can be distressing for patients who gain weight but are not overeating. Early weight gain in recovery is not necessarily a sign of inappropriate eating. It may reflect fluid shifts, metabolic changes, or changes in bowel movements as the body begins to adjust. Reducing the food plan to ease distress may hinder the process of normalizing eating and interrupting the cycle of eating disorder behaviors. Over time, it is expected that the body will regulate itself, but if weight gain continues many months into recovery, it might require further medical evaluation or adjustments to the food plan.

Permission to Return to Exercise

Dysfunctional exercise and eating disorders co-occur with prevalence rates as high as 80% (Quesnel et al; 2023). Dysfunctional exercise is described as an unhealthy relationship with exercise that results in negative physical and/or mental wellbeing. Other terms that fall under this category include compulsive exercise, excessive exercise, exercise addiction, and exercise dependence. Clients struggling with dysfunctional exercise are at greater risk for more severe eating disorder pathology, worse physical health, longer duration of illness, increased risk of relapse, and greater rates of depression. RDs experienced in treating eating disorders are able to provide education on the amount of exercise to maintain health and the dangers of excessive exercise (Hackert et al., 2020).

Until recently, treatment approaches in underweight clients and/or for those engaged in dysfunctional exercise were based on an abstinence approach, with the rationale being to avoid exercise so as not to undermine recovery efforts. Recent treatment recommendations for dysfunctional exercise no longer promote exercise abstinence; rather, they allow exercise throughout treatment based on a client's medical status and ability to nourish themselves. Research has shown that individualized moderate exercise prescriptions during treatment do not significantly interfere with weight restoration, while demonstrating improved physical outcomes, such as improved bone density, and importantly help clients establish a healthy relationship with exercise (Quesnel et al., 2023; Hallward et al., 2022).

Incorporating exercise during the weight restoration process has the positive effect of disassociating movement from calorie burning and weight loss. In fact, research suggests that exercise has a minimal impact on decreasing body weight than what has been commonly believed (Pontzer, 2023). Supporting clients by allowing movement during recovery can provide them with an opportunity to develop a healthy relationship with activity, which may be helpful in preventing relapse. It is important that the decision to return to physical activity or sports is typically made by the primary care physician (or pediatrician) in collaboration with the RD (Cook et al. 2016). We have found it helpful when therapists explore their clients' feelings and beliefs about exercise and figure out ways to cope with reduced exercise if that is recommended by their treatment team. Similarly, it is helpful to communicate to the team when you feel exercise is not being used in healthy or appropriate ways.

RD Interventions and Tools

The goals of nutrition counseling for eating disorders are to interrupt and normalize disordered eating behaviors and reduce distress around eating. Because eating disorder symptoms are deeply connected to biological factors, such as undereating, the focus of nutrition counseling begins with normalizing eating before moving on to cognitive challenges, such as changing negative beliefs about food and weight. While normalizing eating is the priority, these goals often overlap. For instance, to normalize eating, a client might need to start eating carbohydrates that they believe are fattening, or they will likely need to restore weight while grappling with negative body image.

RDs begin the nutrition counseling process with an initial assessment focused on learning more about the client's concerns about eating and reviewing all available medical information, such as recent lab work, vitals, and weight, as well as current eating and exercise habits. During an initial session, RDs provide nutrition education and outline what treatment may look like going forward. Sometimes, sessions end with defined food plans and goals. Frequency of visits varies; however, it usually begins with weekly sessions and decreases in frequency as clients progress toward recovery. It is common for clients to meet with an RD for many months, and in some cases, years.

Each session usually includes a review of eating in-between sessions by asking questions about identified progress and challenges, weight, and goal setting or planning. Topics addressed in nutrition counseling sessions include anxieties related to food, identifying patterns of eating, correlations between eating behaviors and mood, body image, exercise, physical sensations of eating or nutrition related physical symptoms of the eating disorder, cooking and meal planning, conversations related to food and body with peers and family, and any other topics that relate to nourishing the body. If an adolescent is in FBT, RDs may primarily meet with parents to provide the information and coaching they need to restore their child's weight.

Dietary Recall or Food Tracking

To effectively support clients with normalizing eating, RDs need to know what clients are eating. In outpatient settings, the only way to know what a client is eating is through their self-report. RDs will often take a verbal dietary recall in each session, asking clients what they ate over the previous 24 hours or usual intake in the past week. Alternatively (or in addition), some RDs may ask clients to keep a food log, a written inventory of what they ate throughout the day. This can be done with pen and paper, a computer or phone, or using an app specifically designed for eating disorder treatment. Traditional calorie counting apps are typically contraindicated to avoid increasing preoccupation with calories.

It's important to recognize that recalling dietary intake can be difficult for individuals with eating disorders. Cognitive impairments, feelings of shame and guilt, dissociation from eating, and other factors can make it challenging for them to accurately report what they're eating. Clients with restrictive eating disorders often over-report intake, whereas clients with binge eating behaviors often under-report intake (Schebendach et al. 2012). For parents who are reporting intake, there can also be inaccuracies due to secretive behaviors, such as hiding or stealing food. Parental guilt can also skew reporting of their child's intake due to their own guilt, pressure to feed their child right, and more.

Weighing Clients

RDs need to know a client's weight as it provides valuable information, including the appropriateness of the food plan, severity of eating disorder behaviors, and medical complications. Rapid and large fluctuations in weight can signify fluid retention, which can be dangerous and require medical evaluation. In outpatient treatment, weight is usually checked weekly and can be taken by any team member. The RD is often responsible for weekly weights, but psychotherapists may weigh clients, as is common in CBT and FBT. When using telehealth, weights may be done at home by the family or client and reported to the team members. Weights are most accurate when compared on the same scale and taken at a similar time of day in similar clothing.

Weights may be *blind*, where the weight is not shown to the client, *viewed*, where a client sees their weight at the time of weigh-in, or *informed*, where the client does not see the weight at the moment it is taken, but the number is then shared during a treatment session. Scales are available that allow clients to weigh themselves blindly at home, and the data is then delivered directly to the treatment team. It can be helpful to use these blinded scales for virtual weigh-ins to reduce the risk of compulsive weighing out of session. Recent recommendations related to blind versus viewed weights suggest sharing weight information openly with clients is preferable. Both Cognitive Behavioral Therapy (CBT) and FBT utilize open communication about weights. CBT and FBT are associated with positive recovery outcomes (Attia & Walsh, 2025; Austin et al. 2025). In our clinical experience, we recommend sharing weight information with clients for transparency, support for nutrition interventions (such as increasing food plans), and as a tool for challenging the eating disorder; however, if a client does not feel that it is in their best interest, their preference should be respected.

Food Plans

Food plans, commonly referred to as "meal plans," are a tool used to describe normal eating. These plans may provide reassurance to clients who have lost touch with their bodies and are unsure of what "normal" eating looks like; however, not all clients require a food plan during eating disorder treatment. Food plans are designed to ensure clients are eating with structure to interrupt the eating disorder, and so they get the nutrients and calories they need. Food plans are to be used in conjunction with nutrition counseling and are not designed as stand-alone guides. The format of these plans depends on the level of care and the individual needs of the client. For therapists, understanding how different food plans are designed can help to anticipate emotional challenges that may come up when implementing their plan. Importantly, food plans are assessed based on the amount of food eaten, or "completed," in a given meal or snack – this is intended to be an approximate estimate. It is often the case in outpatient treatment that informal language is used to describe how much of something was eaten, such as "I had half a sandwich and four chips" or "I had most of an apple." In higher levels of care, percentages such as 25%, 50%, 75%, and 100% are commonly used.

Adjusting the Food Plan for Weight Restoration

In clients who are underweight, such as those with AN, a focus on weight restoration is paramount to recovery. Food plans need to be continually assessed and adjusted to reach this goal as energy needs increase throughout the re-nourishing phase of treatment. As the body gains weight and restores muscle tissue, metabolism increases. Energy needs for weight restoration can be higher than anticipated with some case reports of calorie needs above 5000 calories per day. A client can be eating 100% of a food plan that seems large and be losing or maintaining weight. When weight restoration slows or plateaus, it is customary to add roughly 300 calories to the food plan (e.g., energy bar and juice), and when weight is down, the increase is recommended to be closer to 500 calories (e.g., bagel with peanut butter). Weight restoration is not always linear. Not everyone restoring weight will do so at a consistent or predictable rate. Some clients' weight restores quickly and then plateaus quickly, whereas others are slow to initially gain weight and then increase in rate later in treatment. Fast initial weight restoration is not necessarily indicative of overfeeding. FBT recommends outpatient weight gains of at least a pound a week (Lock & Le Grange, 2015; Le Grange et al., 2021; Lock & Le Grange, 2025).

Exchange-Based Food Plans

Exchange-based food plans are mostly used in higher levels of care (HLOC), such as inpatient, residential, and partial hospitalization programs. Meals and snacks are broken down into specific food groups, and then those food groups are further categorized into groups that share similar calories, macronutrients, vitamins, and minerals. The food groups are carbohydrates or starches, proteins, fats, fruits, vegetables, and dairy. This method is helpful to HLOC staff to ensure each client is receiving adequate and balanced meals; however, exchange-based plans are too complicated to be useful to clients and caregivers in an outpatient setting.

Rule of Threes

The Rule of Threes is a structured food plan initially developed to help college students navigate dining halls while recovering from disordered eating (Herrin & Larkin, 2013). However, it is now used widely in the outpatient treatment of all eating disordered diagnoses and age groups. The Rule of Three focuses on regular meals and snacks (three meals and up to three snacks per day) with servings of the typical food groups (complex carbohydrates, protein, fruits and vegetables, calcium, and fat) at each meal. As part of this plan, "fun foods" (i.e., desserts) are a requirement at lunch and dinner to help reduce the fear of eating foods in this category. Advice on which foods fall into which food group is provided, as well as typical serving sizes for various food groups. Serving sizes are adjusted to support each client's calorie needs. Meals based on the Rule of Threes plan provide the 40 essential nutrients humans need daily.

Plate by Plate Approach

The Plate by Plate Approach is a visual guide for families plating meals for children recovering from eating disorders (Crosbie & Sterling, 2018). This approach helps create balanced meals by focusing on how to visually fill a plate. No measuring, counting, or tracking is required. There are two versions of the plate: the weight restoration plate, which is divided into 50% starches, 25% protein, and 25% fruit/veggies, and the weight maintenance plate, which is divided into equal thirds for starches, protein, and fruits/veggies. Both plate versions also recommend adding a source of fat and dairy to each meal. The goal is to fill a ten-inch plate with a variety of food groups to create a balanced, normalized meal. The visual nature of the Plate by Plate Approach can simplify creating appropriate meals for recovery and is good to use with culturally and ethnically diverse clients.

Oral Nutrition Supplements

Consuming enough calories and nutrients can be challenging early in treatment. In some cases, drinkable nutrition shakes, also known as oral nutrition supplements, can help support the recovery process. Their main purpose is to provide calories and essential macro and micronutrients in a compact, liquid form. Due to the hyperfocus on protein and avoidance of carbohydrates discussed earlier, many high-protein or low-carb or low-sugar shakes exist, which often feel safer to our clients. Those shakes that are too high in protein and/or low in calories should not be recommended.

Nutrition shakes are often used in cases of unfinished meals to add calories to meet the high energy needs for those requiring weight restoration. In HLOC settings, when clients are unable to eat an entire meal or snack, nutrition shakes are used to replace the missing calories and nutrients. For example, say a meal is equivalent to two nutrition shakes and a client is only about to half of their dinner, then they are asked to drink one shake to "supplement" for the half they didn't eat. This is to ensure they receive the full nutritional value of the meal. Nutrition shakes are also used to add additional calories when eating the volume of solid food needed to meet energy needs is challenging. Lastly, nutrition shakes can also play a role in increasing motivation. For instance, if clients are struggling to complete the last remaining bites of solid food at a meal, the idea of drinking a 250-calorie shake versus finishing the few bites they have left may create motivation to push through their anxiety. Alternatively, a client might do some quick mental math and realize that a 700-calorie meal is more than drinking two supplements at 500 calories, so they opt to drink the shakes instead of eating the food, but this can be easily remedied by requiring three supplements for no solid food intake.

Tube Feeding

Tube feeding, also known as enteral nutrition, can be a life-saving intervention for individuals who cannot consume enough food by mouth. It is typically only available in medical hospitals and some inpatient eating disorder treatment centers. Tube feedings in outpatient settings are very rarely offered. The most common method involves a nasogastric tube (NGT), which is inserted through the nose and into the stomach. Nutrition and fluids are then delivered through the tube.

Special Considerations for ARFID

Below, we will say a few words about how nutrition treatment for ARFID differs from treatment for other eating disorders. As ARFID is a new DSM diagnosis as of 2013 with a significant update in the DSM-5-TR (American Psychiatric Association, 2022), only a small number of studies have been published reporting treatment outcomes. The most promising studies employed either CBT or FBT approaches. ARFID treatment approaches should be individualized and tailored to the specific drivers of the client's food avoidance as described in DSM-5-TR: picky eating (avoidance of foods due to certain sensory characteristics), lack of appetite, and/or fear of adverse consequences. It is also important to consider that autism spectrum disorder (ASD), along with anxiety disorders, obsessive compulsive disorder (OCD), and attention-deficit/hyperactivity disorder (ADHD), are often co-existing with ARFID (American Psychiatric Association, 2022). When a client with ARFID is underweight, the initial focus of treatment is on weight gain and not on expanding food variety (Thomas & Eddy, 2019). This is done by focusing on the client's preferred calorically rich foods at meals and snacks.

Managing Risk of Nutritional Deficiencies

ARFID is often a response to the novelty of food; therefore, processed foods often feel safer for these clients because they taste, look, and feel consistently the same. Given that many of these foods are not high in vitamins and minerals, serious nutrient deficiencies can occur. Consequently, it is recommended that ARFID clients regularly take a multivitamin and mineral supplement. Supplements are available now that are formulated for picky eaters who may not tolerate the taste or texture of standard brands. Nutritional supplements, such as meal replacement drinks and bars, protein drinks and bars, milk shakes, smoothies, and multivitamin/mineral supplements, may initially prove useful in improving calorie and nutritional intake, thereby reducing the detrimental impacts of poor nutrient intake on development and growth. Usefulness of meal replacement drinks and smoothies varies with the degree of the patient's sensitivities to taste and texture differences.

Motivation

In ARFID, utilizing contingency rewards is more effective than the use of consequences or loss of privileges, which is commonly used in the treatment of AN. Urging ARFID clients to eat foods that they find repulsive can cause gagging and vomiting creating more negative associations. Fear of eating or lack of interest in eating itself is in contrast with anorexia, where clients are fearful of the impact eating will have on the body; therefore, interventions need to be gentler than in AN.

In summary, the initial nutrition treatment goals for ARFID include achieving or maintaining a healthy weight, correcting nutritional deficiencies, establishing regular eating patterns, increasing food variety, and consistently consuming foods from each food group. Long-term treatment goals focus on replacing nutritional drinks with food intake, developing the ability to eat with others and outside the home, becoming comfortable eating the same foods as others, and increasing flexibility with regard to food texture, taste, smell, brands, and routines.

Summary

What a psychotherapist needs to know about nutrition counseling in the treatment of eating disorders, in short, is that eating well is simple and much less complex than our culture makes it out to be. And, for our clients, normal eating is extremely complicated, and both physically and psychologically uncomfortable. Supporting clients as they improve food-related behaviors does not require complicated food plans or an in-depth knowledge of nutrition, it takes clear and consistent messaging that the return to normal eating is key to recovery from an eating disorder.

Recommended Resources

Nutrition Counseling in the Treatment of Eating Disorders 2nd Edition
Marcia Herrin & Maria Larkin

Cognitive-Behavioral Therapy for Avoidant/Restrictive Food Intake Disorder
Jennifer Thomas & Kamryn Eddy

The Parent's Guide to Eating Disorders: Supporting Self-Esteem, Healthy
    Eating, and Positive Body Image at Home
Marcia Herrin & Nancy Matsumoto

Treatment Manual for Anorexia Nervosa, Second Edition: A Family-Based
    Approach
James Lock, Daniel Le Grange, Gerald Russel

CDC Child and Teen BMI calculator
https://www.cdc.gov/bmi/child-teen-calculator/

The Plate by Plate Instagram page
https://www.instagram.com/platebyplateapproach/?hl=en

References

Afzal, S., & Salzman, D. (2024, April). Reversible Memory Loss and Brain Fog Associated with Prolonged Ketogenic Diet Use: A Case Report (P5-9.002). In Neurology (Vol. 102, No. 17_supplement_1, p. 6118). Hagerstown, MD: Lippincott Williams & Wilkins.

Agbaje, A. O. (2025). BMI triples overweight prevalence in 7600 children compared with waist-to-height ratio: The ALSPAC Study. Obesity and Endocrinology, wjaf002.

American Psychiatric Association. (2022). Diagnostic and Statistical Manual Of Mental Disorders (5th ed., text rev.). https://doi.org/10.1176/appi.books.9780890425787

Atkins, M., Burton Murray, H., & Staller, K. (2023). Assessment and management of disorders of gut–brain interaction in patients with eating disorders. Journal of Eating Disorders, 11(1), 20.

Attia, E., & Walsh, B. T. (2025). 46. Eating Disorders: A Review; Duggan, H. C., Hardy, G., & Waller, G. (2025). Cognitive-Behavioural Therapy (CBT) for Outpatients with Anorexia Nervosa: A Systematic Review and Meta-Analysis of Clinical Effectiveness. Cognitive behaviour *therapy*, 1–46.

Austin, A., Anderson, A. G., Lee, J., Vander Steen, H., Savard, C., Bergmann, C., ... & Dimitropoulos, G. (2025). Efficacy of eating disorder focused family therapy for adolescents with anorexia nervosa: a systematic review and meta-analysis. International Journal of Eating Disorders, 58(1), 3–36).

Białek-Dratwa, A., Szczepańska, E., Szymańska, D., Grajek, M., Krupa-Kotara, K., & Kowalski, O. (2022). Neophobia – a natural developmental stage or feeding difficulties for children?. Nutrients, 14(7), 1521.

Centers for Disease Control and Prevention (CDC). (2025, February 13). Child and Teen BMI Calculator. U.S. Department of Health & Human Services. https://www.cdc.gov/bmi/child-teen-calculator/

Cook, B., Wonderlich, S. A., Mitchell, J., Thompson, R. O. N., Sherman, R., & Mc-Callum, K. (2016). Exercise in eating disorders treatment: Systematic review and proposal of guidelines. Medicine and Science in Sports and Exercise, 48(7), 1408.

Crosbie, C., & Sterling, W. (2018). How to Nourish Your Child through an Eating Disorder: A Simple, Plate-by-Plate Approach to Rebuilding a Healthy Relationship with Food. The Experiment.

Denniss, E., Lindberg, R., & McNaughton, S. A. (2023). Quality and accuracy of online nutrition-related information: A systematic review of content analysis studies. Public Health Nutrition, 26(7), 1345–1357.

Diekman, C., Ryan, C. D., & Oliver, T. L. (2023). Misinformation and disinformation in food science and nutrition: Impact on practice. The Journal of Nutrition, 153(1), 3–9.

Gauthier, C., Launay, J. M., Thiebaud, M. R., & Godart, N. (2015). The impact of malnutrition on the peripheral serotoninergic system in anorexia nervosa: A systematic review. Current Psychiatry Reviews, 11(1), 8–18.

Georgiou, N., Thompson, M., Bridgland, V., Wade, T., & Balzan, R. (2025). People at-risk of an eating disorder are more likely to endorse dietary misinformation claims and hold rigid beliefs. Journal of Health Psychology, 13591053251324695.

Guisinger, S. (2003). Adapted to flee famine: Adding an evolutionary perspective on anorexia nervosa. Psychological Review, 110(4), 745.

Hackert A. N., Kniskern M. A., & Beasley T. M. (2020 November). Academy of Nutrition and Dietetics: Revised 2020 Standards of Practice and Standards of Professional Performance for Registered Dietitian Nutritionists (Competent, Proficient, and Expert) in Eating Disorders. Journal of the Academy of Nutrition and Dietetics, 120(11), 1902–1919.e54. doi: 10.1016/j.jand.2020.07.014. PMID: 33099403.

Haleem, D. J. (2012). Serotonin neurotransmission in anorexia nervosa. *Behavioural Pharmacology*, 23(5 and 6), 478–495.

Hallward, L., Di Marino, A., & Duncan, L. R. (2022). A systematic review of treatment approaches for compulsive exercise among individuals with eating disorders. Eating Disorders, 30(4), 411–436.

Herrin, M., & Larkin, M. (2013). Nutrition Counseling in the Treatment of Eating Disorders (Chapter 5: Food Planning: The Rule of Threes, pp. 107–139). Routledge, New York, United States.

Hill, L. (2024). Temperament impact on eating disorder symptoms and habit formation: A novel model to inform treatment. Journal of Eating Disorders, 12(1), 40.

Hosseini, F., Jayedi, A., Khan, T. A., & Shab-Bidar, S. (2022). Dietary carbohydrate and the risk of type 2 diabetes: An updated systematic review and dose–response meta-analysis of prospective cohort studies. Scientific Reports, 12(1), 2491.

Hübel, C., Marzi, S. J., Breen, G., & Bulik, C. M. (2019). Epigenetics in eating disorders: A systematic review. Molecular Psychiatry, 24(6), 901–915.

Jary, J. M., Winnie, S. L., Prohaska, N., Bravender, T., & Van Huysse, J. L. (2024). Estimating treatment goal weights in adolescents with anorexia nervosa and atypical anorexia nervosa: Comparison of the median BMI and historical BMI percentile. The International Journal of Eating Disorders, 57, 2491–2496. https://doi.org/10.1002/eat.24298

Kalm, L. M., & Semba, R. D. (2005). They starved so that others be better fed: Remembering Ancel Keys and the Minnesota experiment. The Journal of Nutrition, 135(6), 1347–1352.

Käver, L., Hinney, A., Rajcsanyi, L. S., Maier, H. B., Frieling, H., Steiger, H., ... & Seitz, J. (2024). Epigenetic alterations in patients with anorexia nervosa – a systematic review. Molecular Psychiatry, 29(12), 3900–3914.

Kaye, W. H., Weltzin, T. E., Hsu, L. K., McConaha, C. W., & Bolton, B. (1993). Amount of calories retained after binge eating and vomiting. American Journal of Psychiatry, 150(6), 969–971.

Kreft, M., Smith, B., Hopwood, D., & Blaauw, R. (2023). The use of social media as a source of nutrition information. South African Journal of Clinical Nutrition, 36(4), 162–168.

Le Grange, D., Pradel, M., Pogos, D., Yeo, M., Hughes, E. K., Tompson, A., ... & Sawyer, S. M. (2021). Family-based treatment for adolescent anorexia nervosa: Outcomes of a stepped-care model. International Journal of Eating Disorders, 54(11), 1989–1997.

Lin, J. A., Woods, E. R., & Bern, E. M. (2021). Common and emergent oral and gastrointestinal manifestations of eating disorders. Gastroenterology & Hepatology, 17(4), 157–167.

Lock, J., & Le Grange, D. (2015). Treatment Manual for Anorexia Nervosa: A Family-Based Approach (2nd ed.). Guilford Press.

Lock, J., & Le Grange, D. (2025). Treatment Manual for Anorexia Nervosa: A Family-Based Approach (3rd ed). Guilford Press.

Maguire, E., & Youngson, N. A. (2022). Review on the benefits and drawbacks of ketogenic diet in humans. IDOSR Journal of Experimental Sciences, 7(1), 19–23.

Most, J., & Redman, L. M. (2020). Impact of calorie restriction on energy metabolism in humans. Experimental gerontology, 133, 110875.

National Academies of Sciences, Engineering, and Medicine. (2024). Rethinking the Acceptable Macronutrient Distribution Range for the 21st Century: A Letter Report. National Academies Press, Washington, D.C.

Nitsch, A., Dlugosz, H., Gibson, D., & Mehler, P. S. (2021). Medical complications of bulimia nervosa. Cleveland Clinic Journal of Medicine, 88(6), 333–343.

Ohwada, R., Hotta, M., Oikawa, S., & Takano, K. (2006). Etiology of hypercholesterolemia in patients with anorexia nervosa. International Journal of Eating Disorders, 39(7), 598–601.

Pontzer, H. (2023). Exercise is essential for health but a poor tool for weight loss: A reply to Allison and colleagues. International Journal of Obesity, 47(2), 98–99.

Quesnel, D. A., Cooper, M., Fernandez-Del-Valle, M., Reilly, A., & Calogero, R. M. (2023). Medical and physiological complications of exercise for individuals with an eating disorder: A narrative review. Journal of Eating Disorders, 11(1), 3. https://doi.org/10.1186/s40337-022-00685-9.

Reed, K.K., Silverman, A.E., Abbaspour, A. et al. (2024). Energy expenditure during nutritional rehabilitation: A scoping review to investigate hypermetabolism in individuals with anorexia nervosa. Journal of Eating Disorders, 12, 63. https://doi.org/10.1186/s40337-024-01019-7.

Salvia, M. G., Onteeru, M., Lipson, S. K., & Quatromoni, P. A. (2025). Adopting vegetarian and vegan eating patterns: Associations with disordered eating behaviors among young adult college students. Eating Behaviors, 57, 101967.

Schebendach, J. E., Porter, K. J., Wolper, C., Walsh, B. T., & Mayer, L. E. (2012). Accuracy of self-reported energy intake in weight-restored patients with anorexia nervosa compared with obese and normal weight individuals. International Journal of Eating Disorders, 45(4), 570–574.

Steiger, H., Booij, L., Kahan, E., McGregor, K., Thaler, L., Fletcher, E., ... & Rossi, E. (2019). A longitudinal, epigenome-wide study of DNA methylation in anorexia nervosa: Results in actively ill, partially weight-restored, long-term remitted and non-eating-disordered women. Journal of Psychiatry and Neuroscience, 44(3), 205–213.

Terry, S. M., Barnett, J. A., & Gibson, D. L. (2022). A critical analysis of eating disorders and the gut microbiome. Journal of Eating Disorders, 10(1), 15.

Thomas, J. J., & Eddy, K.T. (2019). Cognitive-Behavioral Therapy for Avoidant/Restrictive Food Intake Disorder: Children, Adolescents, and Adults. Cambridge University Press, Cambridge, UK.

Tybur, J. M., Lieberman, D., Kurzban, R., & DeScioli, P. (2013). Disgust: Evolved function and structure. Psychological Review, 120(1), 65–84.

Włodarczyk, J., Waśniewska, A., Fichna, J., Dziki, A., Dziki, Ł., & Włodarczyk, M. (2021). Current overview on clinical management of chronic constipation. Journal of Clinical Medicine, 10(8), 1738.

Chapter 9

A Physician's Insight into Working with Eating Disorders

Rachel S-D Fortune

People are often surprised to learn that, despite my career focus, I did not set out to treat individuals with eating disorders. Even before embarking on medical school, I knew I wanted to take care of adolescent patients which led me to complete my residency in Pediatrics at Ohio State University (Columbus Children's Hospital) and then pursue a fellowship in Adolescent Medicine at the University of Colorado, where I worked at the Children's Hospital Colorado.

At the start of my career, my goal was to care for adolescent patients with an emphasis on preventive health and building healthy habits in a time of life that contains a multitude of potential pitfalls to wellbeing. My fellowship at the Children's Hospital Colorado had a high volume of adolescents presenting for eating disorder evaluations and, as such, I became quite knowledgeable about these conditions, although I had no intention of making a career out of it. After my fellowship, I was hired at an academic institution that had a specific need to grow inpatient and outpatient eating disorder treatment programs. While working in general adolescent medicine, I undertook the responsibility of developing inpatient and outpatient treatment protocols for those presenting with eating disorders.

From there, I became increasingly involved in a strong and knowledgeable community of eating disorder providers, which solidified my commitment to this special and important population. Over the course of two years, I took further steps to integrate myself into the eating disorder world by expanding the academic hospital's outpatient practice as well as its inpatient protocols. Since that time, I have continued treating those with eating disorders at the inpatient level of care.

I am a board-certified Pediatrician and Adolescent Medicine physician. This means that after medical school, I completed three years of training and obtained board certification in pediatrics, and then completed a three-year fellowship in Adolescent Medicine. In my current position as Executive Medical Director, I oversee the daily clinical care of a 51-bed psychiatric hospital that specializes in treating those with a primary diagnosis of an eating disorder. I work as part of a cohesive multidisciplinary team as we care

DOI: 10.4324/9781003600770-12

for these medically and psychiatrically fragile patients. Due to my experience as an outpatient physician who referred patients into facilities such as this, I know how vital it is to collaborate with outpatient team members.

Individuals with eating disorders are a unique population and should be treated by medical providers who truly understand their needs. Most physicians do not have additional training in eating disorders. A Pediatrician, Family Doctor, or Internist (generally known as "Primary Care Physicians" or PCPs) is often the first professional to become aware that an individual has an eating disorder. This can happen in a myriad of different ways: some patients seek care from their PCP because they are concerned about eating disorder behaviors, whereas others experience medical complications that occur as a result of problematic eating behaviors, although they may not recognize eating to be an issue.

Often, the PCP has built a relationship with their patients over the span of years, which can aid in screening and treatment of an eating disorder. If a referral to a higher level of care is necessary, there is usually a medical work-up that the PCP conducts. PCPs make referrals and work collaboratively with therapists and dietitians and often have a network of local professionals whose clinical expertise they trust and respect. Additionally, sometimes PCP offices will hire social workers or registered dietitians to work in their office, so they can begin to provide the patient with the care they need.

The outpatient physician should complete the initial intake with a focus on medical data. This includes accurate height and weight (ideally, weight is taken in a hospital gown, and after the patient has urinated), orthostatic vital signs, lab work, and a thorough physical examination. The degree of malnutrition will be established by the outpatient physician who works collaboratively with the outpatient dietitian (if there is one involved in the case already) to set goals for weight restoration.

As an outpatient therapist, you should make every effort to collaborate with all other members of the team. This can be tricky, as physicians may work different hours and have busy clinic schedules. When reaching out to a physician, remember that every member of the treatment team holds an essential role – and you have important insights to share. Introduce yourself as the outpatient therapist, outline the work you are doing with the patient, and the frequency that you are meeting with them. Express concerns that you have related to the severity of the eating disorder and behaviors that are being reported to you. You will often have very different information about eating disorder progression than the outpatient physician does. If you feel like the patient is not stable for outpatient care, you should share that concern with the outpatient physician, as well (although the physician is tasked with making the final determination).

It is essential to acknowledge that monitoring patients with eating disorders is not a job you can do alone. For gold standard treatment, these conditions require a multidisciplinary team and, as the therapist, you should never be put in the role of medical monitoring. If you are working with a client who does not have adequate medical care, you should insist on their finding a physician who can monitor them. No matter how much experience, both personal and professional, you have with eating disorders, you should be cautious about offering medical advice or interpreting medical data for your clients. I would encourage you to factor time into your schedule to communicate and collaborate with the medical provider on the team. There will be times when your client may be too medically unwell or unstable to continue in outpatient care, and the medical provider needs to take the lead on guiding them into a higher level of care treatment. While you are not expected to manage the medical complications of eating disorders, it will be helpful for you to be knowledgeable about the medical issues your clients might be experiencing, since they are likely to share symptoms of physical discomfort with you as their therapist.

Medical Considerations in Eating Disorders

Eating disorders can affect every part of the body. The specific eating disorder diagnosis defines what medical complications could arise. The goal of the following section is to familiarize you, the reader, with some of the common and complex medical issues that can arise. My intention is to use plain-English language (as best as possible) to describe these issues for those who may have little or no background knowledge about the medical aspects of the physical body. It is not my goal for you to become a medical expert, and as mentioned earlier, you should never feel like you need to manage medical complications. Patients and their families will hear these terms and use the internet to learn more about them. It is best if all members of the team are familiar with common medical challenges of eating disorders.

In the following sections, I will walk you through the various physical health complications of eating disorders and break them down by diagnosis, and then by body system:

Anorexia Nervosa

Anorexia Nervosa (AN) is defined by an intentional lack of consuming enough calories to support the body's functions. Because Anorexia has two subtypes (e.g., restrictive and binge/purging), the health complications will depend on which subtype is present. Note: the purging subtype of anorexia will overlap with Bulimia Nervosa, outlined later in this chapter.

Cardiovascular System Complications

1 *Bradycardia (Low Heart Rate)*: One of the most common cardiovascular complications of anorexia nervosa is bradycardia, defined as a resting

heart rate below 60 beats per minute. Bradycardia is actually a survival mechanism for the body: the body slows its baseline resting heart rate in order to conserve energy after not receiving enough nutrition. While this may initially be adaptive, prolonged bradycardia can lead to reduced cardiac output and increase the risk of arrhythmias and even sudden cardiac death.

2 *Hypotension (Low Blood Pressure)*: This is another common problem resulting from dehydration and malnutrition. In individuals with anorexia nervosa, low blood pressure can cause dizziness, fainting, and a general sense of fatigue and weakness.

3 *Electrolyte Imbalances and Arrhythmias*: Electrolyte disturbances are often seen in anorexia nervosa, particularly low levels of potassium (hypokalemia), sodium (hyponatremia), magnesium (hypomagnesemia), and phosphorous (hypophosphatemia), to name a few. These imbalances, often exacerbated by vomiting, purging, or excessive use of diuretics (e.g., medications that induce urination), increase the risk of dangerous heart arrhythmias, even sudden cardiac arrest.

4 *Orthostatic Heart Rate or Blood Pressure Changes*: One data point that is often measured by physicians is "orthostatic vital signs." This is a process by which the heart rate and blood pressure are taken in the lying down, sitting, and then standing postures. This process is done to assess the heart's strength and ability to beat more strongly when faced with increased strain on the heart such as going from a less demanding posture to a more demanding one. When an individual goes from lying to standing, a jump in heart rate of more than 20 beats per minute, a decrease of >20 systolic blood pressure points (top number), or >10 diastolic blood pressure points (bottom number) is considered abnormal.

Gastrointestinal Complications

1 *Delayed Gastric Emptying (Slowed Emptying of Stomach Contents into the Small Intestine)*: Malnutrition, as well as the body's adaptive response to malnutrition, can result in delayed emptying of stomach contents and decreased motility of the intestines (e.g., the intestines' ability to move contents along). The resulting symptoms of those issues are early fullness, bloating, constipation, and nausea. Frequently, patients will report continued feelings of gastrointestinal (GI) discomfort throughout the eating disorder treatment process. It is important to reassure them that if their doctor has ruled out any other GI issues, the fullness and bloating are normal and part of the process that needs to be tolerated and worked through.

2 *Hepatic Dysfunction (Liver Dysfunction)*: Malnutrition can impair liver function, potentially leading to hepatomegaly (e.g., enlarged liver) or

abnormal liver enzymes. Liver dysfunction in malnutrition is multifactorial and can lead to severe liver disease.

Endocrine System Complications

1 *Hypothalamic-Pituitary-Gonadal Axis Dysfunction*: Malnutrition can lead to dysfunction of the hypothalamic-pituitary-gonadal (HPG) axis, which results in menstrual irregularities in genetic females and potentially absent menstruation (amenorrhea). The lack of gonadal hormones disrupts ovarian function, leading to reduced fertility. In males, low body weight often leads to reduced testosterone production, causing hypogonadism, which can affect sexual function and contribute to infertility.
2 *Thyroid Dysfunction*: The thyroid is a gland that sits in the neck and affects many functions throughout the body. Malnutrition leads to a decrease in circulating thyroid hormones, particularly triiodothyronine (T3). This condition is called "euthyroid sick syndrome" or "low T3 syndrome," and it is commonly observed in individuals with anorexia nervosa. Although the thyroid-stimulating hormone (TSH) may remain normal or only mildly elevated, the body adapts to lower thyroid hormone levels by reducing metabolic rate, which helps conserve energy in a state of nutrient deprivation.

Renal Complications

1 *Dehydration and Renal Failure*: Dehydration is a significant concern in individuals with anorexia nervosa, often exacerbated by restriction of water intake as well as purging behaviors, such as vomiting or excessive use of diuretics. Severe dehydration can lead to acute kidney failure due to low blood volume. Chronic malnutrition can lead to chronic kidney disease over time.
2 *Electrolyte Imbalances*: The kidneys are responsible for the balance of many electrolytes. Imbalances in potassium, sodium, and other electrolytes can lead to severe and sudden complications, such as cardiac arrhythmias.

Skeletal Complications

1 *Osteopenia and Osteoporosis*: This is one of the most significant and potentially irreversible effects of long-term anorexia. Bone loss occurs as a result of the unavailability of essential nutrients, like calcium and vitamin D, as well as the endocrine system disturbance of low estrogen and/or testosterone. Individuals with AN are at higher risk of developing osteopenia (bone loss) and osteoporosis (severe bone mineral density decrease). Bone mineral density increases over time through the mid-20s,

so when low bone mineral density develops after that timeframe it is often irreversible. Low bone mineral density puts people of all ages at higher risk for bone fractures. Additionally, many patients with AN engage in excessive exercise, which, when paired with low bone mineral density, can cause stress fractures particularly in weight-bearing bones.

Neurological Complications

1 *Cognitive Dysfunction*: Malnutrition affects brain function, leading to cognitive deficits such as difficulty concentrating, poor memory, and slowed reaction times. Severe restriction of nutrients, particularly glucose, impairs brain function and mental clarity. Depression and anxiety are also common co-occurring psychiatric conditions that worsen cognitive and emotional regulation.
2 *Peripheral Neuropathy*: In cases of severe and prolonged malnutrition, nerve damage can occur, resulting in peripheral neuropathy. This condition presents as numbness, tingling, and weakness, particularly in the hands and feet. Nutritional deficiencies in B vitamins, particularly thiamine, contribute to the development of this condition.

Immunological Complications

1 *Increased Risk of Infection*: Chronic malnutrition can lead to decreased production of white blood cells, which weakens the immune system. Individuals with malnutrition can be at higher risk of infection with viral and bacterial infections. The body's ability to heal from wounds or infections is also impaired due to compromised immune function.

The above complications are largely related to AN, restricting type. Again, be sure to note that medical complications associated with Anorexia Nervosa, Purging Type will also include complications as outlined in the section for bulimia below.

Bulimia Nervosa

Bulimia nervosa (BN) is characterized by recurrent episodes of binge eating followed by inappropriate compensatory behaviors such as vomiting, excessive exercise, or misuse of laxatives or diuretics. Unlike anorexia nervosa, individuals with bulimia nervosa may maintain a relatively normal body weight, making the disorder more challenging to recognize. However, despite the normal weight range, the medical complications of bulimia nervosa can be profound and often involve multiple organ systems. These complications arise primarily from the physiological consequences of recurrent episodes of binge eating and purging behaviors. In this section, we will explore the key medical complications of bulimia nervosa, their underlying causes, and their long-term effects on physical health. Refer to the above section on Anorexia Nervosa for many of the overlapping complications, and below are the complications unique to Bulimia Nervosa.

Cardiovascular System Complications

1 *Electrolyte Imbalances and Arrhythmias*: Similar to AN, electrolyte disturbances are often seen in bulimia nervosa, particularly low levels of potassium (hypokalemia), sodium (hyponatremia), magnesium (hypomagnesemia), and phosphorous (hypophosphatemia), to name a few. These imbalances, often exacerbated by vomiting, purging, or excessive use of diuretics, increase the risk of dangerous arrhythmias, such as ventricular tachycardia or even sudden cardiac arrest.

2 *Orthostatic Heart Rate or Blood Pressure Changes*: One data point that is often measured by physicians is "orthostatic vital signs." This is a process by which the heart rate and blood pressure are taken in the lying down, sitting, and then standing postures. This process is done to assess cardiac strength and ability to beat more strongly when faced with increased strain on the heart such as going from a less demanding posture to a more demanding one.

Gastrointestinal Complications

1 *Gastroesophageal Reflux Disease (GERD)*: Repeated episodes of self-induced vomiting can result in damage to the esophagus. When a patient purges, they push the acidic contents of the stomach up into the esophagus causing irritation and inflammation. This can manifest as a burning sensation in the chest and throat, and over time can result in ulcers or bleeding in the esophagus.

2 *Dental Erosion and Oral Health Issues*: Recurrent vomiting exposes the teeth to stomach acid, which can cause significant erosion of dental enamel. In fact, dentists can be the first-line professionals to diagnose an eating disorder that involves purging when the enamel erosion is noted on routine examination. Like the esophageal damage noted above, the acidic contents of the stomach can weaken and eat away at the dental enamel leading to dental discoloration and tooth decay. Prolonged, severe purging can result in dental cavities and gum disease. Additionally, patients who engage in purging behaviors can develop salivary gland dysfunction and present with swollen salivary glands.

3 *Constipation and Abdominal Pain*: Self-induced vomiting will certainly lead to abdominal pain as well as constipation as the GI system becomes

generally dysfunctional when stomach contents are being forced out by purging. In addition to the effects from self-induced vomiting, there are also dangerous effects from laxative abuse, which can result in dangerous electrolyte abnormalities, severe constipation, bloating, dehydration, and abdominal pain.

4 *Pancreatitis*: Chronic purging behaviors, particularly through vomiting, can lead to inflammation of the pancreas (pancreatitis). The repeated exposure of digestive enzymes to the stomach lining may irritate the pancreas, leading to both acute and chronic forms of pancreatitis. Symptoms include severe abdominal pain, nausea, vomiting, and, in extreme cases, organ failure.

Renal Complications

1 *Dehydration and Renal Failure*: Dehydration is a significant concern in individuals with bulimia nervosa, often exacerbated by restriction of water intake as well as purging behaviors such as vomiting or excessive use of diuretics. Severe dehydration can lead to acute kidney failure due to low blood volume. Chronic malnutrition can lead to chronic kidney disease over time.

2 *Electrolyte Imbalances*: The kidneys are responsible for the balance of many electrolytes. Imbalances in potassium, sodium, and other electrolytes can lead to severe and sudden complications such as cardiac arrhythmias.

Skeletal Complications

1 *Osteopenia and Osteoporosis*: Similar to AN, these are some of the most significant and potentially irreversible effects of long-term malnutrition. Bone loss results from the unavailability of essential nutrients such as calcium and vitamin D as well as the endocrine system disturbance of low estrogen and/or testosterone. Individuals with malnutrition secondary to any eating disorder are at higher risk of developing osteopenia (bone loss) and osteoporosis (severe bone mineral density decrease). Bone mineral density increases in childhood, teens, and early 20s, so when low bone mineral density develops after that timeframe it is often irreversible. Low bone mineral density puts people of all ages at higher risk for bone fractures. Additionally, some patients with eating disorders engage in excessive exercise, which, when paired with low bone mineral density, can cause stress fractures particularly in weight-bearing bones.

Neurological Complications

1 *Cognitive Dysfunction*: Malnutrition affects brain function, leading to cognitive deficits such as difficulty concentrating, poor memory, and

slowed reaction times. Severe restriction of nutrients, particularly glucose, impairs brain function and mental clarity. Depression and anxiety are also common co-occurring psychiatric conditions that worsen cognitive and emotional regulation.

2   *Peripheral Neuropathy*: In cases of severe and prolonged malnutrition, nerve damage can occur, resulting in peripheral neuropathy. This condition presents as numbness, tingling, and weakness, particularly in the hands and feet. Nutritional deficiencies in B vitamins, particularly thiamine, contribute to the development of this condition.

Binge Eating Disorder

Binge eating disorder (BED) is characterized by recurrent episodes of eating large quantities of food within a short period, accompanied by a sense of loss of control related to eating. Unlike bulimia nervosa, individuals with BED do not engage in purging behaviors such as vomiting, excessive exercise, or laxative abuse. Despite the absence of compensatory behaviors, BED can still lead to significant medical complications due to its association with metabolic disturbances and other health conditions. The impact of BED on physical health is multifaceted, affecting numerous organ systems, particularly cardiovascular, gastrointestinal, and endocrine. As with all eating disorders, BED occurs in patients with varying body shapes and sizes, and the medical comorbidities vary greatly. People living in larger bodies are undoubtedly treated with bias within the healthcare community. Due to the weight bias that is often implicit in the provision of healthcare, those with BED's health needs are often neglected and delayed, which can lead to medical conditions going untreated. It is also true that those living in larger bodies may be healthy and without any markers of illness, although they often receive misguided messages from their providers that they need to lose weight to be healthy. The following list of medical conditions is possible health complications that have been associated with BED.

Medical Diagnoses Sometimes Associated with Binge Eating Disorder

- *Insulin Resistance*: A hallmark of metabolic syndrome, which increases the risk of developing type 2 diabetes.
- *Dyslipidemia*: Abnormal levels of lipids in the blood, including high cholesterol and triglycerides.
- *Hypertension (High Blood Pressure)*: Increased blood pressure.
- Elevated Blood Sugar: Insulin resistance can lead to higher blood glucose levels, raising the risk of diabetes.
- *Type 2 Diabetes Mellitus*: Individuals with BED can develop insulin resistance, which, if left untreated, progresses to type 2 diabetes.

- *Cardiovascular Disease*: Patients with BED can be at risk for heart disease, including coronary artery disease, heart failure, and arrhythmias. Dyslipidemia, high blood pressure, and inflammation can contribute to the development of atherosclerosis (hardening of the arteries).
- *Sleep Apnea*: Characterized by interruptions in breathing during sleep, is more common in individuals with BED. Sleep apnea can lead to daytime fatigue, cardiovascular complications, and decreased quality of life.
- *Joint and Musculoskeletal Problems*: Excess weight places strain on joints, particularly the knees and hips, increasing the risk of osteoarthritis and other musculoskeletal disorders.
- *GERD*: The frequent overconsumption of food in BED increases the likelihood of developing gastrointestinal problems. One of the most common complications is GERD, a condition in which stomach acid frequently flows back into the esophagus, causing heartburn, regurgitation, and discomfort.
- *Non-Alcoholic Fatty Liver Disease (NAFLD)*: Individuals with BED may be at increased risk of NAFLD. NAFLD is characterized by the accumulation of fat in the liver without the presence of excessive alcohol consumption. The excess calories consumed during binge eating episodes contribute to fat accumulation in the liver. This can lead to inflammation and liver damage over time.
- *Irritable Bowel Syndrome (IBS)* and Digestive Issues: Individuals with BED may also experience digestive issues such as bloating, constipation, diarrhea, and abdominal pain, which are commonly associated with IBS.
- *Menstrual Irregularities*: In biologic females with BED as with all eating disorder diagnoses, a disruption of the typical hormonal cascades can lead to irregularities in the menstrual cycle.

Other Medical Complications for All EDs

Refeeding Syndrome

Refeeding syndrome (RS) is a rare and potentially life-threatening condition that can occur when individuals with severe malnutrition begin to receive nutrition (either orally or by feeding tube). This can happen with any eating disorder. It is most observed in individuals with eating disorders who have been severely restricting their caloric intake and have had significant weight loss. As nutrition is reintroduced into the malnourished body, significant metabolic shifts can occur. These shifts can lead to dangerous electrolyte imbalances, fluid retention, organ dysfunction, and death. Close medical monitoring with frequent blood lab work, preferably at a higher level of care or inpatient setting, is essential during the refeeding process.

Refeeding syndrome occurs due to the body's metabolic response to the sudden availability of nutrients after a period of starvation. When food is re-introduced, the body shifts from a catabolic (breaking down) to an anabolic (building) state. This metabolic shift increases the demand for phosphorus, potassium, magnesium, and other electrolytes to support the synthesis of proteins, lipids, and other essential molecules. Due to a spike in insulin with nutrition reintroduction, glucose and electrolytes will shift from blood plasma into the cells resulting in potentially significant medical complications. Phosphorus is critical for energy metabolism (ATP production) and cellular function. The rapid influx of glucose during refeeding causes insulin release, which drives phosphorous into cells to facilitate energy production and storage, depleting plasma phosphate levels. Furthermore, potassium and magnesium are also driven into cells with the influx of glucose, leading to decreased blood levels of these electrolytes. Potassium and magnesium are essential for muscle function, including the heart, and low levels can result in life-threatening cardiac arrhythmias. Finally, the body's fluid balance may be disturbed due to the rapid reintroduction of nutrition. Insulin secretion, prompted by carbohydrate intake, stimulates sodium retention in the kidneys, which can result in fluid overload and edema (swelling). This can place strain on the heart and lungs, particularly if the individual has pre-existing cardiac or respiratory complications. Edema can be observed on physical examination.

Risk Factors for Refeeding Syndrome

There are certain features of the presentation of an eating disorder that convey a higher risk of refeeding syndrome:

- *Prolonged Starvation or Malnutrition*: The longer the period of food restriction, the more likely electrolyte imbalances and nutrient deficiencies will occur. Individuals with anorexia nervosa are particularly at risk if they have been severely restricting their intake for weeks or months.
- *Low Body Weight or Very Low Body Mass Index (BMI)*: People with a BMI below 16 kg/m² are at increased risk, as they may have minimal fat or muscle stores for nutrient utilization.
- *Severe Electrolyte Imbalances Prior to Refeeding*: Individuals who already have low levels of potassium, phosphorus, or magnesium are more likely to develop refeeding syndrome when reintroducing nutrition.
- *Pre-Existing Medical Conditions*: Those with organ dysfunction or other chronic medical conditions, including alcoholism, could be at higher risk.
- *Rapid Refeeding*: Refeeding that is too rapid, particularly in the first few days, can trigger the syndrome. Gradual reintroduction of nutrition is recommended to minimize the metabolic disturbances.

Clinical Manifestations of Refeeding Syndrome

The signs and symptoms of refeeding syndrome are related to the electrolyte imbalances and fluid shifts caused by the sudden reintroduction of nutrients. They typically manifest within the first 48–72 hours of refeeding, although the risk can be present for 7–10 days or more. Key clinical signs and symptoms include electrolyte imbalances, cardiac abnormalities, respiratory complications primarily from fluid overload, neurological complications, fluid retention, swelling (edema), weakness, and fatigue.

Management of Refeeding Syndrome

While management of refeeding syndrome is outside of the scope of this chapter (and your role as a therapist), it is an important issue that you should be aware of. One way that this can impact an outpatient client is the following scenario: You are working with a motivated patient who has been restricting significantly. On the advice of the outpatient team, the patient abruptly shifts from eating very little to eating their recommended meal plan. This patient can unwittingly put themselves at risk for refeeding syndrome. If this occurs in an outpatient setting, the patient would not be under the correct level of monitoring, which could create a dangerous situation. If you are working with an outpatient who you think is at risk for refeeding syndrome, you should be in touch with their outpatient physician or instruct them to seek care in an emergency department.

Electrolyte Abnormalities in Patients with Eating Disorders

Hypokalemia (Low Potassium)

Potassium is particularly associated with those who engage in purging behaviors such as vomiting or excessive use of laxatives or diuretics. Refeeding syndrome is also associated with low potassium. Symptoms include muscle weakness and cramps, fatigue, cardiac arrhythmias (irregular heartbeats), constipation, respiratory distress (in severe cases), and paralysis (in extreme cases). Hypokalemia can be life-threatening if severe, leading to dangerous heart arrhythmia, which may result in cardiac arrest. The heart's ability to pump blood effectively is compromised, increasing the risk of sudden death.

Hyponatremia (Low Sodium)

Hyponatremia often results from excessive water intake (from "water loading" behaviors), which dilutes sodium levels in the bloodstream, or from purging behaviors (vomiting and diarrhea) that lead to a loss of sodium.

Diuretics, when misused, can also increase the excretion of sodium resulting in low sodium levels. In some cases, individuals with eating disorders may avoid eating sufficient amounts of salt, further contributing to sodium deficiency. Symptoms include nausea, vomiting, headache, confusion, muscle cramps and weakness, seizures (in severe cases), and coma (in extreme cases). Severe hyponatremia can lead to cerebral edema (brain swelling), which can cause seizures, coma, or even death. The central nervous system is particularly sensitive to changes in sodium levels, and the imbalance can lead to severe neurological symptoms, including confusion, lethargy, and altered mental status.

Hypernatremia (High Sodium)

Hypernatremia can occur when there is inadequate water intake – intentional water restriction. This can happen in individuals who restrict fluids or during episodes of severe vomiting and diarrhea, where excessive fluid loss is not adequately replaced. Symptoms include thirst, dry mouth and skin, restlessness or irritability, confusion, muscle twitching or spasms, seizures (in severe cases). In severe cases, hypernatremia can lead to brain damage, especially in children or individuals who are particularly vulnerable. The brain cells shrink as they lose water, and this can cause neurological impairment, including seizures, coma, and death if not corrected promptly.

Hypocalcemia (Low Calcium)

Hypocalcemia is often a result of malnutrition, particularly in individuals with anorexia nervosa who have poor intake of calcium-rich food. Vitamin D deficiency, common in individuals with eating disorders due to poor nutrition and lack of sun exposure, impairs calcium absorption from the digestive tract. Additionally, purging behaviors may cause the loss of calcium from the body, further contributing to its deficiency. Symptoms include muscle cramps and spasms (tetany), numbness and tingling (particularly around the mouth or in the fingers and toes), weakness, seizures (in severe cases), and cardiac arrhythmias (e.g., prolonged QT interval). Severe hypocalcemia can lead to life-threatening conditions, such as seizures, tetany (muscle spasm), and cardiac arrhythmias. Chronic calcium deficiency can also lead to long-term bone demineralization, contributing to osteopenia and osteoporosis, which significantly increase the risk of fractures.

Hypomagnesemia (Low Magnesium)

Hypomagnesemia can result from malnutrition and also from the refeeding process. Low magnesium levels can occur with self-induced vomiting behaviors as well as the use of diuretics and laxatives. Symptoms include muscle weakness, tremors or twitching, cardiac arrhythmias (e.g., torsades de pointes), seizures, nausea, and vomiting. Magnesium deficiency can exacerbate other electrolyte imbalances, particularly potassium and calcium, and can lead to dangerous arrhythmias and seizures. It also increases the risk of sudden cardiac death, especially when combined with hypokalemia.

Chloride Imbalances

Chloride imbalances (typically hypochloremia, low chloride) occur alongside electrolyte disturbances such as hyponatremia and hypokalemia. Vomiting, which causes the loss of stomach acid (which contains chloride), is a key contributor to these imbalances. Dehydration from laxative or diuretic use can also lead to abnormal chloride levels. Symptoms include muscle weakness, respiratory distress, weak pulse, and hypotension (low blood pressure). Chloride imbalances can significantly affect fluid balance and acid-base regulation, contributing to further complications in heart, kidney, and respiratory function. It also increases the risk of arrhythmias when combined with potassium and sodium disturbances.

Electrolyte imbalances are a common and dangerous consequence of eating disorders, particularly in those who engage in purging behaviors. Disturbances in potassium, sodium, calcium, magnesium, chloride, and acid-base balance can lead to a variety of symptoms ranging from mild to life-threatening, including cardiac arrhythmias, seizures, and even sudden death. Early detection and treatment of electrolyte abnormalities are critical to prevent severe complications. Routine blood lab work is necessary to avoid serious, dangerous, and life-threatening electrolyte abnormalities.

Some Thoughts on Psychiatric Medications

There is a potential role for medications in the treatment of eating disorders, and a psychiatrist or psychiatric nurse practitioner should be on the team of professionals taking care of people with eating disorder diagnoses. Many people with eating disorders have found relief from intrusive eating disorder thoughts with the use of antipsychotic medications such as olanzapine. It is important to note that psychiatric medications, particularly SSRIs and SNRIs, are dependent on body weight for efficacy, and as such, many of our patients who are malnourished will not experience desired effects of medications. Pre-existing or co-existing mental health diagnoses should be evaluated for the need for medications with close attention to what the patient can tolerate medically.

To recap, here are a few things to keep in mind: First, eating disorders need to be treated by a multidisciplinary team with every member of the team having a specific role based on their training and expertise. No member of the team should feel pressured to practice outside of their competence. Second, management of medical complications should be done solely by the physician on the team. As the therapist, you should not feel pressured by the family or patient to provide medical advice. And lastly, treatment works; it should be started early and managed aggressively in order to avoid longer-term medical complications.

References

Medical complications of eating disorders: an update. Rome, Ellen S et al. Journal of Adolescent Health, Volume 33, Issue 6, 418–426. https://www.jahonline.org/article/S1054-139X(03)00265-9/abstract
https://www.nationaleatingdisorders.org/health-consequences/

Chapter 10

The Use of Integrative Therapies in the Treatment of Eating Disorders

Lachlan Crawford

Integrative therapies are a collection of healing practices or modalities that extend beyond the conventional Western or standard medical model. These modalities integrate the body; in other words, they include the *experience of being in, or using, the body* as part of treatment. In the field of eating disorders, it is not only helpful but crucial to include embodied practices as a part of treatment.

The types of modalities that fall under the umbrella of integrative therapies include yoga, Tai Chi/Qi Gong, expressive art therapies (dance movement, music, art, drama and writing therapies), acupuncture/acupressure, breathwork, meditation, biofeedback, mindfulness, horticultural therapy, massage therapy and Naturopathic Medicine, Ayurvedic Medicine, Traditional Chinese Medicine, and may even include additional breakthrough therapies like psychedelic-assisted therapy, and more.

These modalities are designed to help regulate the nervous system, cultivate non-stressful body awareness, and process emotions and memories. More than just stress release, these practices are deeply therapeutic in their own way; they invite participants to reprogram their relationships with their bodies and movement to include more compassion and stewardship.

Who Am I?

My passion for integrative therapies comes from witnessing their profound impact on clients struggling with eating disorders and other mental health challenges. As a licensed Naturopathic Doctor (ND) and certified biofeedback practitioner with specialized training in Integrative Psychiatry and Contemplative Psychotherapy, my practice brings a unique blend of knowledge and holistic approaches to treatment. My diverse clinical background has given me a medical understanding of the problems of mental health and eating disorders, while also training me in the use of a broad range of effective evidence-based integrative interventions.

DOI: 10.4324/9781003600770-13

Naturopathic medicine shares fundamental ethical commitments and training with conventional medicine, such as the Hippocratic Oath – First, Do No Harm – and the importance of disease prevention. However, it expands beyond symptom management to emphasize the importance of identifying and addressing root causes of disease (rather than managing symptoms), and the need to treat the whole person – body, mind, and spirit. These principles guide my approach to treating eating disorders in a way that is both scientifically grounded and deeply holistic.

After earning my doctorate in Naturopathic Medicine, I spent years treating eating disorders in collaboration with conventional medical providers across inpatient, residential, and outpatient settings. My experience in integrative psychiatry deepened my ability to bridge whole-person naturopathic and cutting-edge psychiatric approaches, while my training in Contemplative Psychotherapy at the Nalanda Institute for Contemplative Science reinforced the power of embodied and lived practices in healing.

At the core of my work, though, is a profound respect for the mind-body connection and a passion for helping individuals transform their relationship with their bodies. Through years of practice, I have witnessed how integrative therapies – particularly embodied practices – can unlock breakthroughs that traditional approaches sometimes cannot. The body, so often a source of distress for those with eating disorders, can also be a source of strength, healing, and self-efficacy. A proverb I like that reflects this is: "Through practice, what was once your pain is now your power."

On a more philosophical note, these experiences have given me an expansive understanding of what wellness means. Wellness is more than the absence of disease; it means living well, even sometimes learning to "live well" with chronic disease or recurrent symptoms. The more multifaceted a condition, the more multifaceted a treatment must be.

Defining Integrative Therapies

Many of the practices now recognized as integrative therapies were once broadly categorized under the label of "alternative" or "complementary and alternative medicine" (CAM). This wide classification included well-researched treatments alongside therapies with little empirical support, creating confusion about which CAM approaches were truly effective. The more modern shift toward the term "integrative therapies" reflects a growing emphasis on scientific validation, aligning integrative approaches with evidence-based care. As research continues to highlight their efficacy – and as clinicians gain a better understanding of their appropriate use – integrative therapies are becoming an essential part of eating disorder treatment.

This shift has made integrative therapies a new frontier of medicine; a glimpse into the future. As we continue to learn more about the mind-body connection, the field of medicine is embracing a multifaceted, whole-person approach that acknowledges the essential role of somatic healing and mind-body integration. This is an exciting, and necessary, transformation – one that embraces the complexity of healing and recognizes that true wellness is found in the integration of science, compassion, and embodied practice.

Why Integrative Therapies for Eating Disorders? We Tend to Leave Out the Body

Eating disorder treatment often begins with a cognitive emphasis through talk therapy, commonly referred to as a top-down approach. This method aims to address thoughts that may be driving behaviors, helping clients explore motivation, core beliefs, distorted thinking patterns, and identity outside of the eating disorder. While this kind of cognitive work is essential, it often overlooks the lived, physical experience of the body, which is where distress, trauma, and emotions are stored.

Cognitive approaches alone are not always sufficient for full recovery, and several factors can make progress slow or difficult when relying solely on top-down approaches. For example, malnutrition and dehydration impair memory, cognitive function, and emotional regulation, making it harder for clients to engage in talk therapy. A history of trauma can lead to dissociation, fear, and implicit memories surfacing non-verbally in the body, further complicating the recovery process. Chronic stress can also contribute to brain fog, memory lapses, and difficulty concentrating. Avoidance, numbing, or resistance can make it challenging for clients to engage in cognitive processing at all. For clients struggling with these barriers, the recovery journey can feel blocked. Asking clients to give up their eating disorder – a coping mechanism that has perhaps numbed years of emotional pain or created a sense of control – without first creating a felt sense of safety in their body, can feel overwhelming or even impossible. Trauma psychologist Peter Levine writes in *Waking the Tiger*, "We don't *think* our way out of trauma; we learn to feel safe in our bodies again."

This is where integrative, body-based therapies become crucial. These practices help clients develop safety, presence, and tolerance in their bodies – a necessary foundation for meaningful recovery. In fact, Stephen Porges' Polyvagal Theory suggests that true healing begins when the nervous system shifts out of survival mode and into a state of connection. Movement, breathwork, yoga, expressive arts, and other modalities we'll explore in this chapter help facilitate this shift, ultimately making clients more able to engage in traditional talk therapy and cognitive-based treatments as well.

What Does It Mean to Incorporate the Body?

An integrative approach to eating disorder treatment blends both the top-down cognitive strategies and *body-up* methods. While cognitive tools focus on thought patterns and mental frameworks, body-up approaches start with calming and establishing safety in the nervous system. These practices do this by promoting safety in one's body, movement, sensory experiences, and physical engagement with the environment. Focusing on the body helps to reduce barriers to cognitive work, process trauma that lacks a verbal form, and acknowledge the body's role in holding and expressing emotions. Pat Ogden, a pioneer in somatic psychology and founder of the Sensorimotor Psychotherapy Institute, says, "In bottom-up approaches, the body's sensation and movement are the entry points and changes in sensorimotor experience one needs to support self-regulation, memory processing, and success in daily life. Meaning and understanding emerge from new experiences, rather than the other way around" (Ogden et al., 2006).

Two key goals of integrative treatments are somatic integration and non-verbal expression.

Somatic Integration

Somatic integration strengthens the mind-body connection by helping clients develop a more harmonious relationship with their bodies. This includes four parts. The first is developing non-stressful interoception. Interoception refers to the ability to perceive and interpret internal signals, such as physical sensations like hunger, pain, temperature, heart rate, etc., as well as sensations that accompany emotions, such as a tight chest or the energy of excitement. It is involved in decision making and behavior choice, and many individuals with eating disorders struggle with interoception – either feeling disconnected from their bodies or fearing sensations like hunger or fullness. Somatic approaches gently reintroduce bodily awareness in a way that is non-threatening and free from judgment, rejection, or punishment.

The second part of somatic integration is changing the relationship to the body and movement. Clients are encouraged to shift from seeing their bodies as objects of criticism to recognizing them as dynamic, functional systems deserving of respect. For example, instead of using movement as punishment or compulsion, clients can rediscover it as a source of function and freedom. Third, it is processing the physical sensations related to emotions, specifically anxiety, fear, and other emotions that often fuel disordered eating patterns. Engaging the body in therapy helps clients identify, tolerate, and release these emotions rather than letting them drive reactive behaviors. And lastly, it is developing the ability to process traumatic memories, or the imprints of past trauma, that the body holds, which contribute to disordered eating. Somatic approaches can help release these imprints, supporting deeper healing.

Non-Verbal Expression

For many individuals, verbalizing emotions is difficult. Non-verbal expression provides alternative pathways for communication and self-discovery. Alexithymia, or difficulty identifying and expressing emotions, is common among individuals with eating disorders. Expressive practices like movement, art, or dance provide alternative ways for clients to explore and convey emotions that may be difficult to articulate in words. These approaches can help clients bridge the gap between their internal experiences and external expression, fostering a deeper sense of feeling seen, heard, or understood.

Non-verbal expression also helps people act out new ways of being. Through movement, role-playing, and physical expression, clients can experiment with postures, gestures, or behaviors that embody a healthier self-concept and recovery-oriented mindset. Non-verbal activities help individuals construct a more integrated and coherent sense of identity, particularly when verbal processing feels overwhelming. And by integrating these body-focused approaches into eating disorder treatment, clients are not only able to think differently about recovery but also to feel and embody it. Healing is not just about changing thoughts – it's about transforming one's relationship with the body from the inside out.

Benefits and Cautions for Movement: Medical Appropriateness

For some time, the prevailing thought in eating disorder treatment, especially for the treatment of restrictive eating disorders, was that movement had to be limited in order to assist in normalization of the body's metabolism and to speed up medical restoration. On top of this, clients with eating disorders can experience a reduction in bone mineral density and loss of muscle mass. This combination of effects on bones and muscles, coupled with the reduction in daily movements, can increase frailty, risk of falls, impact the heart muscle, and complicate recovery.

As we have learned more about recovery, however, incorporating some gentle movement for clients who have sufficient medical stability is now a recommended part of treatment. This movement has the goals of maintaining mobility, skeletal density, and muscle mass, as well as having the previously discussed therapeutic targets of somatic integration and non-verbal expression.

Officially, assessing the medical appropriateness of a client for any given integrative practice is done by the medical provider. Clients at an outpatient level will usually have sufficient medical stability for gentle movement, but it is important to ask the client's medical provider for confirmation of stable vital signs (such as no severe orthostatic hypotension, cardiac abnormalities, or bradycardia/tachycardia) and record this in your notes before exploring movement-based approaches. In your sessions with the client, you may want to inquire about weakness, dizziness, fainting, or shortness of breath while noting if these are starting or worsening, and encourage the client to disclose any concerns to their medical provider. Finally, you can remind the patient that even when they are cleared for movement, they should have no major change in caloric or fluid intake in the 24 hours prior to movement practice.

For more medically compromised clients who may be admitted or waiting for admission to higher levels of care, even gentle movements might be cautioned. Conditions that require caution before starting movement include severe protein-energy malnutrition, electrolyte imbalances in recent lab blood work, shortness of breath on mild exertion, or acute cardiac issues.

For clients who experience overexercise or compensatory exercise as an eating disorder behavior, treatment may need to begin with reducing excessive physical activity. This can be especially challenging, as providers must navigate both limiting harmful behaviors and supporting clients in relearning movement in a non-compulsive, restorative way. For example, a client who struggles with pacing, excessive running, or an inability to rest could feel as though they are "going stir-crazy" when asked to initially reduce or change their movement for medical restoration. Helping such clients reimagine their relationship with movement through engaging in different activities is a complex but necessary component of treatment.

Understanding the Therapist's Role in Integrative Therapies

Before diving into specific integrative therapies, it is important to clarify the therapist's role in this process. Therapists are not expected to be trained in or facilitate these practices themselves. Instead, your role is to understand the therapeutic potential of these approaches, recognize when they may be beneficial, be able to discuss potential benefits and applications with clients, and help to connect clients with qualified providers. Clients with medical conditions or movement-related concerns should be monitored medically and referred to the appropriate specialists to ensure safe participation when necessary. By being aware of these interventions and how they support recovery, therapists can empower clients to explore new ways of healing while staying within their professional boundaries.

Clinical Vignette: Amanda in Movement Therapy

Amanda walked into a movement therapy session for the first time – clearly unimpressed. Throughout the session, she made it known that this wasn't what she had expected. "I thought this was going to be like a workout group!" she exclaimed, frustrated that the session didn't match her idea of exercise: high intensity, structured, and goal oriented. At first, she resisted the idea of movement outside the rigid, compensatory framework she was used to. But she kept coming back. Over time, she began to engage in movement that prioritized creativity, self-expression, and her own needs rather than those dictated by her eating disorder.

Before the end of her movement therapy, she reflected on how her relationship with movement had shifted. She discovered a way to move that actually felt good; one that brought her joy and connection rather than isolation and self-punishment. This transformation was visible, too. At first, her movements were rigid, quick, and focused on completing a set number of "reps." As time went on, they became more fluid, sustained, and punctuated with pauses – moments of rest that she allowed herself for the first time.

Modalities

Breathwork: The Core Integrative Therapy

Breath is so essential to Integrative Therapies that it merits its own section, although it is included in many other practices like yoga, Tai Chi, and biofeedback. Breathing is unique among autonomic functions in that it can be consciously controlled, allowing clients to directly influence their nervous system. The diaphragm's movement not only impacts breath but also stimulates the vagus nerve, an important part of the parasympathetic nervous system, which plays a key role in relaxation, digestion, and emotional regulation. Similarly, because eating disorders often involve disconnection from the body, breathwork also provides an immediate way for clients to reconnect.

Shallow, restricted breathing – common in stress and trauma – tends to keep the body in fight-or-flight mode, while slow, intentional breaths help shift the system into a state of safety and rest. For example, deep diaphragmatic breathing (pushing the abdomen out on the inhale and letting it fall on the exhale) activates the parasympathetic nervous system and stimulates local muscles, which can help reduce rumination, a repetitive, involuntary regurgitation of food that can be re-chewed or re-swallowed. Diaphragmatic breathing may decrease the frequency and intensity of these symptoms. This is one way of working with the gut-brain connection in eating disorder treatment.

I mention breathwork as a core integrative therapy because it is a part of all the other modalities and can be practiced on its own. Helpful breathing practices include paced breathing, resonance frequency breathing, extended exhale breathing, physiologic sighing, pursed lip breathing, diaphragmatic breathing, alternate nostril breathing, and many more.

Trauma-Informed Yoga for Eating Disorders

Yoga is a relatively well-known breath and movement practice from India that's been popularized for several decades now in Western culture. There are many styles of yoga, ranging in intensity. When thinking about using yoga for recovery, it is important to consider medical appropriateness, style of yoga (including use of a trauma-informed approach), and the environment in which the yoga is practiced.

Slower, gentler practices are best suited for early stages of ED recovery, while moderate styles may be appropriate for those further along. More intense styles require caution and, in many cases, are not recommended. The most relaxing styles, such as Yin, focus on deep relaxation, gentle movement, and nervous system regulation. They are generally well-suited for clients in early recovery. Some popular names include Yoga Nidra (Yogic Sleep), Restorative Yoga, Yin Yoga, and Hatha Yoga. Moderately vigorous styles incorporate movement and mindfulness while maintaining a balanced approach to intensity. They may be appropriate for clients in later stages of recovery and include Viniyoga, Kripalu Yoga, Kundalini Yoga, Sivananda Yoga, and Vinyasa (Flow) Yoga. The most vigorous or challenging styles require significant physical exertion, which may not be appropriate for ED recovery due to potential overexertion, electrolyte imbalances, or compensatory exercise concerns. These can include Hot Yoga, Power Yoga, Rocket Yoga, AcroYoga, Forrest Yoga, Ashtanga Yoga, and Bikram Yoga.

A general guideline for outpatient eating disorder clients is to start with "slow flow," Hatha, gentle Vinyasa, Yin, or Restorative yoga. Clients are generally advised to avoid hot yoga due to its impact on hydration and cardiovascular function. Important minerals and electrolytes are lost in the sweat, which can exacerbate deficiencies and have a serious impact on fluid shifts. This is especially important to watch out for with clients who experience purging and/or restriction as part of the eating disorder behaviors because of the impact on blood chemistry.

Trauma-Informed Yoga Training and Approach

Trauma-informed yoga differs from conventional yoga. It is crucial in reducing the risk of re-traumatization, particularly for individuals with a complex relationship with their bodies, and can be applied to any style of yoga. Registered yoga teachers (RYTs) must complete a 200-hour basic teacher training program to become certified with the Yoga Alliance. In many eating disorder treatment settings, yoga teachers are required to complete an additional 20 hours of trauma-informed yoga training, which goes above and beyond the basic teacher training. By contrast, Yoga Therapists are trained in 800-hour programs that are accredited by the International Association of Yoga Therapists (C-IAYT credentials), which enable them to practice in more one-on-one and smaller-group therapeutic settings. This training is more therapeutic in nature and upholds the trauma-informed training principles.

The core principles of trauma-informed yoga include safety, choice, and repetition. Safety involves creating a physically and emotionally secure environment where clients feel supported. Choice encourages autonomy by offering options for movement and participation, allowing clients to engage at their own pace, while Repetition provides predictability and grounding. While not all clients require exclusively trauma-informed yoga, this approach can be particularly beneficial for those with a history of trauma or body image distress. Outpatient clients seeking yoga studios should inquire about the availability of trauma-informed instructors and class formats.

Evidence Supporting Yoga for Eating Disorder Treatment

Yoga has some of the strongest scientific support among integrative therapies for eating disorders. Research has highlighted its effectiveness in addressing ED symptoms and related mental health conditions.

Effects on Eating Disorder Symptoms

- *Reducing Body Image Concerns*: A meta-analysis of 11 randomized controlled trials found that yoga significantly reduces global ED psychopathology, most significantly through reducing body image concerns (Borden & Cook-Cottone, 2020). Other studies by Hall et al. (2016) and Halliwell et al. (2019) reported that yoga reduces drive for thinness, body dissatisfaction, and weight/shape concerns.
- *Increasing Body Appreciation*: Several studies have demonstrated and discussed an improvement in body appreciation, self-compassion, and embodiment through yoga (Piran & Neumark-Sztainer, 2020; Alleva et al., 2020; Muehlenkamp & Wagner, 2022; Brennan et al., 2022). Interestingly, Mahlo & Tiggemann (2016) showed that these improvements did not vary across different types of yoga; in their study, less strenuous types of yoga contributed similarly to positive body appreciation when compared to more intense types.
- *Weight-Neutral*: Very importantly, yoga interventions have been shown to reduce disordered eating behaviors without significantly impacting weight, reinforcing its role as a physical practice that does not promote compensatory exercise (Carei et al., 2010).

- *Virtual Yoga for Chronic EDs*: A 2024 trial evaluated Eat Breathe Thrive for Recovery (EBT-R), a virtual yoga program for individuals with long-term EDs. Nearly 70% of participants had been living with an eating disorder for over a decade, and they showed reductions in ED symptoms, depression, and anxiety within four weeks, with sustained benefits at follow-up (Cook-Cottone et al., 2024).

Physical Health Benefits

- *Bone Mineral Density (BMD)*: A pilot study (Ziv et al., 2023) found that adolescents with restrictive anorexia who practiced yoga for six months had higher BMD than age-matched peers in treatment who did not engage in yoga. Since ED-related BMD loss is often irreversible, yoga may play an important protective role.

Mental Health Benefits

- Multiple studies have shown reductions in depression, anxiety, and PTSD symptoms with regular yoga practice (Cramer et al., 2018, Streeter et al., 2010, Van der Kolk et al., 2014) as well as increases in interoception for those who struggle with awareness of internal bodily signals (Neumark-Sztainer et al., 2018).

Choosing a Yoga Space

While yoga itself may be very helpful, not all yoga spaces are equally welcoming or appropriate for eating disorder recovery. Clients should seek studios or teachers that are inclusive, use trauma-informed language, and foster a diverse, body-positive community. Considerations include teacher and staff diversity in body shapes and backgrounds, a variety of class styles to suit different needs and recovery stages, and the absence of things that might hinder recovery, such as weight-loss promotions, pseudo-scientific detox/cleanse marketing, or preference for revealing or "purity-focused" all-white clothing, etc. If clients are including yoga in their treatment plan, encourage them to reflect on how they feel after attending a class and remain mindful of any exposure to diet culture. Clients should also wear clothing that feels comfortable and unrestricted, rather than adhering to tight clothing that is popular in some yoga settings.

Yoga provides a holistic, weight-neutral intervention for eating disorder treatment, supporting both physical and mental health. Once clients find a comfortable teacher and/or space, it can open them up to a beautiful, supportive practice that decouples movement from striving and encourages deep mindful presence. With practice, this mindfulness can accompany a yogi both on and off the mat, leading to more mindful engagement in the rest of life as well. As part of an integrative approach, yoga offers a safe and adaptable tool to help clients rebuild a positive relationship with movement and their bodies.

Clinical Vignette: Shar in Yoga

Like many, Shar initially approached yoga with hesitation, expressing discomfort with focusing on her body at all. She engaged in the movements cautiously and struggled with body checking and staying present, frequently redirecting her attention away from bodily sensations.

Over time, as she participated in sessions, she began to shift her focus from how her body looked to how it felt in movement. She started noticing the connection between breath and motion and allowed herself to experience movement without judgment. By the end of her time in the yoga program, she reflected on its impact, stating, "Yoga allowed me a chance to focus on my breath and appreciate my body's ability to make movement, and focus on how different parts work together in movement." This shift marked a significant step in her treatment, as she moved toward a more compassionate and connected relationship with her body.

Tai Chi for Eating Disorders

Tai Chi and its close cousin, Qi Gong, are ancient Chinese practices that combine slow, mindful movements with breath and awareness. These gentle practices have shown promise as treatment for people with eating disorders, as well as common issues like depression, anxiety, and physical challenges such as poor balance and a higher risk of falls. One of the great things about Tai Chi is its adaptability; it can be done standing, seated, or modified for all mobility and capacity levels. Tai Chi emphasizes gentle repetitive stretches and movements, paired with concentration, balance, and familiarity with one's center of balance, called the Dan Tian in Traditional Chinese Medicine (TCM). This helps build familiarity and awareness of the body without judgment. I have seen the Tai Chi program in an eating disorder facility be a bright spot in the day, when clients come with curiosity to experience something new, while their nervous systems get a chance to build efficacy and safety.

Evidence for Tai Chi in Eating Disorders

In a study on stroke recovery and fall protection, Tai Chi was found to aid individuals with frailty or instability against falls (Wayne et al., 2014). Since muscle loss and instability can result from disordered eating patterns, Tai

Chi can be especially beneficial for rebuilding mobility and functionality for activities of daily living (ADLs) after malnutrition. And like yoga, Tai Chi may also help counteract bone mineral density loss, a significant concern for those with restrictive eating patterns during adolescence (Taylor et al., 2012).

Tai Chi's emphasis on non-performative body awareness is particularly relevant for individuals with anorexia nervosa, who often struggle with interoception. Research has shown improvements in interoceptive awareness among adolescents hospitalized with anorexia (Gueguen et al., 2017). Additionally, Tai Chi's slow, deliberate movements and focus on breath coordination can provide a more mindful alternative for individuals who engage in compulsive or excessive exercise. Likewise, it has also been studied for its positive impact on mental well-being and sleep (Yang et al., 2023) with large review studies finding significant reductions in depression and anxiety, as well as increased quality of life across various populations (Wang et al., 2010; Sani et al., 2023; Li et al., 2020).

Tai Chi is not only gaining recognition in the realm of eating disorder treatment but is being embraced more widely in mainstream medicine. Hospitals and healthcare programs across the US are incorporating Tai Chi into their treatment approaches for various conditions. For example, Brigham and Women's Hospital and Boston Medical Center offer Tai Chi for stress reduction and chronic illness management, while Beth Israel Deaconess Medical Center uses it to support patients with Parkinson's disease. Memorial Sloan Kettering Cancer Center provides Tai Chi programs to aid cancer patients in building strength and balance, and the Veterans Health Administration includes Tai Chi as part of its Whole Health initiative to promote overall well-being.

Tai Chi offers a gentle yet powerful healing movement practice that can be an invaluable resource for clients in eating disorder recovery, particularly for those who may not resonate with yoga. With its slow, flowing movements and focus on breath, Tai Chi provides a way to reconnect with the body without pressure, intensity, or competition. Its meditative quality supports stress reduction, emotional balance, and nervous system regulation, making it a deeply restorative practice. As part of an integrative approach, Tai Chi invites clients to move with mindfulness, fostering a sense of peace and presence that can extend far beyond the practice itself.

Biofeedback

Biofeedback uses technology, such as non-invasive wearable sensors, to provide immediate feedback of physiological signals like heart rate variability, brain wave activity, or muscle tension. Clients can watch these signals change in response to grounding and regulation techniques, reinforcing what helps them shift into a calmer state. For individuals with eating disorders, anxiety, or PTSD, biofeedback is particularly valuable because it helps correct chronic autonomic nervous system dysregulation – a state where the body is stuck in fight, flight, or freeze. This can manifest as panic, anxiety, hypervigilance, dissociation, or numbness, all of which often underlie and perpetuate disordered eating behaviors.

For many clients, traditional mindfulness or meditation can feel frustrating, abstract, or inaccessible. Biofeedback offers a science-backed alternative – one that provides real-time visual and numerical feedback – making meditation both tangible and interactive. In essence, biofeedback is like meditation for people who don't like meditation, helping clients develop a sense of self-efficacy in managing their stress response.

At its core, biofeedback empowers clients to recognize what a regulated state feels like by seeing it in real time on a screen, thereby helping build awareness of physiological responses. It allows a client to identify strategies that can effectively bring them back into regulation when stress arises, reinforcing healthy coping mechanisms. With regular practice, biofeedback teaches a client how to shift into a regulated state throughout the day.

It's important to note the "dose" of biofeedback in the evidence listed below: most studies show significant improvement after approximately four weeks of brief daily practice, about ten minutes a day. This is a big impact for something that is non-invasive, non-addictive, with no interactions or side effects, and is relatively inexpensive and empowering for clients. This is why biofeedback is one of my favorite tools for eating disorder treatment.

Types of Biofeedback for Eating Disorders

The two types of biofeedback most common in the psychotherapeutic setting are heart rate variability (HRV) biofeedback and neurofeedback. HRV biofeedback uses a simple heart rate monitor with a software that transforms information into simple visual graphs describing the state of the nervous system. The graphs show a real-time measure of sympathetic vs parasympathetic balance, helping individuals learn to balance sympathetic (fight or flight) and parasympathetic (rest and digest) sides of the nervous system. There are many devices that are commercially available. Neuro-feedback, on the other hand, is a type of biofeedback that measures brain waves with a wearable electroencephalogram (EEG) in a cap or headband. This type helps clients to train their brains to produce neuronal patterns associated with calm, focus, or emotional stability. There are also other biofeedback types that measure functions associated with stress and anxiety, like muscle tension.

Aligned with my experience, the scientific literature suggests that bio-feedback can be helpful at any age, especially for children, adolescents, and young adults. There are ways to "gamify" the training and make the learning fun as part of therapy, helping clients see real-time evidence of their improvement.

Especially important to mention is the proof that is gleaned when using biofeedback. Even clients who feel they have no control over their emotional or physical reactions can see the evidence in real time that their attention and effort impact their internal state. Several times have I heard from clients' comments like "I had no idea I was able to do that" and express interest to keep training. This engagement is what builds the self-efficacy that is so important for those in treatment for eating disorders; clients are building a skill that they can take with them wherever they go.

The biggest benefit I have personally seen come from using biofeedback is its ability to help clients reduce eating disorder behaviors by practicing urge surfing. This is a psychotherapeutic way of saying that clients who are experiencing an intense urge to perform a maladaptive behavior (like purging, restriction, self-harm, or exercise), instead they can engage in biofeedback as a way to reduce that distress. The tool gives clients something to focus on, with visual cues that are directly aimed at reducing the physical distress signal driving the urge. They can help ride the intensity of the urge and then watch it recede. After the urge passes, clients often express surprise and accomplishment in riding it out without acting on the urge.

Heart Rate Variability biofeedback studied in eating disorder settings showed that clients liked it and found it tolerable, which is important because it requires some degree of investment from the client to practice the skills (Scolnick et al., 2014). Multiple studies have shown significant mental health benefits from HRV biofeedback practice on depression, anxiety, PTSD, and insomnia, and anger management (Lehrer et al., 2020, Pizzoli et al., 2021). This is because it helps to address the underlying autonomic dysfunction that can underpin many of these conditions. Lehrer et al. (2020) concluded that practicing biofeedback reduces physiological arousal associated with disordered eating triggers, allowing clients to engage with food and eating with less stress and more regulation. Likewise, research in this area indicates that neurofeedback fosters self-awareness and reduces maladaptive behaviors (Kluetsch et al., 2014).

Practicing Biofeedback Outpatient

For therapists, biofeedback is a powerful tool that can be directly integrated into your treatment session with your client, rather than something that always requires referring out to a specialist. While advanced cases may benefit from a referral, many of the core techniques – especially for HRV biofeedback – are easy to learn and highly effective when used within sessions. Many types of biofeedback sensors are commercially available, and clients can either purchase them themselves or the therapist or clinic can loan them out to clients for a time. You might try starting each session with a brief biofeedback exercise and assigning homework between sessions. For more information about training, see the resources section at the end of this chapter.

Expressive Art Therapies

Expressive Therapies are their own collection of modalities that use forms of art in therapy. Some examples include visual art, dance, movement, drama, music, poetry, and writing. Expressive arts therapies offer non-verbal outlets for emotional expression, allowing clients to externalize and process feelings that may be inaccessible through traditional talk therapy (Abbing et al., 2018). In addition, they breathe life and creativity into a therapeutic process when top-down approaches might feel exhausting or difficult for the client. The term Expressive Arts Therapy is a regulated profession with credentialing by national and international bodies. Accreditation is overseen internationally by the International Expressive Arts Therapy Association (IEATA) and in the US by the Art Therapy Credentials Board (ATCB).

Art Therapy uses practices like drawing, painting, sculpting, and collage to help clients express feelings they may find difficult to verbalize. For those with eating disorders, this can help facilitate exploration of body image issues, identifying and expressing emotions, processing trauma, or developing healthier coping mechanisms. Many individuals with eating disorders have trouble identifying and expressing emotions. In a meta-analysis of studies in populations with eating disorders, Trably et al (2024) suggest that art therapy can aid in emotional expression and recovery.

Dance/Movement Therapy (DMT) uses movement to promote emotional, cognitive, and physical integration and to explore their bi-directional relationship between body and emotions. DMT is particularly relevant for eating disorders as it fosters body awareness by facilitating reconnection with the body and fostering awareness of physical sensations and emotions, which is especially important for clients who may dissociate or struggle with body image (Koch et al., 2019). A small, descriptive study on DMT in eating disorder treatment by Savidaki et al. (2020) wonderfully describes the internal experience of a group of patients in a closed DMT group as part of their eating disorder treatment, allowing insight into the psychotherapeutic mechanisms and how they could apply to larger numbers in bigger programs.

Music Therapy involves actively creating, listening to, or responding to music to explore emotions, promote creativity, and healing. This can be effective in regulating mood, reducing anxiety, and fostering a sense of connection and safety. Music therapy has been shown to reduce anxiety and create a sense of safety, providing a gentle entry point for processing trauma (Freitas et al., 2022).

Poetry and Writing Therapy uses creative writing, poetry, and journaling as tools for self-reflection, expression, and exploration of personal experiences. Both can help clients explore and reframe personal narratives, empowering them to process traumatic experiences in a creative and supportive environment (Pennebaker & Smyth, 2016; Mazza, 2016). Last, Drama Therapy employs storytelling, role-playing, and improvisation to explore personal narratives, develop insight, and rehearse new behaviors. It can help clients externalize inner conflicts, develop empathy for themselves, and experiment with healthier relational dynamics (Pellicciari et al., 2013).

Horticultural Therapy

Horticultural therapy blends psychotherapy with hands-on engagement in gardening, plants, and nature, offering a meaningful way to explore healing through lived experience. Overseen by the American Horticultural Therapy Association (AHTA), it encourages reflection and personal growth through nature-based metaphors. There is so much to be learned from the cycles of nature – how things grow, adapt, and change – mirroring the recovery process itself.

At its core, this practice is about building stewardship, using the senses to foster positive sensory experiences, and challenging the rigidity of an eating disorder – not for growing "healthy" foods. Though there is formal training required to be a certified horticultural therapist, therapists don't need certification to integrate nature into healing; even planting seeds in a windowsill tray can reduce stress and offer lessons (Lee et al., 2015). Through the practice of nourishing, growing, and caring for a plant or natural space, clients develop the empathy and skills needed to nourish, grow, and care for their own bodies. This connection is particularly compelling when viewed through the lens of research on parents with eating disorders, which shows that while self-nourishment may be difficult, they are often able to feed and care for their children with ease. Horticultural therapy can help extend that same compassion inward, reinforcing the idea that bodies – like plants – need care, rest, and nourishment to thrive. A 2025 meta-analysis showed significant benefit in depression and anxiety from engaging in horticultural activities, strengthening the case for their use in mental health settings (Wood et al., 2025; Van Den Berg & Custers, 2011).

Concluding Thoughts: Types of Therapies

All of these approaches give clients a way to process emotions and heal when words fall short. Whether through art, music, movement, or writing, these creative outlets help externalize feelings, build self-compassion, and reconnect with the body in a non-threatening way. Each helps support creativity and learning how to focus on the process of the art, not the product, a skill helpful in building mindfulness, tolerance of emotions, and resilience. I have seen both powerful breakthroughs and small steps forward through creative expression when progress felt otherwise difficult. For those who struggle with traditional talk therapy, expressive arts can be a powerful tool for healing and self-expression.

If your client may benefit from specific expressive therapeutic work, it may be wise to connect or collaborate with a licensed expressive therapist. To find an expressive art therapist, utilize the Art Therapy Credentials Board (ATCB) website or the American Art Therapy Association (AATA) Art Therapist Locator to search for credentialed therapists in your client's area. Look for an ATR (registered art therapist) or an ATR-BC (art therapist board certified who no longer requires supervision). Therapists interested in learning expressive therapy techniques themselves can seek training through recognized institutions.

Clinical Vignette: Alex in Art Therapy

Alex attended art therapy sessions but expressed reluctance to discuss their history of trauma verbally. They frequently stated that talking about past experiences felt overwhelming and unhelpful. Instead, they were encouraged to engage in nonverbal expression through painting, with a focus on exploring emotion through color, movement, and texture. During one session, Alex worked vigorously on a large canvas, using bold, intense strokes and highly saturated colors. Their painting process was dynamic, involving sweeping motions and layers of color. They remained quiet throughout the session but appeared highly engaged in the physicality of the creative process.

At the end of the session, Alex stepped back and observed their work, commenting that the therapist might now understand how they feel. Over time, they began to approach art as a means of processing and externalizing emotions they found difficult to name. This approach provided a valuable outlet for emotional expression and regulation, allowing them to engage with their experiences in a way that felt safe and manageable.

Using Expressive Arts Therapies in Your Practice

A good first step when considering the use of integrative therapies is to think about where your clients are starting from. Each person's relationship with movement and the body is uniquely shaped by personal history, physical conditions, and emotional associations, and many individuals with eating disorders face complex challenges in this area. Some clients may experience dissociation from their bodies due to profound dysmorphia or dysphoria, while others may have chronic conditions or differing abilities that limit physical activity, making it less comfortable to engage in movement. For instance, research suggests a higher prevalence of connective tissue disorders such as Ehlers-Danlos syndrome and autonomic disorders like Postural Orthostatic Tachycardia Syndrome (POTS) among individuals with eating disorders compared to the general population. Each of these associated conditions affects movement in distinct ways, including dizziness, joint hypermobility, and pain (Baeza-Velasco et al., 2022). Trauma can further complicate body awareness, making movement particularly difficult for some clients.

Conversely, athletes with eating disorders may have a deeply ingrained emotional connection to movement, viewing physical performance as a core part of their identity and self-worth. Additionally, many clients have a history of over-exercise, using excessive physical activity as a means of compensation, self-punishment, or emotional numbing. Given these diverse experiences, each client will have different starting points, barriers, and goals when engaging with movement therapeutically.

To be able to discuss and recommend movement-related interventions effectively, it can be helpful to discuss with your client their relationship with movement as part of the therapeutic interview. You may want to ask about how the client feels about movement and what they feel movement does for them, including past history, particularly any physical conditions or tendencies that impact movement. I often ask a client if they can recall a time when they felt differently about movement; when and why did that change? I also ask about frequency and how they feel before, during, or after movement as well as what is the hardest part about movement?

In addition to exploring movement, it may also be beneficial to assess your client's relationship with creative and expressive outlets. Expression through art, music, and other non-verbal forms of communication can provide insight into their internal experiences. You might ask if they connect to art or music as ways to express how they feel, or if they have difficulty finding words to express things but feel more comfortable using music, memes, pictures, or other forms of communication. These conversations can offer valuable context for integrating movement and creative expression into treatment in a way that aligns with each client's needs and comfort level.

Choosing Integrative Therapy Tools

Using your client's responses to the questions above and the information in this chapter, you can begin identifying integrative therapies that may be beneficial and explore where to start incorporating them into treatment.

For instance, for clients who feel numb, "checked out," or disconnected from their body, try to focus on practices that enhance interoception, incorporate breath awareness, encourage slow, mindful movement, and build tolerance for being fully present in the body. Trauma-informed yoga and Tai Chi can be particularly helpful. Art therapy may also be useful for fostering emotional connection and expression.

Or maybe you're working with a client with high baseline anxiety, panic, nightmares, or insomnia. Try biofeedback, a valuable tool for nervous system regulation and supporting sleep. Encourage clients to explore various movement and relaxation practices while using biofeedback to assess what is most regulating for them. For clients with a history of trauma and dissociation, prioritize creating a sense of safety and nervous system regulation before introducing movement. I suggest teaching grounding techniques, vagal nerve exercises, and biofeedback to establish a sense of stability. When movement is introduced, clients should seek out trauma-informed instructors for practices like yoga.

Clients who struggle with Postural Orthostatic Tachycardia Syndrome (POTS) may experience dizziness or fainting when transitioning between positions. It is important to modify movements to avoid rapid changes from sitting to standing and focus on stabilizing movement practices like yin or restorative yoga. Ehlers-Danlos Syndrome (EDS) often involves hyperflexible joints, increasing the risk of injury. Clients should be cautious about overstretching or exploiting flexibility in movement practices like yoga. If clients feel comfortable sharing, encourage them to share their conditions with a yoga or other movement teacher so that movement can be safely modified.

And for athletes or individuals who over-exercise, work to uncouple movement from achievement, pressure, identity, compensation, and obligation. It may be useful to encourage exploration of non-performance-based movement, such as Tai Chi, music making, or horticultural therapy. Working with a dance movement therapist may also help shift the client's relationship with movement in a more exploratory and expressive direction.

Healing Must Include the Body

My goal is for you, the reader, to now have an understanding that integrative therapies are essential for truly effective eating disorder treatment, and for you to have a grasp on how to begin incorporating these practices into your treatment framework. While traditional talk therapy addresses thoughts and behaviors, healing must also happen in the body. As Bessel van der Kolk, author of The Body Keeps the Score, explains, "If the memory of trauma is encoded in the viscera, in gut wrenching sensations, the only way to change these feelings is through the body" (van der Kolk, 2014). This is why practices like yoga, Tai Chi, expressive arts, biofeedback, and breathwork offer clients a way to reconnect, regulate, and reclaim a sense of safety within themselves. These approaches help build resilience in ways that words alone often cannot. By incorporating body-based therapies, we expand the possibilities for healing, offering clients tools that are deeply transformative. As therapists, embracing these methods means meeting clients where they are – not just in their minds, but in their whole being.

Resources

Breathwork Resources

Breath: The New Science of a Lost Art by James Nestor
The Healing Power of the Breath by Richard Brown & Patricia Gerbarg
Just Breathe by Dan Brulé
Helpful Apps: Insight Timer, Headspace, and Calm apps

Yoga Resources

Yoga for Eating Disorders: Ancient Healing for Modern Illness by Carolyn Costin & Joe Kelly

Tai chi Resources

The Harvard Medical School Guide to Tai Chi: 12 Weeks to a Healthy Body, Strong Heart, and Sharp Mind (2013)

Biofeedback Resources

Polyvagal Theory by Stephen Porges
Expressive Art Therapies Resources
Trauma and Expressive Arts Therapy: Brain, Body, and Imagination in the Healing Process by Cathy Malchiodi, PhD
The Art of Recovery: Expressive Therapies for Eating Disorders, edited by Marcia Herrin & Maria L. Sirois

References

Abbing, A., Ponstein, A., van Hooren, S., de Sonneville, L., Swaab, H., & Baars, E. (2018). The effectiveness of art therapy for anxiety in adults: A systematic review of randomised and non-randomised controlled trials. PloS One, 13(12), e0208716.
Alleva, J. M., Tylka, T. L., van Oorsouw, K., Montanaro, E., Perey, I., Bolle, C., ... & Webb, J. B. (2020). The effects of yoga on functionality appreciation and additional facets of positive body image. Body Image, 34, 184–195.

Baeza-Velasco, C., Seneque, M., Courtet, P., Olié, É., Chatenet, C., Espinoza, P., ... & Guillaume, S. (2022). Joint hypermobility and clinical correlates in a group of patients with eating disorders. Frontiers in Psychiatry, 12, 803614.

Borden, A., & Cook-Cottone, C. (2020). Yoga and eating disorder prevention and treatment: A comprehensive review and meta-analysis. Yoga for Positive Embodiment in Eating Disorder Prevention and Treatment, 97–134.

Brennan, M. A., Whelton, W. J., & Sharpe, D. (2022). Benefits of yoga in the treatment of eating disorders: Results of a randomized controlled trial. In Yoga for Positive Embodiment in Eating Disorder Prevention and Treatment (pp. 135–154). Routledge.

Carei, T. R., Fyfe-Johnson, A. L., Breuner, C. C., & Brown, M. A. (2010). Randomized controlled clinical trial of yoga in the treatment of eating disorders. Journal of Adolescent Health, 46(4), 346–351.

Cook-Cottone, C., Roff, C., Perey, I., Lagutaine, M., & Guyker, W. (2024). Efficacy of the eat breathe thrive recovery protocol delivered virtually to adults recovering from eating disorders: A randomized controlled trial. International Journal of Eating Disorders, 58(2), 372–388.

Cramer, H., Anheyer, D., Saha, F. J., & Dobos, G. (2018). Yoga for posttraumatic stress disorder – a systematic review and meta-analysis. BMC Psychiatry, 17(1), 295.

Freitas, C., Fernández-Company, J. F., Pita, M. F., & Garcia-Rodriguez, M. (2022). Music therapy for adolescents with psychiatric disorders: An overview. Clinical Child Psychology and Psychiatry, 27(3), 895–910.

Gueguen, J., Piot, M. A., Orri, M., Gutierre, A., Le Moan, J., Berthoz, S., ... & Godart, N. (2017). Group Qigong for adolescent inpatients with anorexia nervosa: incentives and barriers. PLoS One, 12(2), e0170885.

Hall, A., Ofei-Tenkorang, N. A., Machan, J. T., & Gordon, C. M. (2016). Use of yoga in outpatient eating disorder treatment: A pilot study. Journal of Eating Disorders, 4, 1–8.

Halliwell, E., Dawson, K., & Burkey, S. (2019). A randomized experimental evaluation of a yoga-based body image intervention. Body Image, 28, 119–127.

Kluetsch, R. C., Ros, T., Théberge, J., Frewen, P. A., Calhoun, V. D., Schmahl, C., & Lanius, R. A. (2014). Plastic modulation of PTSD resting-state networks and subjective wellbeing by EEG neurofeedback. Acta Psychiatrica Scandinavica, 130(2), 123–136.

Koch, S. C., Riege, R. F., Tisborn, K., Biondo, J., Martin, L., & Beelmann, A. (2019). Effects of dance movement therapy and dance on health-related psychological outcomes. A meta-analysis update. Frontiers in Psychology, 10, 1806.

Lee, M. S., Lee, J., Park, B. J., & Miyazaki, Y. (2015). Interaction with indoor plants may reduce psychological and physiological stress by suppressing autonomic nervous system activity in young adults: A randomized crossover study. Journal of Physiological Anthropology, 34(1), 1–6.

Lehrer, P., Kaur, K., Sharma, A., Shah, K., Huseby, R., Bhavsar, J., & Zhang, Y. (2020). Heart rate variability biofeedback improves emotional and physical health and performance: A systematic review and meta analysis. Applied Psychophysiology and Biofeedback, 45, 109–129.

Li, H., Chen, J., Xu, G., Duan, Y., Huang, D., Tang, C., & Liu, J. (2020). The effect of Tai Chi for improving sleep quality: A systematic review and meta-analysis. Journal of Affective Disorders, 274, 1102–1112.

Mahlo, L., & Tiggemann, M. (2016). Yoga and positive body image: A test of the embodiment model. Body Image, 18, 135–142. https://doi.org/10.1016/j.bodyim.2016.06.008

Mazza, N. (2016). Poetry therapy: Theory and practice (3rd ed.). Routledge.

Muehlenkamp, J. J., & Wagner, E. M. (2022). Yoga and nonsuicidal self-injury: Mediational effects of self-compassion and body appreciation. *Body image*, 43, 17–24.

Neumark-Sztainer, D., Watts, A. W., & Rydell, S. (2018). Yoga and body image: How do young adults practicing yoga describe its impact on their body image?. Body Image, 27, 156–168.

Ogden, P., Minton, K., & Pain, C. (2006). Trauma and the body: A sensorimotor approach to psychotherapy (Norton series on interpersonal neurobiology). W.W. Norton & Company.

Pellicciari, A., Rossi, F., Iero, L., Di Pietro, E., Verrotti, A., & Franzoni, E. (2013). Drama therapy and eating disorders: A historical perspective and an overview of a Bolognese project for adolescents. The Journal of Alternative and Complementary Medicine, 19(7), 607–612.

Pennebaker, J. W. (2016). Opening up by writing it down: How expressive writing improves health and eases emotional pain. Guilford Publications.

Piran, N., & Neumark-Sztainer, D. (2020). Yoga and the experience of embodiment: A discussion of possible links. In yoga for positive embodiment. Eating Disorders, the Journal of Treatment & Prevention, 29(4), 330–348.

Pizzoli, S. F., Marzorati, C., Gatti, D., Monzani, D., Mazzocco, K., & Pravettoni, G. (2021). A meta-analysis on heart rate variability biofeedback and depressive symptoms. Scientific Reports, 11(1), 6650.

Sani, N. A., Yusoff, S. S. M., Norhayati, M. N., & Zainudin, A. M. (2023). Tai Chi exercise for mental and physical well-being in patients with depressive symptoms: A systematic review and meta-analysis. International Journal of Environmental Research and Public Health, 20(4), 2828.

Savidaki, M., Demirtoka, S., & Rodríguez-Jiménez, R. M. (2020). Re-inhabiting one's body: A pilot study on the effects of dance movement therapy on body image and alexithymia in eating disorders. Journal of Eating Disorders, 8, 1–20. https://doi.org/10.1186/s40337-020-00296-2

Scolnick, B., Mostofsky, D. I., & Keane, R. J. (2014). Pilot study employing heart rate variability biofeedback training to decrease anxiety in patients with eating disorders. Journal of Eating Disorders, 2, 1–3.

Streeter, C. C., Whitfield, T. H., Owen, L., Rein, T., Karri, S. K., Yakhkind, A., Perlmutter, R., Prescot, A., Renshaw, P. F., & Jensen, J. E. (2010). Effects of yoga versus walking on mood, anxiety, and brain GABA levels: A randomized controlled MRS study. The Journal of Alternative and Complementary Medicine, 16(11), 1145–1152.

Taylor, D., Hale, L., Schluter, P., Waters, D. L., Binns, E. E., McCracken, H., … & Wolf, S. L. (2012). Effectiveness of Tai Chi as a community-based falls prevention intervention: A randomized controlled trial. Journal of the American Geriatrics Society, 60(5), 841–848.

Trably, F., Gorwood, P., & Di Lodovico, L. (2024). Art therapy in eating disorders. A systematic review of controlled trials. Journal of Psychopathology, 30(3), 178–186. https://doi.org/10.36148/2284-0249-N466

Van Den Berg, A. E., & Custers, M. H. (2011). Gardening promotes neuroendocrine and affective restoration from stress. Journal of Health Psychology, 16(1), 3–11.

van der Kolk, B. (2014). The body keeps the score: Brain, mind, and body in the healing of trauma (p. 88). Viking.

van der Kolk, B. A., Stone, L., West, J., Rhodes, A., Emerson, D., Suvak, M., & Spinazzola, J. (2014). Yoga as an adjunctive treatment for posttraumatic stress disorder: A randomized controlled trial. *The Journal of Clinical Psychiatry, 75*(6), e559–e565.

Wang, C., Bannuru, R., Ramel, J., Kupelnick, B., Scott, T., & Schmid, C. H. (2010). Tai Chi on psychological well-being: Systematic review and meta-analysis. *BMC Complementary and Alternative Medicine, 10*, 1–16.

Wayne, P. M., Walsh, J. N., Taylor-Piliae, R. E., Wells, R. E., Papp, K. V., Donovan, N. J., & Yeh, G. Y. (2014). Effect of Tai Chi on cognitive performance in older adults: Systematic review and meta-analysis. *Journal of the American Geriatrics Society, 62*(1), 25–39.

Wood, C. J., Barton, J., & Wicks, C. L. (2025). Effectiveness of social and therapeutic horticulture for reducing symptoms of depression and anxiety: A systematic review and meta-analysis. *Frontiers in Psychiatry, 15*, 1507354.

Yang, M., Yang, J., Gong, M., Luo, R., Lin, Q., & Wang, B. (2023). Effects of Tai Chi on sleep quality as well as depression and anxiety in insomnia patients: A meta-analysis of randomized controlled trials. *International Journal of Environmental Research and Public Health, 20*(4), 3074.

Ziv, A., Barnea-Melamed, S., Meisman, A., Ofei-Tenkorang, N. A., O'Donnell, J., Altaye, M., & Gordon, C. M. (2023). Yoga as an intervention to promote bone and mental health in adolescent females with anorexia nervosa: A pilot study. *Eating Disorders, 31*(5), 526–532.

Closing Thoughts

Robert J. Keane and Kameron M. Mendes

We hope that by now, you feel both empowered and equipped to take on the rewarding and challenging work of treating eating disorders. As we've emphasized throughout this book, you already possess many of the foundational skills needed for this work. What we've aimed to provide is a layer of refinement – guidance to help you apply your existing clinical knowledge specifically to the treatment of eating disorders. It is our hope that you now feel not only capable, but invigorated.

Although this book was written with outpatient therapists in mind, the concepts and strategies discussed are applicable across all levels of care. Whether you work in psychiatric inpatient settings, partial hospitalization programs, or intensive outpatient programs, the core ideas remain relevant. Certain aspects – such as communicating within a treatment team or navigating dual roles (e.g., working with both individuals and their families, which is common in higher levels of care) – may require adaptation depending on your setting, but the principles are consistent.

It is also important to acknowledge the limits of this book. Our aim was to offer readers rich insights based on the experiences of seasoned practitioners treating eating disorders, rather than formulaic guidelines derived from quantitative research—treatment is rarely that straightforward. As such, covering the full spectrum of eating disorder knowledge is beyond the scope of this book. Likewise, this work reflects knowledge from a specific point in time. As the field continues to evolve, we anticipate there will be new treatments and innovations to support one's journey toward recovery. Thus, we feel it is essential that readers to stay up to date with ongoing research and developments in clinical practice.

What you do now possess is a strong foundation: the knowledge and clinical orientation necessary to support eating disorder recovery in an outpatient setting, and to function effectively as part of a multidisciplinary team.

With that in mind, here are a few final thoughts we'd like to leave you with:

First, you are not alone. Throughout this book, we have emphasized that eating disorders are not to be treated in isolation, and the multidisciplinary treatment team approach we described is crucial to the successful and safe management of these illnesses. It is best for you to work to establish the components of the treatment team, and to know that the team aspect of ED treatment is one of the things we love most about it – your colleagues are there as a team of trained professionals to help you, should you feel stuck, overwhelmed, or out of your depth.

It's important for you to know that it's OK for the multidisciplinary team to disagree. Of course, disagreements should be based on mutual respect and addressed collaboratively. When team members fail to communicate or align their recommendations, treatment can become fragmented, and clients and families may receive conflicting and confusing messages that inadvertently reinforce the eating disorder. This can have serious consequences. It's clear to us that for treatment to be effective, the team must communicate consistently and move in the same direction. Acting independently or undermining the collective effort not only disrupts treatment, but it also risks reinforcing the very symptoms we are trying to help the client overcome.

Second, don't be afraid to seek out ED-specialized supervision. As you start out, the expertise of an experienced practitioner can be invaluable. We would recommend finding a supervisor who has experience treating eating disorders at multiple levels of care. As mentioned previously in this book, each level of care treats various levels of eating disorder severity, so having someone who can provide that insight can help you to better identify and work through complicated issues. Similarly, a seasoned clinician will be able to guide your work and teach you the tools you'll need to assess for level of care.

Third, know that you will not be able to help everyone who comes into your office. In some cases, the ED pathology is so significant that no matter what you do, you will not be able to "turn the tide" on behaviors. In these cases, treatment at a higher level of care is necessary. Level of care considerations should be made in collaboration with the multidisciplinary team; however, in cases where the team is not established, you should feel empowered to give your recommendation that the client seek treatment at a higher level of care and provide referrals to organizations that specialize in acute care for eating disorders.

Finally, be aware that the power of the therapeutic relationship cannot be understated. This relationship will either constrain your work or open possibilities. How can one provide effective CBT or DBT if the client does not trust them or think they will help? It would be nearly impossible. The therapeutic relationship begins forming the moment you walk through the door – even before you say "hello." Some of this you can control, and some you cannot. However, by understanding this dynamic from the beginning and investing early in the relationship, you'll have your best chance to make meaningful progress.

A part of this is knowing that recovery takes all forms, and that it is not your job to impose recovery on any individual you work with. Because the solution to treating an eating disorder can appear deceptively simple (i.e., stop engaging in ED behaviors), it can be easy to adopt an authoritative stance, direct clients on what to do, and inevitably feel frustrated when they don't follow through. Resist that temptation. Instead, focus on joining with the client to fight alongside them against the eating disorder. For some, directly confronting the eating disorder may feel too overwhelming. In these cases, more indirect approaches can be effective, such as targeting specific behaviors first and gradually expanding to others. Above all, it's important to recognize that recovery takes time and sometimes a great deal of it.

Finally, recovery is not just the cessation of behaviors. True recovery also involves gaining insight, cultivating resilience, developing self-awareness, and fostering meaningful relationships that are no longer governed by food or eating. These deeper shifts are essential to full and lasting healing.

Bob and Kam

Index

For Product Safety Concerns and Information please contact our EU
representative GPSR@taylorandfrancis.com
Taylor & Francis Verlag GmbH, Kaufingerstraße 24, 80331 München, Germany

www.ingramcontent.com/pod-product-compliance
Lightning Source LLC
Chambersburg PA
CBHW070323270326
41926CB00017B/3731

9 781032 980980